D1547027

Handbook of Soils for Landscape Architects

Handbook of Soils for Landscape Architects

ROBERT F. KEEFER

OXFORD
UNIVERSITY PRESS

2000

OXFORD
UNIVERSITY PRESS

Oxford   New York
Athens   Auckland   Bangkok   Bogotá   Buenos Aires   Calcutta
Cape Town   Chennai   Dar es Salaam   Delhi   Florence
Hong Kong   Istanbul   Karachi   Kuala   Lumpur   Madrid
Melbourne   Mexico City   Mumbai   Nairobi   Paris   São Paulo
Singapore   Taipei   Tokyo   Toronto   Warsaw

and associated companies in
Berlin   Ibadan

Copyright © 2000 by Oxford University Press, Inc.

Published by Oxford University Press, Inc.
198 Madison Avenue, New York, New York 10016

Oxford is a registered trademark of Oxford University Press

All rights reserved. No part of this publication may be produced,
stored in a retrieval system, or transmitted, in any form or by any means,
electronic, mechanical photocopying, recording, or otherwise,
without the prior permission of Oxford University Press.

Library of Congress Cataloging-in-Publication Data
Keefer, Robert F.
Handbook of soils for landscape architects / by Robert F. Keefer.
p.   cm.
Includes bibliographical references and index.
ISBN 0-19-512102-3
1. Soil science. 2. Landscape architecture. I. Title.
S591.K385   2000
631.4—dc21   98-29581

9 8 7 6 5 4 3 2

Printed in the United States of America
on acid-free paper

Preface

Landscape Architecture curriculum at colleges and universities often requires a course in soils. During my teaching in the College of Agriculture and Forestry at West Virginia University, I was requested to teach a course specifically for Landscape Architects. The faculty and students were concerned that the general course in soils at WVU was not providing them with their needs. After gathering the information required to teach this course, it occurred to me that students in Landscape Architecture throughout the country could use a simplified handbook of soils information written specifically for them. The students and faculty were pleased with the course, and when I asked them if a text for such a course would be accepted, they thought it would. The number of students who could use such a book was calculated to be from 1200 to 1500 annually. Therefore, I undertook the task of writing and illustrating this book.

Sincere thanks are extended to the West Virginia University landscape architecture professor, Mr. George Longenecker, for his suggestions, encouragement, and for providing names of several reviewers. My son, Brian Douglas Keefer, graduated with a B.S.L.A. degree in landscape architecture from West Virginia University in 1988; presently, he is involved in land planning for golf course development and design of golf courses in many places throughout the world. He was generous in giving some of his time to redraw by hand many of the graphics so they would be acceptable to the intended readers. Helping him in this endeavor were two of his friends, Jennifer Oliviera and Russell Oliviera. Jennifer Oliviera graduated in 1998 with honors from the Landscape Architecture Program, California Polytechnic State University, San Luis Obispo, California. Russell Oliviera, her husband, has a natural ability for drawing cartoons and a witty sense of humor that added interest to the figures. Brian also provided me with names of several reviewers. Lastly, I want to thank my wife for her patience and encouragement during the writing and editing of the manuscript.

R.F.K.

Contents

1: Use of Soil Surveys for Landscape Architecture   3

    Modern Soil Survey Reports   3

2: Basic Information About Soils and Plants   9

    Plant Requirements for Growth   9
    What Is Soil?   9

3: Parts of a Soil (Soil Constituents)—Air, Water,
  Minerals, and Organic Matter   21

    Physical Parts of a Soil   21
    Chemical Parts of a Soil   22
    Biological Parts of a Soil   22

4: Physical Properties of Soils   27

    Soil Texture   27
    Soil Structure   30
    Soil Bulk Density   32
    Soil Depth   32
    Soil Aeration   35
    Soil Water   40

5: Movement of Water Across Soils (Erosion)   53

    Erosion Defined   53
    Types of Water Erosion   53
    Types of Accelerated Erosion   54
    Factors That Determine Extent of Erosion   57

6: Nature of Soil Erodibility   61

    Soil Texture   61
    Soil Structure   62

Soil Organic Matter   64
Soil Permeability   65
Use of a Nomograph to Evaluate Soil
    Erodibility Using the Four Factors Above   65

7: Controlling Erosion   69

Improving Soil Structure   69
Covering Soil With Plants   72
Covering Soil With Mulch   72
Using Special Structures   78

8: Effective Water Use—Irrigation   83

Which Soils Are Suitable for Irrigation?   83
When Should Water Be Applied?   83
How Much Water to Add?   85
Kinds of Irrigation Systems   86

9: Chemical Properties of Soils for Growing Plants   91

Soil Reaction (pH)   91
Factors That Cause Acids to Form in Soils   96
Correcting Soil Acidity   99
Base-Forming Factors   101
Correcting Alkalinity in Arid Regions   103

10: Soil Nutrients (Soil Fertility)   107

Respiration vs. Photosynthesis   107
Elements Required by Plants (Essential Nutrients)   107

11: Macronutrients—Nitrogen   113

Nitrogen in Plants   113
Nitrogen in Soils   117
Transformations of Nitrogen in Soils   118
Decomposition (Mineralization) Processes   118
Nitrification = Formation of Nitrates   119
Nitrogen Fixation in Soils   122
Nitrogen Added to Soils From the Atmosphere   125
Losses of Nitrogen from Soils   125

12: Macronutrients—Phosphorus and Potassium   131

Phosphorus in Plants   131
Phosphorus in Soils   133

Factors Affecting Availability of Phosphorus in Soils   135
Practical Control of Phosphorus Availability   139
Potassium in Plants   140
Potassium in Soils   141

13: Macronutrients—Calcium, Magnesium, and Sulfur   147

Calcium and Magnesium in Soil Is Related to Liming   147
Amount of Limestone to Apply   148
Kinds of Lime   149
Neutralizing Power of Liming Materials   150
Fineness of a Limestone   150
When and How to Apply Lime   151
Soil Calcium and Magnesium Per Se   152
Plant Calcium and Magnesium   153
Sulfur in Plants   154
Sulfur in Soils   155

14: Micronutrients   157

Forms of Micronutrients Present in Soils   157
Factors Affecting Availability of Micronutrients   161
Anions—Boron, Chlorine, and Molybdenum   164
Soil Management and Micronutrient Needs   166

15: Fertilizers   169

Nitrogen Fertilizers   169
Phosphorus Fertilizers   173
Potassium Fertilizers   174
Sulfur Fertilizers   175
Micronutrient Fertilizers   175
Mixed Fertilizers   175
Farmyard Manures   176
Methods of Fertilizer Application   177
Movement of Fertilizers in Soils   179

16: Soil Organic Matter   183

Importance of Soil Organic Matter   183
Definition of Soil Organic Matter   183
Composition of Soil Organic Matter   183
Soil Changes When Organic Matter Is Added   184
Decomposition of Soil Organic Matter   186
Sources of Organic Matter   188

17: Diagnosing Plant Disorders   191

   Plant Appearance   191
   Plant Tissue Testing and Analysis   207
   Total Plant Analysis   209
   Soil Sampling and Analysis   209
   Soil and Root Problems   211
   Alteration of the Environment by Man   212

18: Engineering Aspects of Soils   217

   Physical Properties Used in Engineering
      Classification of Soils   217
   Engineering Classification of Soils   218
   Soil Engineering Properties   220
   Engineering Geotechnical Applications   222
   Geotechnical Aspects   223

19: Satellite Imaging, Laser Technology, and
   Computer Programs   227

   Definition of Geographic Information System   228
   Operation of GIS   229
   Recent Developments in 3-Dimensional Models   244
   Remote Sensing Using an Airborne Laser Altimeter   247

References   253

Index   257

Handbook of Soils for Landscape Architects

1

Use of Soil Surveys for Landscape Architecture

MODERN SOIL SURVEY REPORTS

Modern soil survey reports, published since about 1959, have a wealth of information that could be useful for landscape architects. Characteristics of each specific soil are detailed in the text of the soil survey. Distinct kinds of soils for a specific site can be identified from the soil designation on the aerial photographs at the back of the report. Considerable specific information is provided in tables, including data on temperature, precipitation, freeze dates in spring and fall, woodland management and productivity, recreational development capabilities, wildlife habitat potentials, building site development possibilities, sanitary disposal potentials, engineering properties, value of materials for construction, water management limitations, physical and chemical properties of specific soils, and soil and water features. Modern soil survey reports consist of text, tables, soil maps, and often a glossary. These reports are available free to the public and are usually found in county extension services offices, soil conservation district offices, or state agricultural colleges.

Text

The text of a soil survey report describes the general nature of the county as to location in the state, climate, physiography, relief and drainage, geology, farming, natural resources, industries, history of settlement, and how the survey was conducted. Soil associations and individual soils are described in detail. Formation of soils is usually discussed in relation to the factors of soil formation. A glossary of terms is often provided for the nonscientific person.

Maps

The whole county or counties in the report is shown on a *soil association map*, which is designed to be used to compare the suitability of large areas for general land use. The county is divided into large areas, each of which contains an association of several soils grouped by similar management. Usually from 5 to 15 soil associations are shown with a legend describing each of the specific associations. This type of information could be used for zoning purposes, county management, or other governmental activities.

Aerial photos are provided on sheets showing the location of each individual soil in the county. Comprising about half of the soil survey report, this is one of the most useful sections. An index of map sheets is shown on a general map of the county so any exact location can be found on a specific map sheet. Each soil is designated on the map sheets by a symbol, and a map legend is provided showing names and symbols for all the soils. Roads, cemeteries, railroads, dams, farmsteads, churches, schools, and other specific features are indicated on the aerial photos as well.

Soil Descriptions

A "typical" profile of each individual soil is described in detail as to topography, depth, internal drainage, amount of rock fragments, depth to subsoil, presence of a hardpan, and profile horizons as to color, friability, structure, number of roots, and acidity.

Tables

The tables in a soil survey report can provide a wide array of valuable data. Typically these tables include the following information:

Physical and Chemical Properties of Soils

Individual soils are listed by name, thickness of horizons, percent clay, bulk density, permeability, available water-holding capacity, pH range, shrink-swell potential (stability), erosion factors (soil erodibility index and soil loss tolerance), and presence of organic matter. This table can be used to compare individual soils in the county in relation to properties that are important for growing plants.

Recreational Development

Soils are listed by suitability in terms of slight, moderate, or severe limitations for camp areas (slope, flooding, percolation, and wetness), picnic areas (slope, wetness, percolation, stones, and flooding), playgrounds (slope, flooding, stones, percolation, acidity, and wetness), paths and trails (slope, stones, clay content, percolation, wetness, and floods), and golf fairways (slope, stones, thin layer, flooding, drought, and wetness). This table can be used to show which soils are best for recreational development and the limitations of other soils for camping, picnicking, playgrounds, hiking, and golf.

Wildlife Habitat Potentials

Soils are rated for wildlife as to good, fair, poor, or very poor for limitations in the categories of grain and seed crops, grasses and legumes, wild herbaceous plants, hardwood trees, coniferous plants, wetland plants, shallow water areas, openland wildlife, woodland wildlife, and wetland wildlife. This table is useful for showing soils adapted for wildlife management with regard to planting crops for wildlife food, providing shelter and offering hiding places in shrubs and trees, and indicating suitability for wildlife as to aquatic, woodland, and openland areas.

Building Site Development

Soils are rated for site development limitations as to slight, moderate, or severe for the categories of shallow excavations (wetness, floods, slope, slippage, clay content, and depth to rock); dwellings with or without basements (slope, shrink-swell, slippage, wetness, floods, large stones, and depth to rock); small commercial buildings (slope, floods, large stones, slippage, shrink-swell, wetness, and depth to rock); local roads and streets (frost action, low strength, floods, slippage, slope, wetness, and depth to rock); and lawns and landscaping (slope, floods, small or large stones, thin layers, drought, and wetness). This table shows adaptability of a particular soil as support for shallow excavations, buildings with or without basements, small commercial buildings, roads and streets, and suitability for lawns and landscaping.

Sanitary Facilities

Soils are rated for usefulness for sanitary facilities as to slight, moderate, or severe limitations and good, fair, or poor ratings for the categories: septic tank absorption fields (slope, wetness, floods, large stones, slippage, slow percolation, and depth to rock), sewage lagoon areas (slope, wetness, seepage, floods, large stones, and depth to rock), trench sanitary landfill (wetness, floods, acidic seepage, slippage, clay content, large stones, and depth to rock), area sanitary landfill (slope, clay content, wetness, seepage, floods, and depth to rock), daily cover for landfill (slope, wetness, clay content, small or large stones, acidity, hard to pack, thin layer, seepage, and difficult to reclaim).

All of the above situations are related to permeability, hydraulic conductivity rate, percolation rate, depth to water table, extent of flooding, degree of slope, depth to bedrock or impervious layer, and extent of stoniness or rockiness. Care must be taken to prevent undue seepage from a septic field, especially if there are nearby water supplies, streams, ponds, lakes, or water courses.

Construction Materials

Soils are rated for use for construction as to good, fair, poor, or unsuited for the following categories: roadfill (low strength, large stones, slope, shrink-swell, thin layer, wetness, and difficult to reclaim), sand (excess fines, large stones, and thin layer), gravel (excess fines, large stones, and thin layer), and topsoil (slope, thin layer, small stones, acidity, clay content, wetness, and difficult to reclaim). Often there is a need to have a supply of material for construction purposes. This table indicates the suitability of different soils in supplying topsoil, gravel, or material for roads, lawns, or backfills for housing.

Water Management

Soils are evaluated as to slight, moderate, or severe with regard to limitations for pond reservoirs (slope, seepage, slippage, and depth to rock); embankments, dikes, and levees (thin layer, wetness, hard to pack, seepage, large stones, seepage around pipes laid in soil causing erosion or "piping"); aquifer-fed excavated ponds (depth to water, slow refill, no water, cutbank cave-ins, and depth to rock). Also listed are features affecting drainage (frost action, slope, depth to water, favorable, floods, cutbank cave-in, and slow percolation), terraces and diversions (slope, wetness, ease of erosion, sandiness, large stones, slippage, favorable, slow percolation, rooting depth, and depth to rock), and grassed waterways (slope, ease of erosion, rooting depth, slow percolation, wetness, drought, favorable, large stones, and depth to rock). This table lists soil limitations when used for reservoirs, levees, ponds, terraces, grassed waterways, and internal and surface drainage aspects.

Soil and Water Features

Soil problems are listed with respect to flooding frequency (none, occasional, and frequent), flooding duration (very brief, brief, or very long), flooding months (specified), high water table for depth (specified in feet or range of feet), high water table kind (apparent or perched), high water table months (specified), depth to bedrock (range in inches), hardness of bedrock (soft or hard), potential frost action (low, moderate, high), risk of corrosion of uncoated steel (low, moderate, or high), and risk of corrosion of concrete (low, moderate, or high). Estimation of corrosivity is based on (1) resistance to flow of electrical current, (2) total acidity, (3) soil drainage, (4) soil texture, and (5) conductivity of the saturation extract. This table can be used by architects to evaluate soils with respect to flooding, shallowness, hardness of bedrock, possibility of heaving by frost action, and extent of corrosion for specific soils.

SUMMARY

A modern soil survey consists of text, tables, and maps. The two types of maps are soil association and aerial photo, which list specific soils for the whole county. The soil association map is useful for broad-based county management purposes, whereas the aerial photo maps are useful for delineating soils in specific areas. Soils are described as to typography where located and specific horizons as to depth, internal drainage, color, texture, structure, friability, acidity, presence of a pan, and number of roots. Physical and chemical properties of soils are useful for providing limitations, if any, for growing plants. Suitability of soils for recreation includes camping, picnicking, hiking, and golf. Soils for wildlife management involve usefulness for growing plants for food, shelter, and adaptability to different kinds of wildlife. Soils for building sites relate to limitations for excavations, construction of houses with and without basements, commercial buildings, roads and streets, and lawns and landscaping. Many soil factors are related to their use for sanitary lagoons, septic fields, sanitary landfills, and cover for landfills. Soils can also provide material for construction such as gravel, topsoil, and fill. Water management includes information on soils adapted to ponds, embankments, terraces, diversions, grassed waterways, and drainage. Landscape architects can use information from the soil and water features table to help in siting buildings to prevent flooding, to prevent damage to pipes by corrosion, and to help in excavations by depth to and hardness of bedrock.

REVIEW

What are the parts of a modern Soil Survey
  Report?
What are the two different maps presented in
  a Soil Survey Report?
For what purpose is the soil association map
  used?
How are the individual soils shown on a map
  and what is the background for the map?
What terms are used for soil descriptions?
Of what use is the table for physical and
  chemical properties of soils?
What types of recreation are covered in the
  table on recreational development?
What different wildlife potentials are present
  in the table on wildlife habitat potentials?
How is the table for building site development important for landscape architects?
How can the table on sanitary facilities be
  useful in architectural planning?
What type of information for landscaping is
  provided in the table on construction
  materials?
What type of structures and water management is covered in the table on water
  management?
What type of landscape features is covered in
  the table on soil and water features?

2

Basic Information About Soils and Plants

PLANT REQUIREMENTS FOR GROWTH

All higher plants require the following factors for growth:

1. Light
2. Heat*
3. Water*
4. Carbon Dioxide*
5. Oxygen*
6. Nutrients*
7. Mechanical Support*
   *Supplied by Soil or Soil Substitute.

Except for light, all of these requirements are supplied by soil or a soil substitute; however, they must be supplied in the proper combination for best plant growth (Fig. 2. 1). Whichever of these is supplied below the optimum level will limit plant growth. Landscape architects need to determine which factor or factors limit growth and take measures to correct it.

WHAT IS SOIL?

"The soil" is a general term for the layer of the earth's crust above the bedrock that has been weathered (physically and biochemically) by destructive and synthetic sources (Fig. 2.2).

"A soil" denotes a specific well-defined part of "the soil" with recognized properties and characteristics (Fig. 2.3). There are thousands of different kinds of soils, and each individual soil has its own characteristics and responds to specific management. The

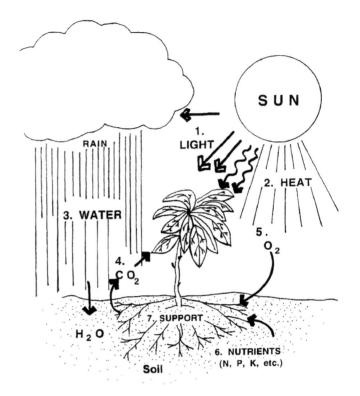

Figure 2.1 Plant growth requirements.

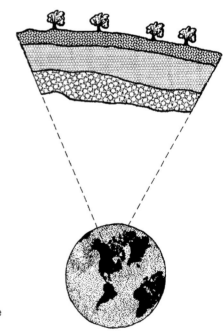

Figure 2.2 The soil as the
outer layer of the earth.

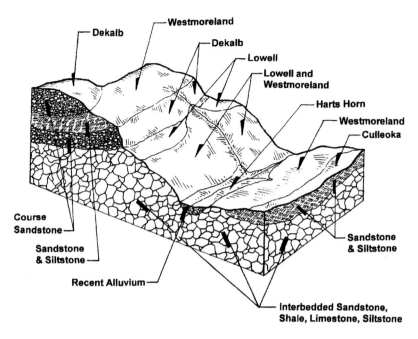

Figure 2.3 Soils as part of a landscape.

name of a soil is associated with specified soil properties within stated limits. A few examples are Cecil clay loam, Marshall silt loam, and Norfolk sand.

SOIL FORMATION

A number of factors have been involved in the formation of the soil and also of individual soils (Fig. 2.4). The type of soils that have been formed depend on the nature of parent material (rocks and minerals), topography (lay of the land), climate (temperature and precipitation) whether or not living organisms are present, and geological time for formation. A change in any one or more of these soil-forming factors can have a profound effect on the specific "soil" that is formed. Is it any wonder that many diverse kinds of soil have been formed? In fact, branches of soil science called soil genesis and soil classification delve into this diversity in great detail.

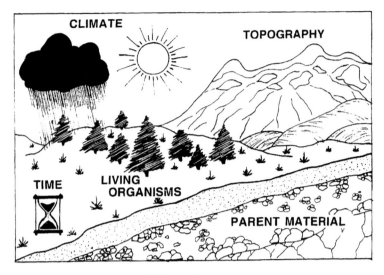

Figure 2.4 Factors of soil formation.

Factors Affecting Soil Formation

Soil Parent Material.   Most soils are derived from the weathering of rocks and minerals. Exceptions to this are man-made soils and organic soils that are almost exclusively developed from organic matter. Information about soil precursors (rocks and minerals) is the study of geology. The three main kinds of rocks—igneous, sedimentary, and metamorphic—undergo weathering into minerals that may become clays with the final product of soils (Fig. 2.5). Parent materials that are high in silica, such as sandstones or quartzites, or are coarse-grained, such as granite, produce sandy soils. These sandy soils have much inert quartz and are often less fertile than soils developed from basic rocks with more clay. Rocks containing large amounts of calcium, magnesium, and potassium generally produce young fertile soils. With time and weathering, these soils lose their nutrients, resulting in low fertility. Fine-grained rocks, such as basalt, produce soils high in clays and may be stony.

Topography.   Topography indicates elevations on the earth with the sea level as zero. Broadly speaking, it is the way the land lays in a three-dimensional aspect (Fig. 2.3). Topography has been formed by geological processes of uplifting; natural erosion by water, wind, and ice; sedimentation; and volcanic reactions all operating over geologic time.

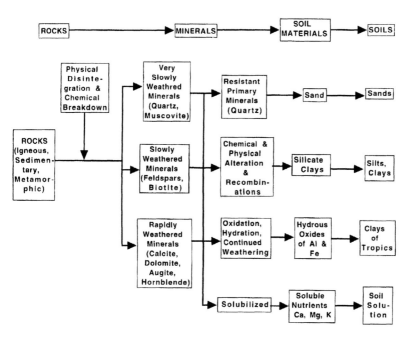

Figure 2.5 Breakdown of rocks to form parts of soils.

Climate. Climate is the average of weather experienced in a location over time. Climate directly affects soils by temperature and moisture through weathering processes and indirectly through the effects of vegetation and topography (Fig. 2.4).

Living Organisms. Organisms living in or on the soil change the soil with time. A good example of this is the beginning stages of a soil when mosses and lichens (algae and fungi acting together) gain a foothold. As the mosses and lichens grow they gain sustenance from the dissolving rocks. In return, the mosses and lichens secrete exudates to dissolve more rocks to make soil. When the mosses and lichens die they provide a source of organic matter to the new soil. With time other organisms, beginning with bacteria, fungi, and actinomycetes, start inhabiting the newly formed soil, giving their input into further soil development. At later stages, seeds of higher plants start to germinate and grow. They ultimately are returned to the developing soil through their contribution of organic matter. Soil-inhabiting animals such as earthworms churn and digest soil parts, producing excrement (casts) that also helps soil development (Fig. 2.6). Larger animals eventually enter the cycle and cause churning and soil movement, thereby providing channels

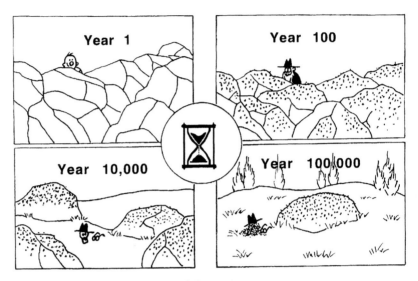

Figure 2.6 Geologic time in soil formation.

for air and water to enter. All of these living organisms act upon parent material to produce soil along with topography, climate, time, and weathering processes.

Time. Soil formation is related to geological time—meaning hundreds, thousands, even millions of years—for soil to be formed (Fig. 2.6).

Weathering Processes

Weathering of soils includes those processes that also affect rocks. These processes include physical weathering, that is the actual mechanical breaking apart of the rock into smaller parts; chemical weathering, whereby the rocks are changed by water, acids, and oxidation; and biological weathering, in which living organisms are involved. Physical weathering is directly related to changes in temperature, changes in state of water (i.e., freezing and thawing) amount of wearing away by water, action of ice (glaciers), and abrasive forces of wind. Chemical weathering also involves changes in the water molecule; formation of acids and their attack on rocks; and reaction of oxygen in the oxidation process. Biological weathering can also affect soil weathering by action of any living organism, especially microorganisms, in which organic material changes from living material into recognized organic portions of the soil and higher plant exudates. Biological weathering results in the formation of soil organic matter.

Physical Weathering.   Physical weathering is the breakdown or disintegration (Fig. 2.7) of rocks (destructive) that results in decrease in size of rocks and minerals, with no change in composition, and eventually results in formation of sand, silts, and clays that become a soil. Physical weathering can be affected by:

1. Temperature
   Heating and cooling—Differential expansion of minerals
   Freezing and thawing—May move soil
   Exfoliation—Peeling away of surface layers; accelerated
      by freezing
2. Water—Raindrops and water run over the surface of
   rocks and minerals.
3. Ice—Glaciers are formed by abrasive action that causes
   grinding and mixing.
4. Wind—Wind is abrasive and picks up dust.

Chemical Weathering.   When rocks or soil break down by definite chemical change, chemical weathering occurs. In this process soluble materials are released and new materials can be synthesized (Fig. 2.8).

1. Action of water
   Hydrolysis—When a water molecule breaks in two, one
      or both parts may combine with materials present.
   Hydration—When an *intact* water molecule attaches di-
      rectly to minerals, hydration occurs and the material
      becomes hydrated, often changing its properties.
2. Acidification—Acidification is the formation of acids
   which attack rocks (primary minerals), dissolving them
   to form clays (secondary minerals).

Figure 2.7 Physical breakdown (disintegration) of rocks.

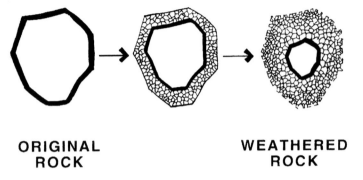

**ORIGINAL
ROCK**

**WEATHERED
ROCK**

Figure 2.8 Chemical weathering of rocks.

3. Dissolution—Rocks or minerals partly dissolve and go into solution. This is usually associated with acidification.
4. Oxidation—Oxidation occurs when oxygen combines with elements or minerals. The oxides formed have different properties than the original material.

Biological Weathering.   Biological weathering causes changes in rocks or soil parent material by the action of living organisms, such as microorganisms and excretions of higher plants. Biological weathering can be either destructive or synthetic.

Formation of Soil Organic Matter.   Soils begin to be formed when mosses and lichens (algae and fungi) secrete chemicals that dissolve the rocks (by acidification and/or dissolution) allowing these lower life forms to gain a foothold and grow.

Microorganisms (microscopic plants and animals) and remains of plants or other microbes by organic decomposition result in the formation of soil organic matter. Higher plants are also involved in biological weathering as they excrete chemicals into the growing medium dissolving rocks and minerals, thereby releasing nutrients needed by plants to grow. Furthermore, as roots grow through soil they exert hydraulic pressure that can distort walkways of brick, stone, or concrete.

SOIL APPEARANCE

Soil Profile

A soil profile is a vertical cut through a soil exposing horizontal layers. A soil profile (Fig. 2.9) consists of the following elements:

Horizons

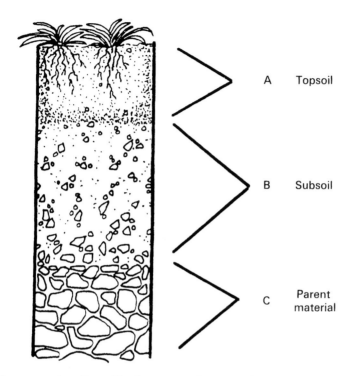

Figure 2.9 A soil profile showing and naming horizons.

Topsoil.   Topsoil is the upper layer of a soil in which organic matter accumulates along with water, air, living microorganisms, and plant nutrients. Landscape architects use topsoil as a growth medium for plantings around homes and buildings or for planters within commercial or residential areas. Topsoil is also called the "A" horizon.

Subsoil.   Subsoil is the lower layer of a soil having much less organic matter, microorganisms, and nutrients than the topsoil and is important as a reserve supply of water and nutrients in a relatively unavailable form. Subsoil is important in providing (a) a reserve water supply, (b) a place for large roots to anchor, (c) material for fill around building sites, (d) leach beds for septic systems, (e) a base for roadways, (f) fill for construction, and (g) movement of water into aquifers. Subsoil is also called the "B" horizon.

Parent Material. Parent material consists of the partially disintegrating and decomposing rocks that are in the beginning stages of soil formation. It is also called the "C" horizon. The primary rocks that lie below this (the "D" horizon) eventually develop into soils.

MAN-MADE SOILS

In the last fifty years, with the production of heavy machinery, man has moved great volumes of earth. In this process, there now exists a number of man-made soils. Some of these have been the result of road cuts and fills for transportation systems, shopping centers, housing developments, mining operations, and landfills. When soils are purposely developed using recent technology they are called "technogenic soils."

Fly Ash—A Soil Substitute

Fly ash produced by electrical power generating plants has been used to improve surface-mined land. Certain properties of fly ash, such as the presence of many plant nutrients and neutralizing ability, make it a desirable material that can substitute for much of the topsoil. Fly ash consists mainly of silt-sized hollow spherical particles. These spheres can absorb water and hold it in a form that is available for plant use. This is highly desirable for reclaiming soils that have been disturbed during mining operations because these soils tend to be droughty, due to water moving through them quickly. Fly ash that is used for landscaping has limitations of (a) high concentrations of boron, (b) lack of organic matter, (c) high susceptibility to erosion, and (d) sometimes concentrations of undesirable metalloids, such as arsenic (As) or selenium (Se). These limitations can be overcome by growing boron-tolerant plants or waiting for a year for the boron to be leached, by mixing organic materials with the fly ash to provide a healthy soil, and by using fly ash on areas that are flat enough to keep erosion down or by providing for erosion-controlling measures.

TROPICAL SOILS

The minor fluctuations of high temperatures in the tropics is a common aspect of most tropical soils. Tropical soils show as much variety as do soils from temperate regions, so individual soil series need to be managed on an individual basis. For details on specific management practices for tropical soils, see the book by P. A. Sanchez in the References section of this handbook. Some tropical soils are considerably different from temperate region soils because the clays are mainly hydrous oxides instead of the temperate silicate clays. Thus, the properties of hydrous oxides require different techniques in soil management.

Hydrous oxide clays have a very low capacity to hold nutrients so require continual frequent renewal of nutrients by additions of fertilizers or amendments containing the necessary nutrients for adequate plant growth. The low capacity to hold nutrients also requires careful use of lime, as overliming can easily occur resulting in certain nutrient deficiencies or toxicities. An advantage of hydrous oxides is their ability to be worked shortly after a rain. Most silicate clay minerals become very sticky when wet, whereas the hydrous oxides can be worked within a few hours after a rain.

Often weather conditions of high temperatures and abundant rainfall result in tropical rain forests. The soils developed under these conditions are highly weathered and much of the nutrients have been leached to lower layers within the soil. In the rain forest abundant tree growth results in nutrients at lower depths being absorbed and translocated to the above ground leaves and stems. When the leaves and stems fall periodically, the nutrients are returned to the surface soil for use by the present plants growing there. This creates a recycling process of nutrients from lower depths to the vegetation to the topsoil then leached again to the lower layers. Some well-meaning people clear the rain forests and do not consider that the hydrous oxides are fragile. Unless protected from the hot sun, they will soon bake into very hard material (plinthite) that cannot be easily worked. This rapid weathering causes any organic material in the soil to become quickly oxidized, and the organic matter then becomes depleted from the topsoil rather quickly. Unless the organic material is replenished fairly soon and the topsoil is protected from drying, the soil can become ruined and useless for further plant growth.

SUMMARY

We have learned that plants need light, water, oxygen, heat, nutrients, and a means of support. All but light are provided by a soil or soil substitute. Soil is the outer layer of the earth's crust that is able to support plant growth. Soils are formed by physical, chemical, and biological weathering processes, including disintegration, chemical and biological decomposition, hydrolysis, hydration, acidification, dissolution, and oxidation.

The kind of soil that develops depends on the parent material (rocks), topography, climate, living organisms, and time of development. A profile of a vertical cut through a soil usually shows distinct layers or horizons of (A) a topsoil where microorganisms thrive, plant roots grow, and organic matter is present, (B) a subsoil providing reserve water, a place for deep plant roots to anchor, and useful for construction, and (C) parent material just beginning to form soil material. New soils begin to develop when original soils are disturbed and reclaimed during highway construction, landfills, and mining operations. Some tropical soils require management that differs from that of temperate region soils.

REVIEW

What do plants need to grow?
What is soil? How do soils form?
How do the soils appear below the surface?

3

Parts of a Soil
(Soil Constituents)

Air, Water, Minerals, and Organic Matter

PHYSICAL PARTS OF A SOIL

Soils physically consist of soil solids and pore space (Fig. 3.1).
Soil solids are composed of (a) mineral matter such as sand
(coarse particles), silt (fine particles), and clay (very fine particles), and (b) soil organic matter, like decaying plant, animal,
and microbial remains, along with microbial synthates. The pore
space is occupied by soil air and soil water, each of which has a
different makeup than atmospheric air and rainwater. Soil air
often has more carbon dioxide and gases of nitrogen and sulfur
compounds. Soil water has much more dissolved substances in
it than rainwater.

Soil Solids

Soil solids occupy about 50% of a soil. They are made up of about
45% mineral matter and about 5% organic matter, but these proportions vary greatly.

Soil mineral matter consists of very coarse rocks (primary
minerals) and the three main soil parts:

1. *Coarse—Sand* (a primary mineral, silicon dioxide)
2. *Fine—Silts* (both primary or secondary minerals)
3. *Very Fine—Clays* (secondary minerals)

Soil organic matter consists of plant and animal remains
(in various stages of decomposition), microorganisms, and
compounds synthesized by microorganisms.

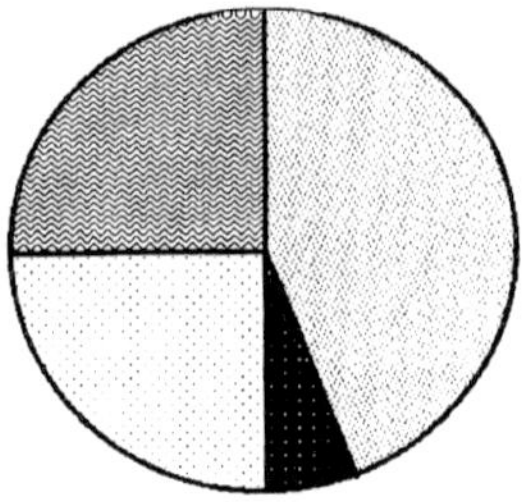

Figure 3.1 Soil volume showing pore space (water and air) and solids (mineral matter and organic matter).

Water

Mineral Matter

Air

Organic Matter

Soil Pore Space

Soil pore space occupies about 50% of a soil and consists of the open space occupied by either air or water. The proportions of air and water that are present can greatly influence plant growth.

Soil air is necessary for plants to grow, but if this component dominates, drought occurs and plant growth suffers.

Soil water is also necessary for plant growth, but if this component dominates, flooding occurs and plant growth also suffers as most plants require a supply of oxygen.

CHEMICAL PARTS OF A SOIL

Soil consists of natural elements, for example, Si, Al, Fe, Ca, Mg, Na, K, Ti, P, and others. Often the elements are present in oxides, sulfides, silicates, and other combinations. These elements or their combined form are present as rocks (primary minerals), clays (secondary minerals), and available nutrients for plants.

BIOLOGICAL PARTS OF A SOIL

Soil contains many life forms (Table 3.1). These can range from large animals, such as ground hogs, snakes, and chipmunks, to small ones, such as moles, earthworms, slugs, centipedes, spiders, mites, and insects (Fig. 3.2), and even to microscopic animals, such as nematodes, protozoa, and rotifers (Fig.3.3).

Plant organisms are also components of the soil and can range from large—roots of trees, shrubs, and all higher plants—to

Table 3.1 Kind, Size, Number, and Weight of Organisms Present in Soils

Organism	Relative Size	Approximate Numbers Found	Biomass Weight (kg/ha)
Microorganisms			
Bacteria	0.1μ–10μ	1–3 billion/g	300–6,000
Fungi	2μ–30μ	10–20 million/g	2,000
Actinomycetes	up to 600μ	400 million/g	1,000
Algae	10μ × 50μ	10,000–3 million/g	5–550
Protozoa	5μ–20μ	up to 1 million/g	200
Rotifers	160μ–2mm	up to 150/g	—
Nematodes	160μ–183cm	up to 1 million/g	10–180
Macroorganisms			
Ants			—
Workers	0.2cm–1.5cm	many thousands/nest	
Queen	5cm	one/nest	
Termites			—
Workers	0.2cm–2.3cm	millions/nest	
Queen	10cm	one/nest	
Earthworms	0.2cm–6.8m	30,000–3 million/g	15–1,100
Collembola (Springtails)	0.2mm–6.0mm	2.5 billion/ha	—
Other insects	1mm–25mm	12,500/ha	—
Slugs (Mollusca)	2mm–80mm	up to 1.5 million/ha	—
Spiders	0.8mm–10mm	2,500/ha	—
Miscellaneous	Varies	Varies	Varies

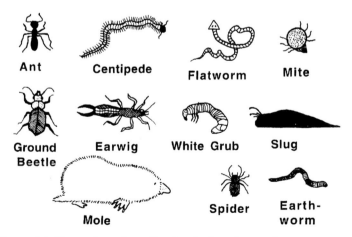

Figure 3.2 Examples of small animals found in soils.

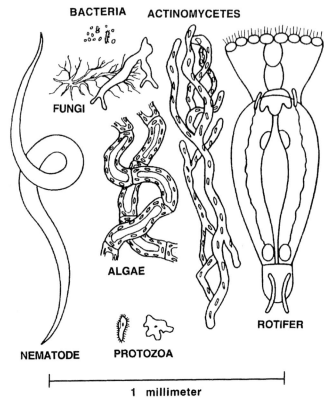

Figure 3.3 Microscopic animals and plants found in soils.

small—microscopic algae, bacteria, fungi (e.g., mycorrhizae), actinomycetes, and viruses (Fig. 3.3).

Considering all this, soil can be visualized as a complicated "living organism." The many diverse organisms that live in or on the soil definitely contribute to soil formation along with the other factors of parent material, topography, climate, and time.

SUMMARY

Soils often consist of solids and spaces (pores) in approximately equal portions. The soil solids are about 5% organic matter and 45% mineral matter, but this varies widely. The organic portion is the decaying plant or animal remains that have been acted on by microbes (the living part of a soil). The mineral matter consists of rocks, sand, silts, and clays. Soil pore space is occupied by water and air with the proportion depending on the weather. Chemically, the soil consists of many natural elements in the form of rocks, clays, and available nutrients. Many kinds of animals and plants grow in or on soils. These are present from microscopic size to very large creatures. The very small plants, such as algae, bacteria, actinomycetes, and fungi are active in soil transformations.

REVIEW

What are the physical parts of a soil?
What is the makeup of the solids in a soil?
What is present in the soil pore spaces?
What are the components of the chemical and
  biological parts of a soil?

4

Physical Properties
of Soils

SOIL TEXTURE

Soil Texture Defined

Soil texture can be defined as the *size and proportion* of the soil particles—sand, silt, and clay (Fig. 4.1)—that are present in a soil.

Sand is the largest—from 0.05 to 2mm—and considered coarse texture; consists of angular spheres or cubes.

Silt is intermediate—from 0.002 to 0.05mm—and considered medium texture; consists of properties between sand and clay.

Clay is the smallest, being less than 0.002mm, and considered fine texture; appears as plate-like or flakes.

Soil Textural Classes

Any individual soil can be placed on the soil textural diagram (Fig. 4.2) when relative amounts of sand, silt, and clay are specified. As a general rule, the type of soil can be determined by feel when squeezed between the fingers. If the soil feels harsh and gritty it would be classified as a sandy soil. One that feels smooth and not sticky or plastic would be a silt soil, and one that is sticky or plastic would be a clay.

Another way to distinguish between soils is their ability to form a ribbon. Soils that will not form a ribbon are sands. Those that form a fragile ribbon are loams; those that easily form a thick

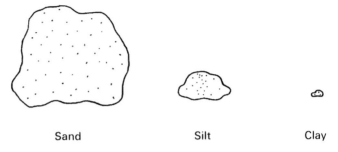

Sand   Silt   Clay

Figure 4.1 Relative size of three main soil solids.

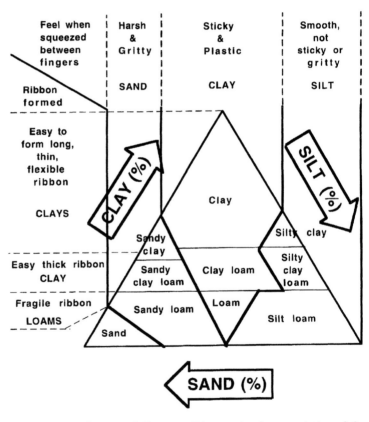

Figure 4.2 Soil textural diagram. Diagnostic characteristics of the various groups of soils are shown.

ribbon are clay loams; and those that easily form a long, thin, flexible ribbon are clays.

To be classified a *sand*, the soil must have more than 45% sand.

To be classified a *clay*, the soil must have more than 20% clay.

Loam is a mixture of sand, silt, and clay in about equal proportions. It is considered "ideal" for growing plants.

Weight of Soils

Particle Density

Weight of the soil solids is called "particle density." For most common mineral soils (soils in which organic matter is usually less than 20%), particle density is about 2.65 g/cm^3. Organic soils (where organic matter is greater than 20%) are usually about half as heavy, with particle density between 1.1 to 1.4 g/cm^3. This measurement would be an important factor to consider if much material was to be transported for topsoiling. Often it would be more economical to transport some form of organic material rather than the heavier mineral soil, especially if one were trying to improve the soil in a landscape area. Also the organic material would be more beneficial for water and nutrient relations for successful plant establishment.

Alteration of Soil Texture

In the field, soil texture is not easily changed. A "typical soil" is considered to have 2,000,000 pounds (or 1,000 tons) in the top six inches over an acre (43,560 sq. ft.). If this soil is categorized as a "loam," it might have 40% sand, 40% silt, and 20% clay. Thus it would contain 400 tons of sand, 400 tons of silt, and 200 tons of clay. To change the texture by five percent, that is, to 45% sand, would require more than 100 tons of sand (four large triaxle truckloads) to be spread and worked into the ground. Even after all this, the soil would still be considered a "loam," and it is doubtful that there would be any noticeable change in the appearance or characteristics of that soil.

On the other hand, for greenhouse conditions (where soil substitute mixtures are made up and altered for use in pots or greenhouse benches) or in containers used for landscape aesthetics, a change in texture is possible and may be desirable to provide adequate aeration and drainage for specialized pot culture. By working with limited amounts of material, soil texture can be changed.

Importance of Soil Texture

Soil texture affects plant growth primarily through air and water relations. Plant roots require oxygen (air) and water in proper proportions to survive and thrive. Movement of air and water into the soil (infiltration) and through the soil (permeability) is essential. Infiltration and permeability are generally higher for sands than silts or clays and should be better for air and water movement. An exception to this would be a sand with a hardpan below the surface preventing free movement of air and water (discussed later in this chapter). A problem with sands, however, is that they do not hold water as long as clays; consequently, sands may drain too rapidly and cause lack of sufficient water for the plants to grow (Fig. 4.3). Therefore, sandy soils require frequent watering or plants growing there will wilt and die. Some clay or silt should be present in a mixture to retain the water for use by plants and make it more convenient for watering. Organic matter holds water even better than clays, so this might be a more desirable alternative in providing plants with a constant supply of water. Organic matter usually has a more open structure than clays and would thereby provide a supply of oxygen needed by the plant roots.

Another factor to consider is the ability of the textural classes to hold nutrients. Sand has no ability for this, silt is low, clay is higher, but organic matter is the highest in ability to hold and supply nutrients for living plants. Consequently, one would be wise to provide sufficient sand to permit adequate aeration and water drainage, some clay for stability, and considerable amounts of organic matter to retain water and nutrients, especially if one is making up a mixture for potting growing plants.

SOIL STRUCTURE

Soil structure is the arrangement of soil particles. The type of soil structure influences the amount and distribution of soil pores that are important in movement of air and water to plants growing in a soil.

Some examples of soil structure are (Fig. 4.4):

a. massive—no definite shape; running together
b. blocky—cube-like, with or without angles

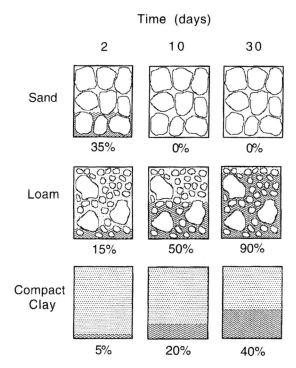

Figure 4.3 Amount of water held by soils. Relative amount of water held by soils depends on amount of sand, loam, and compact clay present.

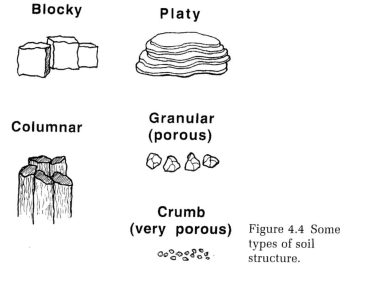

Figure 4.4 Some types of soil structure.

c. platy—flat-like plates, or leaves
d. columnar—columns with rounded tops, or prismatic with level tops
e. granular—rounded porous particles
f. crumb—small rounded, very porous particles

SOIL BULK DENSITY

Soil bulk density is a measure of the weight per unit volume of a soil that includes both solids and pore space. Bulk density is a specific property of a soil and can be best indicated as a range for general soils:

Sandy topsoils have bulk density of about 1.2 to 1.8g/cm³.

Clay topsoils have a bulk density of about 1.0 to 1.6g/cm³.

Compact subsoils may have a bulk density of more than 2.0g/cm³.

Bulk density can initially be decreased by any method of cultivation such as plowing, cultivating, or turning a soil with a shovel; however, with time bulk density usually increases to the maximum indicated.

Pore space is affected by the soil structure (arrangement of soil particles) and is inversely related to bulk density. Plant roots can only grow in the soil pore spaces. Also, the air and water in a soil can only pass through the soil pores. Therefore proper size and distribution of pore spaces are essential for desirable plant growth.

SOIL DEPTH

Soil depth can be considered the "effective root depth" or the area that is favorable for roots. Soil depth varies from very shallow, as in soils close to bedrock and a hard layer (hardpan), to very deep as in soils along streams (Fig. 4.5).

Soil depth is classified by inches into:

very shallow = less than 10 inches

shallow = from 10 to 20 inches

moderately deep = from 20 to 36 inches

deep = from 36 to 60 inches

very deep = more than 60 inches

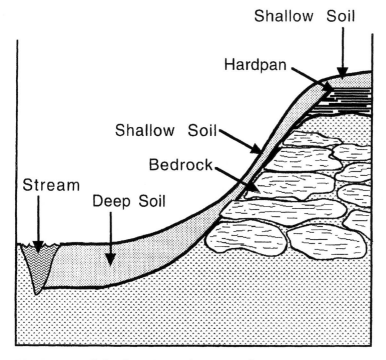

Figure 4.5 Soil depth varies with topography.

Interrupted Water Flow

Hardpans, at any depth, resist root and water penetration and may result in water accumulating on the surface (water logging) (Fig. 4.6). Similar conditions may arise when sand or gravel are placed below soil in pots causing interrupted water flow (Fig. 4.7). Water does not pass from the soil into the sand or gravel until the upper layer is saturated. This could cause root damage.

Can Soil Depth Be Changed?

Soil depth results from soil weathering in place, with the movement of soil from the top of hills to lower portions, or the transport of soil by water (through erosion) followed by deposition along streams. Some of the deepest soils are found along streams. Soil depth can be increased by putting soil into raised planters or by mounding soil on top of other soil.

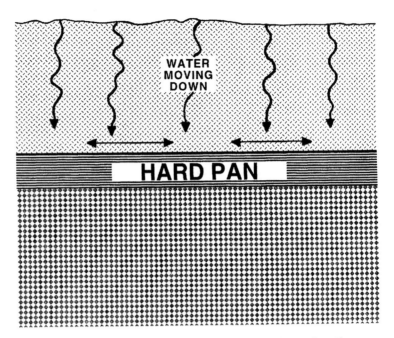

Figure 4.6 Hardpans restrict water movement through soil.

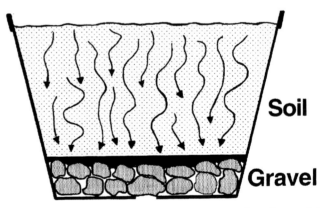

Figure 4.7 Discontinuous boundary between soil and gravel in pots prevents rapid flow of water.

Importance of Soil Depth

Soil depth is important in that it determines water- and nutrient-holding capacities affecting rooting. Usually deep soils have more water, nutrients, and plant roots than shallow soils. However, water relations vary with soil depth. Water is held in the bottom six-inch layer of a container at the same percentage whether the soil depth is 12 inches, 24 inches, or 36 inches (Fig. 4.8). This means that deeper soils, especially in containers, require more frequent watering to keep the upper roots functioning than those in shallow containers.

SOIL AERATION

Respiration

All living organisms, including plants, respire, that is, use oxygen (O_2) and release carbon dioxide (CO_2):

$$\text{Food} + O_2 \rightarrow CO_2 + H_2O + \ldots$$

Decomposition

Oxygen is also used during the process of organic matter decomposition:

$$\text{Plant or Animal Remains} + O_2 \rightarrow CO_2 + H_2O + \ldots$$

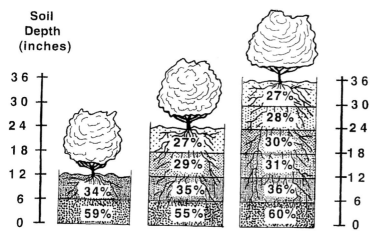

Soil Depth (inches)

Figure 4.8 Soil depth determines amount of water held (*Arbori-culture* by Harris, R. W., 1983. Reprinted by permission of Prentice-Hall, Inc., Upper Saddle River, NJ.)

Gaseous Exchange—
Why Is It Important?

Gases move by diffusion from an area of high concentration toward an area of low concentration (Fig. 4.9). Gases present in soil include nitrogen, oxygen, carbon dioxide, and a few others. An exchange of these gases in soils is important for healthy plant growth (Fig. 4.10). In well-aerated (well-drained) soil, gaseous exchange between soil air and the atmosphere must be rapid enough to prevent deficiency of oxygen or toxicity of carbon dioxide for normal root functions. Soils that are dry permit CO_2 and O_2 to move easily, whereas wet or flooded soils restrict gaseous movement (Fig. 4.11).

Relation of Pore Size
to Gaseous Exchange

The size of soil pores becomes important in this gaseous exchange (Fig. 4.12). Ideal gaseous movement would occur in sands that have

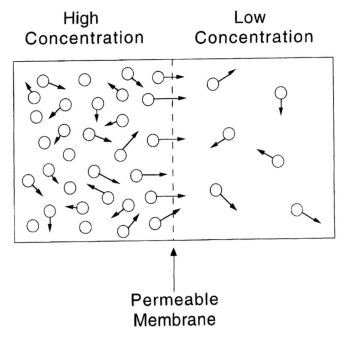

Figure 4.9 Diffusion illustrated. Diagrammatical sketch of gas molecules moving from areas of high concentration to areas of low concentration (diffusion).

Plant Root Hair

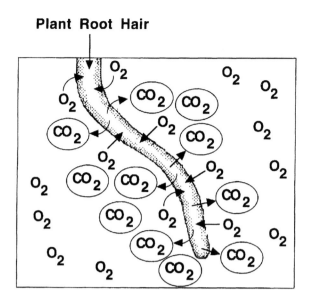

Figure 4.10 Plant root respiration. Plant roots absorb oxygen gas (O_2) needed for growth in exchange for carbon dioxide gas (CO_2) given off during respiration.

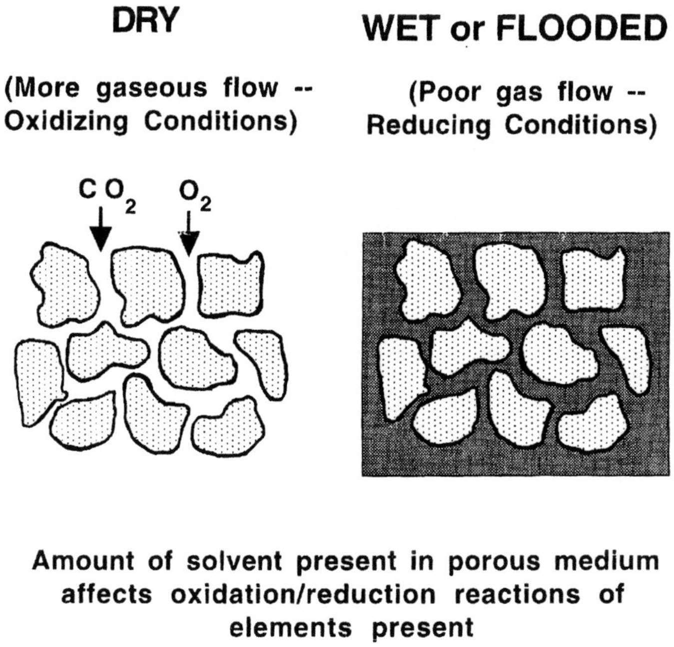

DRY

(More gaseous flow -- Oxidizing Conditions)

CO_2 O_2

WET or FLOODED

(Poor gas flow -- Reducing Conditions)

Amount of solvent present in porous medium affects oxidation/reduction reactions of elements present

Figure 4.11 Flow of gas in dry versus flooded soils.

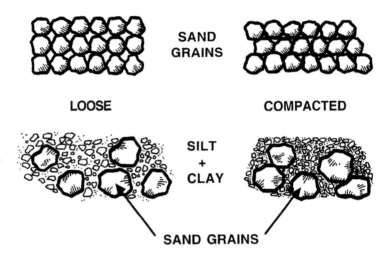

Figure 4.12 Diagram comparing loose versus compacted sand grains and loose soil versus compacted soil.

an abundance (i.e., 30–50%) of macropores (large size); very little gaseous exchange can occur in clays that are dominated by micropores (small size).

How Soil Heterogeneity Affects Aeration

Within a well-aerated soil there may be areas that are poorly aerated. This would be where soil has been compacted under a lot of traffic or where clay has accumulated. Most soils have three main horizons:

A   Horizon = the biochemically active topsoil

B   Horizon = the subsoil, where clays often accumulate, and

C   Horizon = which has been recently developed from underlying rocks

Usually, these three horizons have considerably different characteristics and would vary greatly with respect to aeration.

Seasonal Variation of Soil Aeration

Soils in winter and spring usually have high amounts of moisture that would favor low oxygen and high carbon dioxide. Conversely, soils in summer and fall are often dry, favoring high amounts of oxygen. However, this may be offset by soils being warmer, resulting in greater amounts of carbon dioxide from organic matter decomposition.

Effects of Aeration on Higher Plants and Microbes

Both higher plants and microbes need oxygen for root growth, water absorption, and nutrient absorption. Poor aeration may cause accumulation of toxins that could result in a nutrient deficiency developing, even though adequate amounts of the specific nutrient were present.

Compaction

Soil compaction develops any time soil is compressed (Fig. 4. 12). The amount that develops depends on (1) the pressure exerted, (2) duration, and (3) frequency. For instance, compaction is aggravated by heavy machinery; when the machine remains on the soil for a period of time; and repeated pressure, such as constant walking, even by dogs. Soils are particularly susceptible to compaction when they contain large amounts of water. Therefore, whenever a soil is wet, avoid compaction by keeping off of it.

Farmland that has been converted to uses by landscape architects may have had plow pans developed by repeated plowing with tractors at the same depth. This causes a hard layer called a "hardpan" that interferes with movement of air, water, nutrients, and plant roots (Fig. 4.6). A soil should be examined for plow pans, and if found, these pans must be broken with rippers to prevent problems of flooding, drought, or nutrient deficiencies.

Prevention of Soil Compaction

Prevention of soil compaction is easier than the means of remedying it. Specific suggestions include:

- Do not cultivate a wet soil.
- Do not till a soil after loosening.
- Schedule landscape maintenance when soil is as dry as possible.
- Keep travel on paths—away from plantings.
- Use lightweight vehicles with large, smooth, low-pressure tires.

- Spread thick, coarse mulch on the soil surface to disperse the load.

Rejuvenating Poor Soil Structure

A number of techniques can be used to improve poor soil structure:

1. Compacted soil when dry could be ripped or deep plowed, then rough graded.
2. Addition of organic matter is fine, but often too little is added to be beneficial; in warm climates decomposition is very rapid and may require larger amounts of organic materials than in temperate climates.
3. If extra soil is needed, the soil texture should be the same or coarser (more sand) than the indigenous soil.
4. Fill soil should not be placed on compacted soil without loosening the compacted portion; otherwise, moisture and aeration problems, such as wet spots, may develop.

Amending a Soil
to Improve Aeration

A soil can be amended to improve aeration only in pots or planters, but is not practical on a large scale. Amendments are only effective if material is added in the amount of 25 to 50% of the soil volume. When sand is used it must be added at more than 45% to be effective. Mineral amendments, such as perlite or vermiculite, can be effectively used. Also organic amendments of peat moss, peat (muck), sawdust, bark, manure, or composts can be incorporated into the soil, but these decompose with time and may require additional nitrogen to prevent nitrogen deficiencies of plants to be grown.

SOIL WATER

Kinds of Soil Water Related
to Plant Growth

Water in soils for plant growth can be divided into available and unavailable. These two conditions depend on how much water is present and how it is held in the soil.

Permanent Wilting Point.   As the amount of water is withdrawn from a soil, there comes a point, called the "permanent wilting point," or "wilting coefficient" at which plants can no longer use the water (Fig. 4.13). All water below this point is held so strongly that plants are not able to use it.

Field Capacity.   As water is added to a soil, there comes a point, called the "field capacity," above which plants can no longer use the water (Fig. 4. 13).

Gravitational Water.   All water present in amounts more than field capacity is considered "saturated" (Fig. 4. 13) or an excess, that is, gravitational water, that must be drained from a soil fairly quickly or plant growth will suffer.

Plant Available Water

Plant available water is that held in the soil *between permanent wilting point and field capacity* (Fig. 4.14). A soil can be adjusted to field capacity (maximum amount of water available for plants)

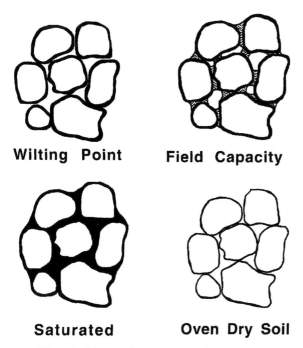

Wilting Point   **Field Capacity**

Saturated   **Oven Dry Soil**

Figure 4.13 Water held in soil. Extent to which water is held in soils under conditions of oven dry, wilting point, field capacity, and saturated.

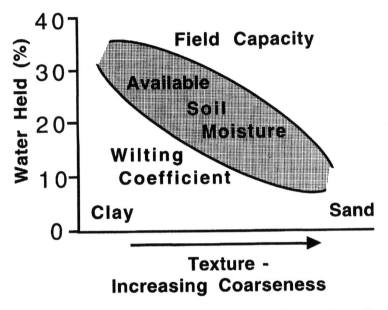

Figure 4.14 Plant available soil water. Diagram showing that soil moisture available for plants is water held between the wilting coefficient and field capacity.

quite easily by saturating the soil with water. After allowing all excess water to drain out by gravity, the remaining water will be at field capacity. Water that is held in soil at field capacity is present in small pores (capillaries), adsorbed onto soil particles, or held between the clay layers. There is some capillary water that is held below the permanent wilting point.

Effect of Water on Plants and Microbes

Water is required for many plant processes, such as (a) photosynthesis—the process whereby plants manufacture their own food supply to grow and reproduce; (b) solvent water for holding nutrients so they can be absorbed by plant roots; (c) solvent water for keeping nutrients in solution within a plant and transported to all plant parts (translocation); (d) water for the air-conditioning system of a plant (transpiration); and (e) water for maintaining turgor (keeping cell contents from drying out), important in growth of shoot tips and extension of roots.

Water, also required by microorganisms, regulates the number and types of microbes present along with the extent of their activity. In a healthy soil, many biochemical reactions require microbial activities.

Landscape plants are more affected by water than any other factor. Problems arise from floods, lack of water (drought), adequate aeration, lack of air (suffocation), or unacceptable, salty water. Excess gravitational water cannot be used by plants and may be detrimental if present for more than a few days.

Plants grown in containers frequently suffer from water problems. Pots usually have a drainage hole at the bottom and sometimes sand or gravel is used at the bottom, supposedly to aid in draining out excess water. According to hydrologic principles, these conditions create a boundary that prevents the normal flow of water out of the pot. The sand or gravel creates a distinct layer that is different from the potting medium above. Before water can flow into the sand or gravel, the medium above must be oversaturated with water (Fig. 4.7). This creates anaerobic conditions throughout the pot and plants suffer from lack of oxygen. To prevent these problems, one should use a potting mix that contains mixtures of coarse organic ma-terials, such as peat, sphagnum peat moss, or sawdust, and inorganic materials, such as sand, vermiculite, perlite, or porous volcanic rock, but no gravel in the bottom of containers.

Importance of Water at Planting or Transplanting

Seeding a Lawn

When growing grass for ground cover, the grass seeds must be kept moist for germination and early growth. Seeds can be kept moist either by frequent irrigation or by applying a mulch that will hold the moisture for the new plants. Often grass seeds, especially Kentucky bluegrass, require up to four weeks to germinate. A mulch applied at seeding helps to maintain adequate moisture, but frequent sprinkling with water, particularly if the weather is hot and dry, may be needed. The newly germinated grass seeds must not be allowed to dry out during the early stages of growth. If they do happen to dry, they will die and further watering will be of no benefit. Timeliness of watering is critical to establishing a desirable lawn.

Planting or Transplanting Flowers, Trees, or Shrubs

A critical time in the life of a plant is at planting or transplanting. The best time to plant trees or shrubs is when they are dormant; however, there may be difficulty in digging the plants and replanting them when the ground is frozen or very wet. A very important part of planting or transplanting is to be sure to *thoroughly water the new planting immediately after setting.* This ensures proper settling of the soil around the plants and improves contact of the roots with the soil. If landscape plants are transplanted during the growing season, it is advisable to remove some of the upper parts of the plant when first set. This is necessary as the plant requires time for the roots to become intimately associated with the soil particles so that water can be absorbed by the plant. If this is not done, there may be substantial wilting from the large number of leaves on the plant tops, resulting in a setback of growth or even death of the plant.

Movement of Water Within a Soil (Internal Drainage)

Water needed by plants moves in a soil either by capillary movement, saturated flow, or unsaturated flow. Each of these types can be important to plant growth.

Capillary Movement

The small pores in a soil (*capillaries*) hold considerable water that is available for plants (Fig. 4.15). Usually one considers a capillary as a small tube; however, in soils many capillary pores are not straight. Water held in the capillaries is attracted to the soil particles by adhesion. The number and extent of capillaries are related to soil texture and structure. Clay soils have very many capillaries, but sands often have very few, if any. Soil structures that are granular, crumb, or columnar usually have more capillaries than other types.

Saturated Flow

When all the soil pores are filled with water, water moves by saturated flow (Fig. 4.16). How quickly the water flows is related to (a) the *hydraulic force*, often called the "water head" or "height" (the greater the water height, the more saturated flow will occur)

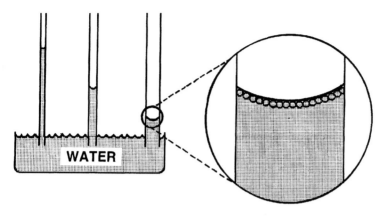

Figure 4.15 Capillary water flow. Diagram showing how water rises more in small capillaries than in large ones.

Water Movement Beginning

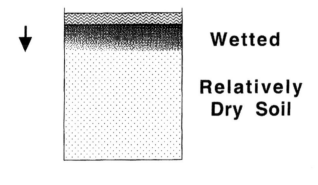

Wetted

Relatively
Dry Soil

Water Movement With Time

Wetted
Area

Figure 4.16 Saturated flow in soils. Diagram depicting water movement by saturated flow.

(Fig. 4.17), and (b) the *hydraulic conductivity* or ease of travel of the water through the pores. The saturated flow is also governed by the soil texture and structure. Coarse textured sandy soils are open with large pores, resulting in faster saturated flow than in fine textured soils (clays); however, the flow will probably be more direct and downward. Saturated movement through a fine textured soil is often slow, but more water will move laterally with time than would occur in a coarse textured soil.

Unsaturated Flow

Unsaturated flow of water in a soil only occurs when the macropores (large) are mostly filled with air and the micropores (capillaries) are filled with both water and air (Fig. 4.18). There will be few to many air space voids present with unsaturated flow. These voids of air result in very slow movement by unsaturated flow. Soil texture and structure also are important in this type of water movement.

Stratified Soils

Hardpans

A soil that has a hard layer will restrict water movement downward (Fig. 4.6). This often occurs in fine textured clays but can also occur in sands. When downward movement of water is prevented, the water flows horizontally from the center of applica-

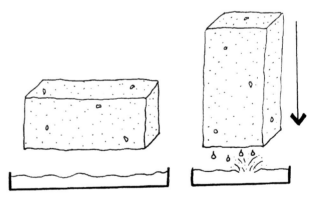

Figure 4.17 Water head illustrated. Two sponges showing how head of water in a vertical sponge results in flow out while lesser water head of the horizontal sponge remains in place.

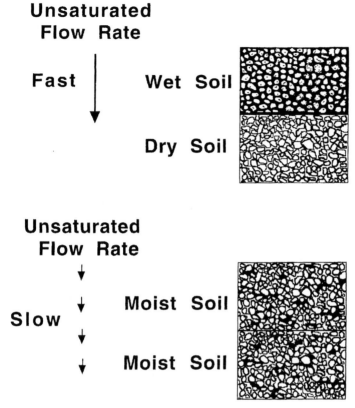

Figure 4.18 Water flow through unsaturated soils. Unsaturated flow rate is fast from wet soil to dry soil, but slow through thoroughly moist soil.

tion and may eventually penetrate the hardpan. Hardpans may result in flooding, if more water is applied than the soil can hold above the pan. Likewise, when drought occurs on soils with hardpans, no reserve water can be obtained from the lower depths, resulting in undesirable wilting of plants.

Soil Over Gravel in Pots

Often people place sand or gravel in the bottom of pots below the soil or soil substitute thinking that this will improve drainage (Fig. 4.7). On the contrary, this creates a distinct layer between the soil and the coarse material below causing drainage problems. Flow through this disjointed layer only begins after the above soil becomes saturated. But the soil no longer drains freely, resulting in a "perched water table" that excludes needed oxygen for adequate root growth and absorption of water and nutrients. Sometimes roots resist penetrating this zone.

These conditions of disjointed substances can occur in (a) pots having sand or gravel below the soil; (b) bottoms of planters covered with gravel; and (c) drainage pipes lined with gravel.

Artificial Drainage of Soils

Subsurface or Underground Drains

Underground drains can be constructed of many substances, including (a) air (mole drains)—formed by pulling a pointed cylinder plug, usually 7–10 inches in diameter, through a soil at a desired depth (inexpensive, but clogs readily); (b) clay tiles (older and not used now); (c) perforated plastic pipes (Fig. 4.19) (usually the desired type of drain today). All drains are placed in the zone of maximum water accumulation. If installed correctly, the water entering the drain moves downward to an outlet usually into a nearby stream. The spacing of drains within a field will depend on soil characteristics. When drainage is required, engineers should design the system. If drains are improperly installed, they will not remove the undesirable gravitational water.

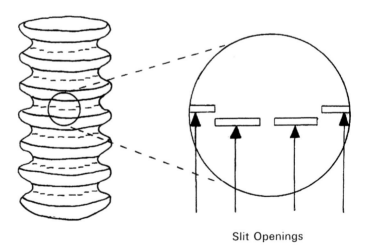

Slit Openings

Figure 4.19 Perforated plastic pipes for drainage.

Drains Around Buildings

During construction of a building with a basement wall below grade, provision must be made to keep water from building pressure against the external wall. This is usually accomplished by installing an underground drain near the footer of the basement wall so that any water coming against the wall will be directed away from the building to a satisfactory outlet. Without adequate drains, foundation walls may crack and if enough pressure is exerted may even break, resulting in expensive repairs. Be sure that no material that will restrict drainage, such as compacted clay, is placed near the foundation wall.

Benefits of Internal Drainage of Soils

Alternate freezing and thawing, resulting from poorly drained sites, can crack foundations, disrupt roadbeds resulting in "potholes," and can push plants upward or "heave" them out of the soil. This often breaks the plant root system and can even cause death of certain plants.

Proper internal drainage of soils eliminates water logging. Adequately drained soils contain more oxygen for plant roots, more available water for plants, more available nutrients for plants, better conditions for organic matter decomposition with release of nutrients, and less chance for accumulation of toxic elements than poorly drained soils. All these conditions present in well-drained soils are beneficial for more efficient growth of plants.

Natural Wetlands

Some soils are naturally wet and are often called bogs, swamps, or marshes. Many are now classified as "natural wetlands." There is an increasing concern about preserving these areas as habitats for wildlife, for grazing of livestock, for catch basins permitting recharge of water aquifers, and for collecting sediment that would otherwise end up in streams. In the last few years, wetlands have been found beneficial for detoxifying and purifying water from acid mine drainage. Recent governmental regulations require that any natural wetland must remain as such and cannot be drained for agricultural or other purposes. For the size required for this designation, check the latest federal regulations. More information on wetlands can be found in the references under Horowitz (1978), U.S. Department of Agriculture (1996), Cowardin et al. (1979), "Special Issue on Wetlands" (1995), and Wentz (1981).

SUMMARY

Soil texture means the size of soil particles, that is, sand, silt, and clay (from largest to smallest), and proportions of each present. The proportions of textural sizes divide specific soils into sands, loams, and clays. Weight of the individual soil particles is the particle density and is important in indicating soil properties and ease of transport for construction. Soil texture is difficult to change in the field, but in greenhouse conditions, clay soils can economically be amended with sand to correct drainage. Soil texture is important for plants in water/aeration relations, particularly movement of water into and through a soil, and in providing a storehouse for plant nutrients.

In contrast to soil texture, soil structure is the arrangement of soil particles into categories of platy, columnar, blocky, or granular. Soil bulk density is a weight measurement of soils and includes both the solids and pores which are important in movement of air and water through a soil. The depth of a soil is the effective root growth area and is classified from very shallow to very deep. Soil aeration is essential for respiration and plant growth as oxygen (O_2) moves through soil pores to plant roots.

Respiration and decomposition are similar in that both use oxygen and a food source and produce water and carbon dioxide as end products, but decomposition differs in that microorganisms are involved in the process and can produce other distinctly different by-products. Gaseous exchange in soils is important for roots to have a supply of oxygen and to remove carbon dioxide (CO_2) formed during respiration away from the plant root. This gaseous movement is affected by the size and distribution of the soil pores. Usually more moisture is present in soils during winter and spring causing lower amounts of air, whereas, in warmer and drier seasons O_2 is more abundant for plant growth. However, greater microbial activity also occurs in the summer creating more CO_2 than in the colder seasons.

Soils become compacted by frequent movement of man, animals, or equipment over them, especially when the soils are wet. This compaction results in restriction of plant roots with less growth. Compaction can be reduced by keeping off of the soil as much as possible. Soil structure can be improved by ripping compacted layers, adding organic matter and sand, and providing drainage. Soil aeration can be improved economically only on a small scale as in greenhouse or landscape pots.

Water for plant growth is classified as available (water between permanent wilting point and field capacity) and unavailable (below the permanent wilting point and above field capacity as gravitational water). Water is essential for most plant metabolic processes, including photosynthesis, nutrient and water absorption, translocation, and transpiration, in growing plants and is also required for microbial growth and reproduction. At seeding, water is essential to maintain growth of the early seedlings until they can produce their own food and develop roots adequate to absorb water. Water is very important during transplanting as the plant is undergoing shock until its roots can be once again established for water and nutrient absorption.

Water moves in soils as capillary (very small pores), saturated flow (pores filled with water), and unsaturated flow (pores partially filled with water). Capillary water is the form usually absorbed by plant roots; saturated flow is important in removing excess gravitational water that could be detrimental to plants; and unsaturated flow provides water to plants during "normal" conditions. Stratified soils occur as hardpans or where soil is placed over sand or gravel in pots; both of these conditions restrict water movement and would be undesirable for plant growth. Subsurface drains include mole drains, clay tile, and plastic pipes. Proper internal drainage of soils results in better conditions for plant growth and decomposition processes.

REVIEW

What is meant by soil texture?
Are the soil textural classes used in identifying a soil different from "soil texture?"
How is soil weight important?
Can soil texture be changed?
Why is soil texture important?
How does soil structure differ from soil texture?
What are the different types of soil structure?
What is soil bulk density? How is this important?
What is meant by soil depth? How is it classified?
How is water flowing through a soil interrupted?

(continued) ➡

REVIEW (continued)

What is involved in soil aeration? Why is it important?

How do respiration and decomposition differ?

Why is gaseous exchange important in soils?

How do pore size and soil heterogeneity affect gaseous exchange?

How do changing seasons affect soil aeration?

What is soil compaction, why is it important, and how can it be prevented?

Can poor soil structure be improved? How?

Can soil aeration be improved? How?

What kinds of water affecting plant growth are present in soils?

What is meant by wilting point, field capacity, or gravitational water? How does each of these affect plant growth?

Why is water so important to plants and microbes?

Why is water so important at seeding or planting?

What are the types of water movement within a soil? How are these important to plants?

Explain the difference between saturated and unsaturated flow in soils?

How do soils become stratified? Why is this important?

Describe the different kinds of artificial soil drainage and indicate the desirable and undesirable effects of each.

Why is soil internal drainage so important?

5

Movement of Water
Across Soils (Erosion)

Erosion is the physical wearing away of the land surface by running water, wind, or ice. Soil or rock is initially detached by falling water, running water, wind, ice or freezing conditions, or gravity. Movement of the rock or soil may follow. Erosion is the combination of detachment and movement of soil or rock.

TYPES OF WATER EROSION

Water erosion can be subdivided into either natural or man-made.

Natural or Geological Erosion

Natural or geologic erosion does not require the presence of man. This process has been going on from the moment that land masses were uplifted. An example of geologic erosion is the Grand Canyon in Arizona.

Accelerated Erosion

Man-made erosion is also called "accelerated erosion" as it is more rapid than natural erosion. Changes that man or animals have made to the soil by cultivation, construction, or any movement of earth often result in loss of soil by erosion.

TYPES OF ACCELERATED EROSION

Accelerated erosion involves raindrop erosion, sheet erosion, surface flow, and landscapes. For raindrop erosion to occur, there must be detachment of soil particles followed by either transportation or compaction. Sheet erosion is the slow wearing away of the surface of soil. Surface flow occurs when sufficient water collects to run downhill, resulting in small soil cuts (rills) that often develop into large ruts (gullies). Landslides or slips occur when large chunks of soil move as a unit downhill, often resulting in drops of several feet or more.

Raindrop Erosion

As rain falls, the drops strike the soil surface moving the soil particles with energy being expended in three kinds of ways: (a) *detachment*—soil particles are broken into smaller pieces, (b) *transportation*—small soil grains are moved to a new location as they splash into the air; movement can be downward, to sides, or up eventually acting as a smoothing agent, or (c) *compaction*—raindrops compact soil surface on bare soil forming a crust, resulting in running the soil particles together (puddling) so that air and water can no longer enter the soil. This causes loss of infiltration and results in runoff.

Sheet Erosion

Sheet erosion describes loss of soil over a wide area. This type of erosion occurs so gradual that it is hardly noticeable from day to day. However, with time the soil eventually disappears and is lost for use.

Surface Flow

Rill Formation.   When enough rain falls to accumulate, the water on the soil surface concentrates and begins to flow downhill toward the oceans. Flowing of the concentrated water begins with small channels (*rills*) that show distinct cuts on the soil surface (Fig. 5.1). These small cuts can be covered by normal cultivation.

Gully Formation.   If much rain falls, the accumulated water flows through the rills, cutting deeper channels (*gullies*) that are too large to be covered by normal cultivation (Fig. 5.1).

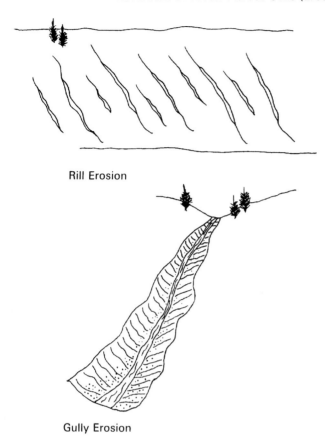

Rill Erosion

Gully Erosion

Figure 5.1 Sketch of erosion by small rill channels and deep gullies.

Gullies can be classified as to activity or shape.

Gullies Based on Activity

Active gullies are those that have their sides bare of vegetation and are subject to further erosion at the next rainfall.

Inactive gullies are those that have their sides covered with sufficient vegetation so that they will be stabilized and not erode further.

Gullies Based on Shape

V-shaped gullies have sides of subsoil that resist cutting. Usually these are soils with a clay base.

U-shaped gullies have sides of subsoil that is friable, result-ing in vertical wall cuts that easily collapse as erosion progresses.

Landslides (Slips)

Certain soils are susceptible to slipping or movement downhill. Three conditions are necessary for this to occur (Fig. 5.2):

1. *Slope steep enough to slide,*
2. Slowly permeable or *impermeable* (impervious) *subsoil layer,* and
3. Enough water in the soil to *fully saturate the soil layer above the impermeable layer.*

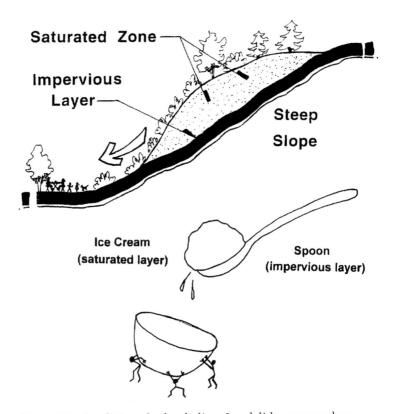

Figure 5.2 Conditions for land slips. Landslides occur when soils on steep slopes become saturated with water above an impervious layer.

Remedies for this condition are to regrade the slope to be less steep or redirect the water entering above the slip so that it does not saturate the upper soil.

FACTORS THAT DETERMINE
EXTENT OF EROSION

The extent of erosion that occurs in a soil depends on five factors, that is, the *amount of rainfall*, the *intensity of rainfall*, the *duration of rainfall*, the *seasonal distribution of rainfall*, and the *amount of surface flow*. All of these factors interact and must be considered collectively to properly evaluate the anticipated erosion that may occur or the erosion that has already happened.

Amount of Rainfall

Amount of rainfall is probably most important in determining the extent of erosion. This is measured by the volume of water falling on a given area, expressed as acre-inches or hectare-millimeters fallen.

Intensity of Rainfall

Intensity of rainfall is the amount of rain fallen over a certain time period (rate). A given rate may last only a short time, for example, 3 inches per hour for a two-minute duration equals one-tenth of an inch rain total. Thus, intensity of rainfall is not always a good indicator of runoff or erosion from a storm.

Terms used for rate in inches of rainfall per hour:

Gentle rain   less than 0.25 inches

Moderate rain   from 0.25 to 0.50 inches

Heavy rain   from 0.5 to 2.0 inches

Severe rain   more than 2.0 inches

Duration of Rainfall

Duration of rainfall is the amount of time that rain actually falls. An "excessive storm" is one that lasts less than an hour with the total amount of rainfall of more than 0.8 inches. Duration and intensity will determine the total amount of rain that falls.

Duration (minutes)	Average Intensity (inches/hour)	Total Amount (inches/hour)
8	6.00	0.80
20	2.40	0.80
40	1.20	0.80
60	0.80	0.80
120	0.70	1.40
180	0.67	2.00

Seasonal Distribution of Rainfall

The part of the year that rain falls will partially determine the extent of erosion. If a lot of rain falls when the soil is exposed (just after clearing or plowing), much erosion will occur. If the soil is covered with plants during a certain time of year, erosion is retarded.

Amount of Surface Flow

How much surface flow occurs depends on the mass (weight) of water present and the velocity (speed) of the downhill movement. The mass of water present is represented by the amount of rainfall and the velocity is related to the steepness and length of slope over which the water is flowing. Water tends to concentrate more on long slopes.

SUMMARY

Erosion is the removal of soil by running water, wind, or ice. Erosion by man (accelerated erosion) is either by raindrop, sheet, or surface flow into rills or gullies. Gullies are classified by the amount of vegetation covering them into active, with no vegetation, or inactive, being covered with vegetation and no longer subject to erosion. Gullies are also classified by shape, that is, V-shaped or U-shaped according to the resistance of the soil to cutting action by the running water. Land slips occur when three conditions are met: steep slope, an impermeable soil layer, and soil above this layer being saturated with water. The extent that erosion occurs is related to amount, intensity, duration, and seasonal distribution of rainfall, resulting in the amount of water flowing across the soil surface.

REVIEW

What is erosion?
What are the different kinds of accelerated
   erosion?
How are gullies classified?
What conditions cause land to slip?
What determines the extent of erosion that
   occurs?

6

Nature of Soil Erodibility

Inherent properties of a soil determine the extent to which that soil will erode. These properties are soil texture, soil structure, soil permeability, and the amount of soil organic matter.

SOIL TEXTURE

Soil texture consists of a mixture of soil particle sizes of sand, silt, and clay. Soil texture is also related to water movement into the soil (*infiltration*) and water movement through a soil (*permeability*).

Particle Sizes

Sand grains are large and difficult to move; however, they are easily detached.

Clay particles often stick together and therefore are difficult to detach; however, once detached the clays remain suspended and are easily carried and separated from the original soil mass by water.

Silt is intermediate in size between sand and clay, but silt is both easily detached and easily transported. Thus, any soil that has large amounts of silt will erode easily.

Water Movement Through Soils

Infiltration. Water moves into and within a soil through the large macropores and only a very limited amount in the small micropores (Fig. 6. 1). Sandy soils have many large pores allowing water to move into the soils by infiltration. Conversely, clay soils have many microspores through which water passes only very slowly (Fig. 6.2). Therefore, during a moderate storm, runoff and erosion would be greater from a soil with more fine textured clays than from a soil where coarse texture dominates.

Permeability.   Once water enters a soil, it flows within the soil. The extent of internal movement of water in a soil is the permeability of that soil.

SOIL STRUCTURE

Soil Aggregate and Aggregation Defined

A soil aggregate is a soil granule or soil crumb consisting of a number of soil grains, that is, silt or clay, held together by a cementing substance. Aggregation is the condition of a soil having many individual aggregates (Fig. 6.3). Soils that have many large stable aggregate are more permeable and are difficult to detach and erode. An aggregate has stability when it is not broken easily by water. Soil aggregates help keep the soil receptive to rapid infiltration of water and keep water from moving over the soil and eroding it.

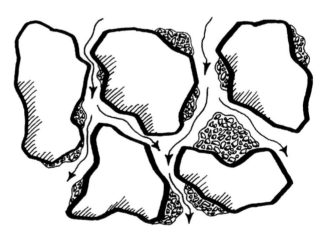

Figure 6.1. Ease of water movement through large pores (macropores) in a soil. In dry conditions water is held in small pores. Any flow would be through the large pores.

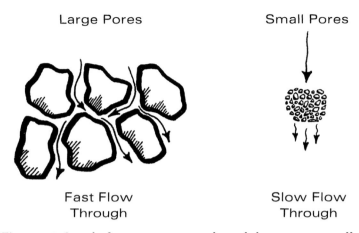

Figure 6.2 Speed of water movement through large versus small pores.

Factors Affecting Size and Stability of Aggregates

The size and stability of soil aggregates are affected by soil texture, kinds of ions present, types of clays present, presence of soil organic matter, presence of cementing substances, and the cropping history of the soil.

Soil Texture.   Usually a soil that has large amounts of clay will have large aggregates. The ability of aggregates to clump together (*flocculation*) is also important as this permits water to infiltrate and not runoff, thereby reducing erosion.

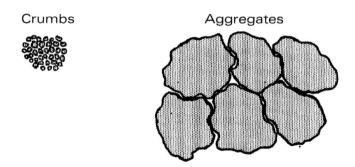

Figure 6.3 Small soil crumbs can become large aggregates by cementation in soils.

Kinds of Ions Present in Soils.   The presence of large amounts of calcium (Ca) in a soil produces great flocculation which is desirable for deterring erosion and providing a suitable medium for root growth. Calcium is often added to soils in the form of limestone. On the other hand, presence of large amounts of potassium (K), magnesium (Mg), and especially sodium (Na) are detrimental for adequate flocculation.

Type of Clay Mineral Present.   Clays in soils can be either hydrous oxides (in the tropics) or silicate clays (in temperate regions). Hydrous oxides of aluminum (Al) or iron (Fe) in the tropics are well aggregated. The aggregates of this type of clay do not stick together when wet. Shortly after a rain one can step onto these tropical soils without getting the shoes muddy.

Silicate clays consist of crystal units of silica and alumina sheets. A silica layer has four oxygen atoms surrounding each silicon atom, whereas an alumina layer has six oxygen atoms around each aluminum atom. Silicate clays are classified on the basis of the ratio of number of silica to alumina layers as a general means of grouping soil that have similar inherent properties. The 1:1 clays, that is, one layer of silica to one layer of alumina, are generally well aggregated. The 2:1 clays, with two layers of silica to one layer of alumina, are generally poorly aggregated.

Presence of Organic Matter.   The amount of organic matter in soils greatly affects soil erodibility. The more organic matter that is present the larger the size and stability of the aggregates. This is directly related to the amount of cementing substances present.

Presence of Cementing Substances.   Cementing substances that improve aggregate formation include organic matter, microbial synthates, clay, limestone, or Ca, and sometimes Fe.

Cropping History of the Soil.   A soil that has been idle for years will have large stable aggregates along with root and plant residues that will resist erosion. Also, any soil mixed with organic matter that is decomposing will produce stable aggregates that resist erosion. However, repeated cultivation of a soil will break apart aggregates and will erode easily.

SOIL ORGANIC MATTER

As the amount of organic matter present in a soil increases, the number of stable aggregates also increase. This results in increased permeability, increased infiltration, and consequently, decreased runoff and erosion. Under very hot and dry environments, the compounds in soil organic matter rearrange creating a water repellent condition. This can be prevented by keeping the soil moist, by mulching, or sometimes by applying lime.

SOIL PERMEABILITY

Soil permeability is classified by the rate of water flowing through a saturated soil. These soil permeability classes are very slow, slow, moderately slow, moderate, moderately rapid, rapid, and very rapid (Table 6. 1). If the permeability of a soil increases, more water can flow into the soil and there would be less flowing across the soil, meaning less runoff and erosion.

USE OF A NOMOGRAPH TO
EVALUATE SOIL ERODIBILITY
USING THE FOUR FACTORS ABOVE

A nomograph has been devised (Wischmeier and Smith, USDA Agriculture Handbook #537) to evaluate the erodibility of a specific soil when sufficient information about that soil is available (Fig. 6.4). The information needed is texture (percent silt and very fine sand and percent sand), amount of organic matter, kind of soil structure, and the permeability. The soil erodibility (or K) factor can then be read directly. These erodibility factors can be compared from one soil to another and will directly influence how easily a specific soil will erode with respect to other soils. Soil structure in the nomograph is rated from good to poor as very fine granular, fine granular, medium or coarse granular, and blocky, platy, or massive. Soil permeability is indicated as good to poor, specifically, rapid, moderate to rapid, moderate, slow to moderate, slow, and very slow.

Table 6.1 Soil Permeability Class Related to
Flow of Water through a Saturated Soil

Permeability Class	Rate of Flow (inches per hour)
Very slow	Less than 0.06
Slow	0.06–0.2
Moderately slow	0.2–0.6
Moderate	0.6–2.0
Moderately rapid	2.0–6.0
Rapid	6.0–20.0
Very rapid	More than 20

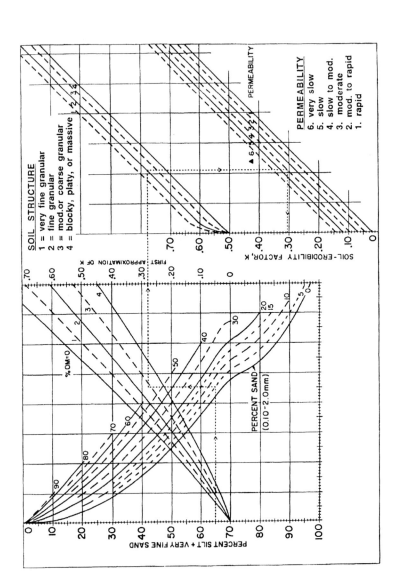

Figure 6.4 Nomograph to evaluate soil erodibility of a specific soil.

Procedure

Enter the appropriate data from a particular soil on the scale at the left for percent silt + very fine sand. Proceed to the right horizontally until coming to the percent sand curves (which are presented from upper left to lower right). For your soil choose the data for percent sand (0.1 to 2.0mm) as shown on the curve representing that soil. At that point go upward vertically until the curves for percent organic matter are reached. For your soil choose the data for percent organic matter. Proceed from that point to the right horizontally until reaching the curves for soil structure. For your soil choose the soil structure represented. At that point proceed downward vertically to the curves representing permeability. For your soil choose the permeability of that soil. At that point proceed left horizontally to the left vertical row that will show the soil erodibility (K factor) for your specific soil.

Percent sand values are plotted from zero to 90% on lines for 0, 5, 10, 15, 20, 30, 40, 50, 60, 70, 80, and 90%.

Percent organic matter (OM) values are plotted from zero to 4% percent on lines for 0, 1, 2, 3, and 4%.

Soil structure values are plotted in approximately parallel lines with the numbers represented as 1 = very fine granular; 2 = fine granular; 3 = medium or coarse granular; and 4 = blocky, platy, or massive.

Permeability values are plotted in parallel lines with the numbers represented as: 1 = rapid; 2 = moderate to rapid; 3 = moderate; 4 = slow to moderate; 5 = slow; and 6 = very slow. Soil permeability classes have been defined earlier (Table 6.1).

The Soil Erodibility Nomograph is used where the silt fraction does not exceed 70%. The nomograph is based on the equation:

$$100 \ K = 2.1 \ M^{1.14} \ (10^{-4}) \ (12 - a) + 3.25 \ (b - 2) + 2.5 \ (c - 3)$$

where M = (percent silt + very fine sand)(100 − percent c)
a = percent organic matter
b = structure code
c = profile permeability class.

SUMMARY

Soil erodibility is determined by soil texture, soil structure, soil permeability, and the amount of soil organic matter. Sand is easy to detach but difficult to move and therefore resists erosion. Silts are easy to detach and easy to transport and therefore are highly erodible. Clays initially resist erosion as they are difficult to detach, but once detached will flow readily with moving water causing much erosion. Water flows into a soil by infiltration and through a soil by the permeability of that soil.

A soil aggregate consists of soil grains clumped into a granule or crumb that is important in providing an open soil into which water will infiltrate quickly in a rain thereby reducing erosion. The size and stability of soil aggregates determine their effectiveness in permitting rain to infiltrate into a soil and retard erosion. The size and stability of soil aggregates are affected by the soil texture and presence of certain kinds of ions, type of clay minerals, amount of organic matter, amount of cementing substances, and cropping history of that soil. A nomograph has been devised to evaluate the erodibility of a specific soil, provided soil properties of texture, organic matter, structure, and permeability are known for that soil.

REVIEW

What factors affect soil erodibility?

To what extent is sand, silt, and clay eroded?

What are the two processes where water flows into and through a soil?

What is a soil aggregate and why is this important for soil erodibility?

What two properties of soil aggregates determine their effectiveness in the amount of infiltration?

What affects the size and stability of soil aggregates?

What information is needed to evaluate soil erodibility by the nomograph that has been devised?

7

Controlling Erosion

Erosion can be controlled by four main means, that is, improving soil structure, covering soil with plants, covering soil with mulch, and using special structures.

IMPROVING SOIL STRUCTURE

Soil structure is related to the soil tilth, or physical condition of a soil, with respect to ease of tillage or workability as shown by the fitness of a soil as a seedbed and the ease of root penetration. Other terms relating to soil structure improvement are soil aggregation and the formation of aggregates. Aggregates form when a cementing substance is present in a soil. The most important cementing substances in soil are soil polysaccharides and soil polyuronides produced as by-products from microorganisms during decomposition of organic matter. Other less important cementing substances in soil include clays, Ca, and Fe. Formation of aggregates results in improved water infiltration with reduction in erosion.

Organic Decomposition

Decomposition of organic matter in soils can be shown as an equation:

Plant and animal remains + O_2 + soil microorganisms →
CO_2 + H_2O + elements + humus + synthates + energy

The decomposition process has the following features:

1. Oxygen is required; thus soil aeration is important. Anytime a soil is stirred or mixed by cultivation, spading, plowing, some organic matter decomposition occurs.
2. Readily available decomposable organic material is required for the microbes to work on. Green organic material, such as grass clippings, is an excellent substrate.
3. Many different types of soil microorganisms are involved in this process. Decomposition is more rapid in soils at pH 7 (neutral).
4. A product of organic decomposition is humus. Humus has many desirable features that improve a soil for plant growth.
5. Plant or animal remains are not effective in soil aggregation until they begin to decompose.
6. The more rapid the decomposition, the greater effect of soil aggregation.

Definition of Microbial Synthates

Microbial synthates consist of polymers called "polysaccharides" and "polyuronides." A polymer is a long-chain compound made up of single monomer units hooked together acting as a unit. The term "poly" means "many" and "saccharide" means "sugar." Therefore, a polysaccharide is a substance made from many sugars. A "uronide" is a sugar molecule that has been partially oxidized to a sugar-acid. These microbial synthates are the cementing substances important in the formation and stabilization of aggregates (Fig. 7.1).

Aggregate Stabilization

In order for aggregates to be stabilized in soils the following must be considered:

1. A stable aggregate is relatively resistant to breakdown in water. To determine if an aggregate is stable, a number of aggregates are placed together on a sieve, then repeatedly lowered into water and raised out. The stable aggregates do not disintegrate, but the unstable ones fall apart.

2. The effect of aggregate stability is only temporary, with a peak in stability occurring in 20 to 30 days after the aggregate is formed.

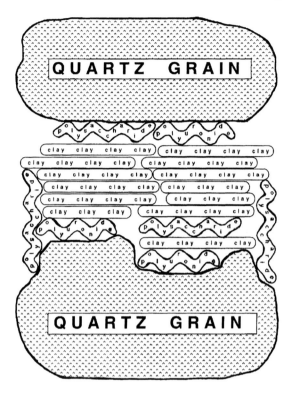

Figure 7.1 Soil crumb formation. Diagram showing how soil crumbs form from quartz grains, clay sheets, and cementing polysaccharides and polyuronides.

3. Effective aggregates must be continually renewed by addition of more organic material to a soil. This happens naturally in a forest as the leaves and twigs fall to the forest floor. Likewise, in a natural uncut grassland, as the grass leaves senesce and die they fall to the ground and decompose there.

4. Polysaccharides and polyuronides are used as a food source by certain microorganisms and thus are destroyed and are no longer aggregators. This is another reason that they must be constantly renewed.

5. Cultivation of a soil destroys the structure and breaks down the stable aggregates. This, in turn, increases the chance of crusting of the soil surface.

6. Plant growth habits influence soil structure. Grasses that have many fine, fibrous roots promote stable aggregates. Trees

and shrubs, with their larger roots, are less effective in encouraging stable aggregates than grasses.

COVERING SOIL WITH PLANTS

The extent that plants cover the soil is determined by how well the plants thrive. A complete cover of the soil surface by plant leaves considerably reduces erosion that would occur from raindrops striking the ground. Therefore, when the raindrops strike the leaves, they may soon fall to the ground, but the distance of fall is reduced considerably. Plant cover is much more important in those areas where intensity of erosive forces is severe. The severity of the erosion forces, called the "rainfall erosion index," has been mapped for the United States (Fig. 7.2) (Wischmeier and Smith, USDA, Agriculture Handbook #537). The most hazardous area for erosion in the United States is the area around the Gulf of Mexico, including the whole state of Florida.

COVERING SOIL WITH MULCH

Sources of Mulch

Mulches for use on soils can come from a number of sources.

Straw or stubble is an excellent mulch for cover of lawn grasses just seeded.

Leaves tend to pack down when used as a mulch and are better to use in a compost pile.

Wood products of sawdust, chips, or shavings all generally take longer to decompose and will persist more than other mulches. Plants growing in the mulch may show nitrogen deficiency and may require extra nitrogen fertilizer.

Animal manures are excellent as mulches as they are high in organic matter and many available plant nutrients but may have strong odor; for landscape use, it is better to have aged, dried, or well-rotted manures (less odors but less nutrients). Manures slowly release nutrients which is desirable for landscape plantings.

Peat and peat mosses are excellent sources of organic matter; good for water holding properties; improve soil aggre-

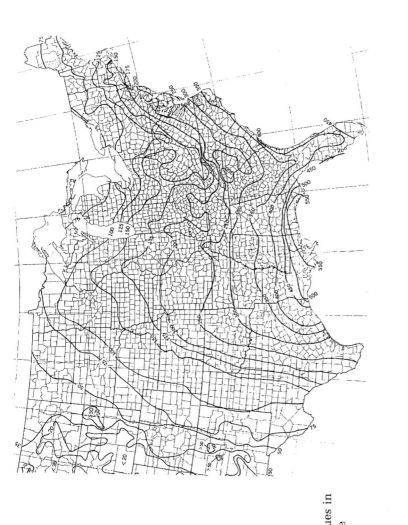

Figure 7.2 Rainfall erosion index values in eastern United States used to evaluate erosion severity.

gation; but either of these may be easily washed away. Peat mosses are very light and fluffy; they are difficult to wet, but once wetted, hold water well. An easy way to wet these is to place them in a container, add water, and mix until they become thoroughly wetted.

Paper products, such as newspapers, generally decompose slowly and may mat down and restrict water and air movement into the soil.

Polyethylene plastic films are partially decomposed by sunlight, but will persist in soil. The kind of plastic film to select for plants should be porous or water may not reach the plant roots. Black plastic should be used, as it will prevent weed seeds from sprouting and growing under the plastic. Clear plastic encourages weed germination and growth. Any holes cut in either type of plastic (for placing plants) will create an opening through which weed seeds can germinate and grow.

Stones, rocks, and sand are inert materials that can be used to cover plastic films to prevent photodisintegration.

Composts consist of a mixture of decayed organic material and are excellent for landscape purposes. Composts are generally produced in small areas by stacking successive layers of carbonaceous material (mature or dead plant material), green plant material, small amounts of soil (act as microorganism inoculant), water (sufficient to moisten, but must not be too dry or too wet), and small amounts of lime and fertilizer (optional but highly desirable) (Fig. 7.3). Soon the microorganisms start the decay process and in a few days, the pile should heat. This heat will kill most insect eggs, disease organisms, and weed seeds. The pile needs to be turned every week or so for more rapid decomposition. After about six to eight weeks, there should be no more heat released and the compost is ready to use.

Methods of Mulch Application

Mulches applied as a soil cover are generally effective against raindrop impact and often retard runoff and erosion. As long as the ground is kept covered, erosion is reduced. If the mulch is partially mixed with the soil, it becomes less effective against

Mix all layers well every 3-4 days

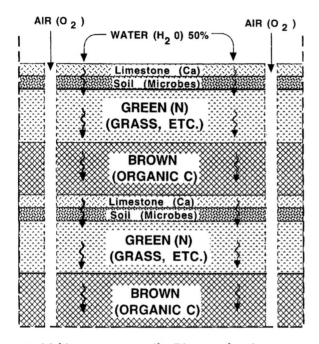

Figure 7.3 Making a compost pile. Diagram showing cross-section of layers and requirements for a typical compost pile.

raindrop damage, but may be more effective in retarding runoff and erosion. Mixing mulch with the soil encourages faster decomposition with more rapid aggregation.

Rate of Mulch Application

For effectiveness in controlling raindrop impact, mulches should be applied thick enough to cover from ⅔ to ¾ of the soil from view. This will amount to about 1½ to 2 tons of straw per acre or 4 to 5 tons of manure per acre. Very thick layers of mulch may absorb water that could be evaporated and lost for plant use. Also, too thick layers could retard newly seeded grass growth.

At planting time for trees and shrubs, at least three inches of peat, compost, or well-rotted manure should be applied around each plant.

Time of Mulching

Mulch should be applied to a bare soil as soon as possible to protect the soil from raindrop impact, runoff, and erosion. As long as the ground is kept covered, erosion is prevented. Many mulches are low in nitrogen (N) and high in carbon (C), producing a high C/N ratio. This condition favors slow decomposition, slow aggregation, and may create problems of N deficiency in plants that have been mulched. If plants are mulched, they should receive supplemental N *after* they have become established. Fertilizing during transplanting is not advisable as the fertilizer salts may slow the plants in becoming established or may even kill the plants.

Effects of Mulching

Physical Effects

Soil physical properties are affected by mulching.

1. Mulches result in *less raindrop splash, impact, and crusting*, which reduce the effect of runoff and erosion.

2. Presence of a mulch helps to *keep down wind erosion*. Dry soils, in certain parts of the country, are subject to wind erosion. The wind can pick up small soil particles and transport them many hundreds of miles. Unfortunately, during wind erosion the small particles picked up by wind have the best properties for plant growth. When the wind diminishes, the soil load falls and is deposited on top of an area. Organic soils are also subject to wind erosion. When organic soils are dry, they are very fluffy and wind can easily pick up the particles and transport them away. Damp soils are not eroded by wind.

3. A soil is protected and will have *no rapid temperature changes* when mulched. The mulched soil will be cooler in hot weather than bare soil.

4. Mulched soils usually have *improved aggregation* through decomposition of the mulch.

5. The improved aggregation from a mulch results in *increased soil porosity* with rapid infiltration of water. The added organic matter from a mulch also increases the water-holding capacity of a soil that can benefit plants.

6. Mulches generally *reduce evaporation* by holding more moisture in the soil itself. Exceptions to this occur if mulches are applied in large amounts.

Chemical Effects

1. *Available soil N is tied up* in organic form shortly after a mulch is applied as microbial decomposition begins. Mulches are chemically unbalanced, that is, containing much more carbonaceous (carbon-containing) than proteinaceous (N-containing) material. This type of material causes a reduced rate of decomposition during which any N in the material quickly becomes immobilized in the bodies of the decomposing microbes. Any soil N is also consumed by (i.e., immobilized in) the microbial biomass. If plants are growing in the mulch, they often suffer from N deficiency, which can be corrected by applying N fertilizer when the mulch is first applied. After the initial surge in microbial growth, the decomposition begins to wane. At this time the microbes begin to die and the N that was incorporated into their bodies is released into the soil as available N. After decomposition, available N is often present in larger amounts than before. Available N is released about 6 to 8 weeks after decomposition begins. If one can wait until after 6 to 8 weeks before planting, then there will be no problem of N deficiency. If one needs to plant seeds or put plants in the soil while decomposition is proceeding, then supplemental N is needed for desirable plant growth.

2. There is also an abundance of potassium (K) present in plant and animal remains that undergo decomposition. This *K then becomes available for plant growth.* However, if certain soils are subjected to cycles of wetting and drying, the K may become unavailable by being tied into part of the clay crystal units. This unavailable K will only be released slowly with time, often by cycles of freezing and thawing. Usually, there will be an abundance of K in these soils in the early spring of the year.

3. Mulches in soils generally cause *more water infiltration,* followed by water moving through the soil (percolation). Any soluble nutrients present could be removed and lost by leaching from the soils.

4. Mulches often keep soil particles from being dislodged thereby *retarding water runoff and erosion.* If an erodible soil is held in place, then any nutrients present within or attached to the soil particles remain available for plant use.

Biological Effects

Biological effects of mulching are related to the activity of microorganisms that decompose the mulch and create conditions for seedling establishment.

1. Mulching generally results in increased microbial activity. Mulches act as food (an energy source) for the microbial decomposition. A mulch also creates more uniform moisture and temperature—conditions under which soil microorganisms thrive.

2. Presence of a mulch creates ideal germination and growth conditions for new seedlings. Thus, lawn grass seedings are more likely to succeed when mulched. However, weed seeds are also encouraged to germinate and grow, so these may need to be controlled. Once the new desirable seedlings are well established, weeds can be controlled by judicious mowing and using herbicides sprays.

Problems Associated with Mulching

Unless black plastic films are used, other mulches may *encourage weed growth*. The high C/N ratio of many mulches may make *soil N temporarily unavailable* for plants as the microorganisms use any available N for decomposition purposes, resulting in none available for higher plants. This may lead to *N deficiencies* and could be *remedied by adding supplemental N fertilizer* when mulches are used.

USING SPECIAL STRUCTURES

Landscape architects often need to use special structures to retard erosion. Two of these are breast walls and brush layering; another is terraces.

Breast Walls

Breast walls are constructed of loosely laid rock placed on undisturbed soil with soil added on the uphill side of the wall (Fig. 7.4). This type of earthwork will have only small amounts of force pushing against the rocks. If a wall is constructed of concrete blocks or stone that has mortar between the joints, water can build up behind the wall and may cause the wall to fail. To avoid this, one must place drain pipes at the bottom and through the wall every few feet to prevent a buildup of water behind the wall. Small branches or easily rooted trees or shrubs can be placed within the rock wall to stabilize the structure.

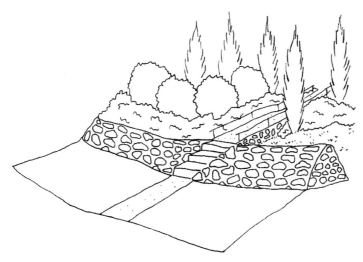

Figure 7.4 Breast walls. Erosion can be retarded on sloping areas by constructing breast walls.

Brush Layering

Brush layering is when branches of easy-to-root ground cover, shrubs, or trees are planted on the contour of a steep slope (Fig. 7.5). The tips of the plants should remain exposed while fill is placed in successive layers around them. Once the plants grow, the slope is stabilized, which is highly desirable on steep slopes on which grass would be difficult to maintain.

Terraces

Terraces are constructed by moving earth so that nearly level areas are formed on slight to moderate slopes. The terrace should be designed by an engineer and must have a gradual slope downwards toward the back (uphill side) to allow water to drain away from the steeper downhill portion. Water is drained away with a gradual slope to one or both sides of the terrace emptying into a well vegetated drainageway. Sometimes rock riprap (large rocks) is placed in the drainageway if the slope would cause fast drainage. This riprap slows down the running water to keep erosion to a minimum. The main disadvantage of terraces is the expense of constructing; however, a well-constructed and maintained terrace will last for years.

Figure 7.5 Brush layering. Erosion on steep slopes can be retarded by growth of ground cover, shrubs, or trees with brush layering.

SUMMARY

Methods for controlling erosion are improving soil structure, covering soil with plants, covering soil with mulch, and use of special structures. The presence of soil aggregates allow for greater infiltration of rainwater into a soil with reduction in erosion. Decomposition of organic material in a soil results in production of microbial synthates of polysaccharides and polyuronides that help in the formation and stability of soil aggregates. A stable aggregate is one that will not break up easily when placed in water. The extent of this stability is related to the amount of microbial synthates that are produced during decomposition. Cultivation by man destroys aggregates and creates undesirable soil structure, whereas growth of grasses increases the amount of soil crumbs by stimulating soil microbes.

Plant growth that covers a soil surface keeps the raindrops from striking the surface avoiding compaction and movement of soil particles. Mulches can be straw, leaves, sawdust, manures, peat, paper, plastic films, stones, or composts. Their effectiveness depends on how well they prevent raindrops from striking the surface. Mixing a mulch into the soil surface will help prevent runoff water and erosion, but surface mulch protects the soil better from raindrop impact. Mulches are usually applied as soon as possible after the soil is exposed and sufficiently thick enough to cover from two thirds to three fourths of the soil from view.

Mulches physically prevent raindrop impact, crusting of soil surface, wind erosion, rapid temperature changes, promote aggregation formation and stability, increase soil porosity, and improve water retention in soils. Chemically, mulches may temporarily tie up N, may cause some loss of nutrients by leaching, but do provide K for plant growth, improve water infiltration into the soil, and retard water runoff that may encourage erosion with loss of nutrients. Biologically, mulches encourage microbiological activity by improving conditions for decomposition besides creating ideal conditions for seed germination and growth of seedlings.

Special structures, such as breast walls, brush layering, or terraces can be used effectively in retarding erosion.

REVIEW

What are the main means of controlling soil
  erosion?
How is soil aggregation important in controlling erosion?
How is organic decomposition related to
  improving soil tilth?
Can you name the two microbial synthates
  useful in holding the soil grains together
  into aggregates?
What is meant by a stable aggregate?
What determines aggregate stability?
What practice of man causes increases in soil
  runoff and erosion?
What natural processes help soil resist
  erosion?

(continued) ➡

REVIEW (*continued*)

How does covering the soil with plants help
to control erosion?
What different types of materials can be used
as a mulch?
To what extent are mulches effective in
controlling erosion?
Should mulches be placed on the soil surface
or mixed in?
What is the "rule-of-thumb" used to determine how much mulch to apply to a soil?
When is the best time to cover soil with a
mulch?
How do applying mulches affect the soil
physically? Chemically? Biologically?
What are some special structures that are
useful for controlling erosion during
landscaping?

8

Effective Water Use

Irrigation

Soils that are suitable for irrigation are deep soils that are permeable and have a high available water-holding capacity (usually containing much organic matter). Limitations for irrigation include presence of restrictive layers (pans), erodible soils, sloping land, susceptibility to stream overflow, salinity or alkalinity, stoniness, and hazard of soil blowing.

WHEN SHOULD WATER BE APPLIED?

Plant-Available Water

The amount of plant-available water in a soil depends on rooting depth (Fig. 4.8) and soil texture (Fig. 4.14).

Soil Texture

Coarse textured sands hold much less available water than finer textured clayey soils (Fig. 4.3). Available water increases as the texture becomes finer up to a silt loam. Any soil texture finer than that results in no additional increase in available water (Fig. 4.14).

Rooting Depth

In shallow soils, the rooting depth is limited by the soil depth. In deep soils, root depth is determined by the kind of plants present:

Trees and large shrubs   48 inches depth

Medium shrubs and vines   40 inches depth

Small shrubs and ground cover   24 inches depth

Techniques to Determine When
a Soil Needs Water

A number of techniques can be used to determine when water should be applied to soil in which plants are growing. These techniques include observing the plants, especially for wilting; feeling the soil; using tensiometers or electrical resistance meters installed in the soil; and measuring temperatures of plant leaves.

Observation of Plants

Wilting—When plants begin to lose water they droop and wilting results (Fig. 8.1). If plants remain in this condition very long, they soon die. It is better to water plants before they become wilted. Any plant that is wilted will require some time to reestablish its water equilibrium, thereby slowing the growth of that plant.

Feel the Soil

The amount of moisture in a soil can be roughly estimated by the "feel method" (Fig. 4.2). The degree of moisture can be determined by rolling or squeezing the soil into a ball. The soil moisture condition can be divided into six categories from dry to very wet (Table 8.1):

   a. If a ball will not form → soil is too dry for plants.
   b. If the ball formed will not crumble when rubbed → soil is too wet for plants. However, if the soil is sandy, it will crumble even if wet.
   c. If a ball can be molded and it will crumble when rubbed → plants will grow fine.

Tensiometer

A tensiometer is a closed tube containing water and a ceramic cup on the tip. A gauge attached measures water tension. Some tensiometers have electrical contacts connected to timers for automatic operation.

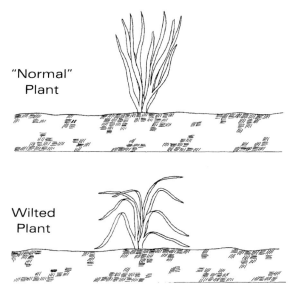

Figure 8.1 Wilting. Inadequate moisture causes plants to droop and wilt.

Electrical Resistance Meters

Electrical resistance meters use the ability of a soil to conduct electricity. This is related to the moisture content of a soil.

Foliar Temperature

Measurement of foliar temperature is a relatively new technique that is based on the premise that when a leaf is under water stress, less transpiration occurs and the leaf temperature rises. This is especially useful for mature plants. The device uses infrared sensing instrumentation.

HOW MUCH WATER TO ADD?

Apply Enough Water to Wet the Root Zone

Applying sufficient water to wet the root zone encourages deep rooting, minimizes crown rot, and aids water-holding ability. Water should be applied slowly enough for even distribution (Fig.

Table 8.1 Determining Soil Moisture by the "Feel" Method

Degree of Moisture	How It Feels	Amount of Moisture
Dry	Powder dry	None
Low	Crumbly; will not hold together	25% or less (critical)
Fair	Somewhat crumbly, but will hold together	25 to 50%
Good	Forms ball; will stick slightly with pressure	50 to 75%
Excellent	Forms a ball and is pliable; sticks readily, a clear water sheen will come to the surface when the ball is squeezed in the hand	75 to 100%
Very wet (too wet)	Can squeeze out free water	Over field capacity

4.18). Care must be taken to prevent applying too much water as this is not economical and can cause plants to suffer from flooding and lack of oxygen for proper plant growth. Water applied to a deep soil will hold more water initially, but will quickly drain out (Fig. 4.8). The upper portion of the deep soil will establish field capacity sooner than a shallow one.

KINDS OF IRRIGATION SYSTEMS

Irrigation schemes include basin (for level land), furrow (on level or slightly sloping land), sprinkler (water applied in an overhead spray), and drip. Drip irrigation is supplied by pipes to individual plants through emitters (small devices that meter water out slowly).

Basin

The basin system is used on level land that will not be used for recreation or traffic. The whole area is flooded until the required amount of water is added (Fig. 8.2). This is useful only on level land but may be uneconomical, as much water may evaporate and be lost to plant use.

Furrow

Irrigation water is diverted into furrows created in the ground at intervals over the field (Fig. 8.3). The amount of water the area

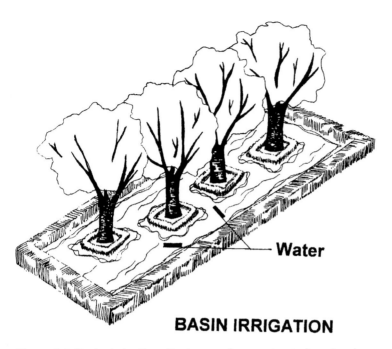

BASIN IRRIGATION

Water

Figure 8.2 Basin irrigation. Basins can be constructed on level soil to hold water around plantings.

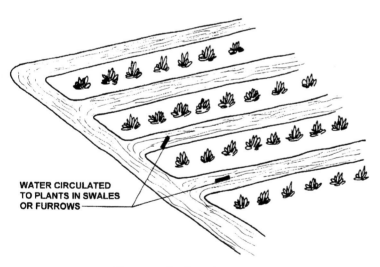

WATER CIRCULATED
TO PLANTS IN SWALES
OR FURROWS

Furrow Irrigation

Figure 8.3 Furrow irrigation. Slightly sloping areas can use furrows for irrigation.

receives is regulated by the infiltration rate of the soil, slope of the furrows, and rate of flow. Infiltration rate may be increased by adding organic matter, keeping cultivation to a minimum, and irrigating adequately but infrequently. Caution must be used with this system as erosion may occur unless the land is nearly level. One can shorten the furrow rows if there are more inlets.

Sprinkler

Irrigation water is sprinkled overhead either on raised pipes or on risers from pipes on the ground (Fig. 8.4). A common problem is nonuniformity of application. This depends on the design of the system, water pressure used, and amount of wind. The overhead view (Fig. 8.4) shows square spacing, which is acceptable; however, for large areas triangular spacing is preferred for

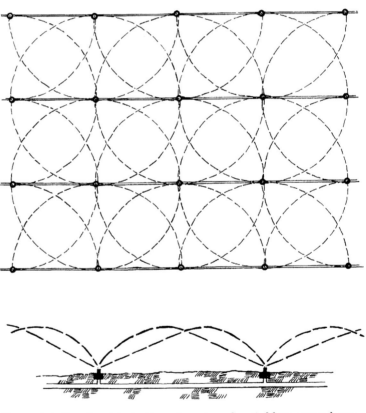

Figure 8.4 Overhead irrigation. A series of sprinklers cover large soil areas but encourage weed growth.

greater coverage, especially for golf courses. Water should be applied no faster than the soil will absorb it. Downslope movement can be retarded by having turf between plants, use of mulch, or presence of ground cover. Since water is indiscriminately applied over a large area, weed growth is also encouraged.

Drip

Drip irrigation consists of plastic pipes with special emitters that are placed close to the plants that require the water (Fig. 8.5). The goal of this system is to supply water only to the root area needing it, thereby increasing efficiency of water use. Water is dripped slowly through emitters with the amount applied being regulated by the kind of emitter used. The amount of soil that is wetted depends on the soil characteristics, the duration of irrigation, and number and kind of emitters used. The emitters should be exposed so their operation can be checked for leaks and defective emitters. For example, the emitters may plug if below the surface and

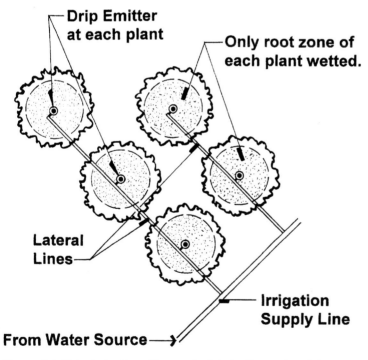

Figure 8.5 Drip irrigation. Economical irrigation using drippers at each plant efficiently wets only the desired plant soil area.

some do become defective by allowing too much water to flow. This system may require more frequent irrigation as plants deplete the water faster than if the entire root zone is wetted. Irrigation lines should be flushed periodically to keep the emitters free from plugging with soil particles, Ca and Fe precipitates, bacterial slimes, and algae. These problems can usually be prevented by installing a filter before water enters the system.

SUMMARY

Soils used for irrigation should be deep and able to absorb water quickly with a high water-holding capacity. The presence of adequate amounts of organic matter is highly desirable. Techniques used to determine when to irrigate a dry soil include observing the plants for wilting, squeezing soil into a ball, using a tensiometer or electrical resistance meters, or measuring foliar temperatures. Water for irrigation should be applied slowly enough to provide sufficient water in the root zone. Care must be taken not to overwater as it is wasteful and may be detrimental to plant growth.

Irrigation methods for watering plants include basin, furrow, sprinkler, and drip. Basin systems are used where whole fields are flooded, but water may be lost by evaporation. Furrow systems control placement of water, but erosion may occur on sloping land. Overhead sprinkler systems can be effectively used on level or sloping land, but problems may arise from increased weed growth and uneven application over the area. Drip irrigation is the most efficient use of water to reach the root zone and is desirable in very dry locations where water is limited, but it may require more maintenance than the other types.

REVIEW

Which soils are suitable for irrigation?
How does one determine when to irrigate?
What is the correct amount of water to use for irrigation?
Can you name four kinds of water irrigation systems?
Can you describe the advantages and disadvantages of each of the irrigation systems?

9

Chemical Properties of Soils for Growing Plants

SOIL REACTION (pH)

Definition of pH

Soil reaction is the amount of acids (acidity) or bases (alkalinity) present in a soil and is indicated by a term called "pH" (Table 9.1). By definition, pH is the logarithm of the reciprocal of the hydrogen ion (H^+) concentration, or

$$pH = \log \frac{1}{[H^+]}$$

When a number has a smaller superscript number with it, the number is raised to that power which is called the "logarithm." Raising a number to a power means multiplying that number by itself the number of times indicated by the superscript.

Examples: 10^2 means 10 x 10 = 100; 10^3 means 10 x 10 x 10 = 1,000. The logarithm (log) is 2 for the first example and 3 for the second.

Logarithms are used as these are more convenient in expressing the amount of hydrogen ions present. Under neutral solutions the pH is 7.0. Any pH that is less than 7 is acid and any pH above is alkaline (Table 9.1). When changing from a pH of 7 to a pH of 6, the H ion concentration increases ten times, and when going from a pH of 7 to a pH of 5, the H ion concentration increases 100 times because pH uses a geometric scale and not an arithmetic scale. Thus, pH changes by steps of ten times the next adjacent number (Fig. 9.1).

Table 9.1 Soil Reaction (pH) Categories

Soil Reaction Description	pH Range
Extremely acid	Below 4.5
Very strongly acid	4.5–5.0
Strongly acid	5.0–5.5
Medium acid	5.5–6.0
Slightly acid	6.0–6.5
Neutral	6.6–7.3
Mildly alkaline	7.4–7.8
Moderately alkaline	7.9–8.4
Strongly alkaline	8.5–9.0
Very strongly alkaline	Above 9.0

The logarithmic scale used for pH is the same type, but opposite in direction, as that used to measure earthquakes. For each larger number of earthquake, the severity increases ten times; for each smaller number of pH, the acidity increases ten times.

Range of pH for Most Plants and Microbes

Optimum Range is pH 6 to 7

Some plants can tolerate very low pH (4.5) and others can withstand a pH of 8.3, but the optimum range for growth of most plants (Table 9.2) and microbes is between 6 and 7.

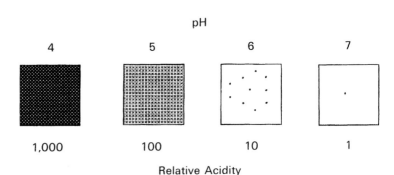

Figure 9.1 Acidity changes illustrated. Relative acidity changes logarithmically from 1 at pH 7 to 1,000 at pH 4.

Table 9.2 Optimum pH Range of Selected Landscape Plants

Plant	pH	Plant	pH
Ageratum houstonianum	6.0–7.0	Cinquefoil	6.0–7.0
Anemone patens	5.0–6.0	*Potentilla fruticosa*	
Apple	5.0–6.5	Cockscomb	6.0–7.5
Malus pumila		*Celosia argentea cristata*	
Ash, White	6.0–7.5	*Coleus blumei*	6.0–7.0
Fraxinus americana		Columbine, Colorado	6.0–7.0
Aspen, Bigtooth	3.8–5.5	*Aquilegia caerulea*	
Populus tremuloides		Coral bells	6.0–7.0
Aster, alpine	5.5–7.0	*Huechera sanguinea*	
Aster aplinus		*Cosmos bipinnatus*	5.0–8.0
Aster, New England	6.0–8.0	Cottonwood, Fremont	6.0–8.0
Aster novae-angliae		*Populus fremontii*	
Azalea	4.5–6.0	*Crocus vernus*	6.0–8.0
Rhododentrum obtusum		Currant, red	5.5–7.0
Baby's breath	6.0–7.5	*Ribes sativum*	
Gypsophila paniculata		Daisy, ox-eye	6.0–7.5
Bachelor's button	6.0–7.5	*Chrysanthemum*	
Balloon flower	5.0–6.0	*leucanthemum*	
Platycodon grandiflorum		Daisy, Shasta	6.0–8.0
Barberry, Japanese	6.0–7.5	*Chrysanthemum*	
Berberis thungergii		*maximum*	
Basswood (Linden)	6.0–7.5	*Delphinium grandiflorum*	6.0–7.5
Tilia glabra		Dogwood, flowering	5.0–7.0
Bearberry (kinnickninnick)	4.5–6.0	*Cornus florida*	
Arctostraphylos uvaursi		Dogwood, yellow twig	6.0–7.0
Beautybush	6.0–7.5	*Cornus sericea*	
Kolkwitzia amabilis		*Euonymus alatus*	5.5–7.0
Birch, European	4.5–6.0	Fern, maidenhair	6.0–8.0
Betual verrucosa		*Adiantum pedatum*	
Bleedingheart	6.0–7.5	Firethorn	6.0–8.0
Dicentra spectabilis		*Pyracantha coccinea*	
Blueberry, highbush	4.0–5.0	Foxglove	6.0–7.5
Vaccinium corymbosum		*Digitalis purpurea*	
Boxwood	6.0–7.5	*Gaillardia aristata*	6.0–7.5
Buxus sempervirens		Geranium, domestic	6.0–8.0
Buffaloberry	6.0–8.0	*Pelargonium domesticum*	
Shepherdia argentia		Hackberry	6.0–8.0
Calendula officinalis	5.5–7.0	*Celtis pumila*	
Candytuft, perennial	5.5–7.0	Hawthorn, English	6.0–7.0
Iberis sempervirens		*Crataegus oxyacantha*	
Canterberry bells	6.0–7.5	Hemlock, Canada	5.0–6.0
Campanula medium		*Tsuga canadensis*	
Cherry, sour	6.0–7.0	Hen & chickens	6.0–8.0
Prunus cerasus		*Sempervivum tectorum*	
Chokeberry	5.0–6.0	Holly, American	5.0–6.0
Arenia arbutifolia		*Ilex opaca*	
Chrysanthemum x	6.0–7.5	Honeylocust	6.0–8.0
morifolium		*Gleditsia triacanthos*	

(*continued*)

Table 9.2 (*Continued*)

Plant	pH	Plant	pH
Honeysuckle, tartarian	6.5–8.0	Pine, mugho	5.0–6.5
Lonicera tatarica		*Pinus mugo*	
Iris germanica	6.5–7.5	Pine, white	4.5–6.0
Iris, Japanese	5.5–6.5	*Pinus strobus*	
Iris kaempferi		Poppy, oriental	6.0–7.5
Juniper, common	5.0–6.5	*Papaver orientale*	
Juniperus chinensis		Primrose	5.5–7.0
Juniper, creeping	5.0–6.0	*Primula* x *polyantha*	
Juniperus chinensis		Pyrethrum	6.0–7.5
"Sargentii"		*Chrysanthemum*	
Kentucky coffeetree	6.0–8.0	*atrosanquineum*	
Gymnocladus dioicus		Rhododendron	4.5–6.0
Lilac, common	6.0–7.5	*carolinianum*	
Syringa vulgaris		Rose, hybrid tea	5.5–7.0
Lilac, Persian	6.0–8.0	*Rosa* spp.	
Syringa x *persica*		Rosemary, bog	3.0–5.0
Lily, regal	6.0–7.0	*Andromeda glaucophylla*	
Lilium regale		Snapdragon	6.0–7.5
Lobelia cardinalis	6.0–7.5	*Antirrhinum majus*	
Lupine, garden	6.5–7.5	*Spirea bumalda*	6.0–7.0
Lupinus polyphyllus		Spruce, Colorado	6.0–7.0
Magnolia, saucer	5.0–6.0	*Picea pungens*	
Magnolia soulangiana		Spruce, Norway	5.0–6.0
Maple, striped	5.0–6.0	*Picea abies*	
Acer pennsylvanicum		Stonecrop, showy	5.5–7.0
Maple, sugar	6.0–7.5	*Sedum spectabile*	
Acer saccharum		Sumac. staghorn	5.0–6.0
Mint	7.0–8.0	*Rhus typhina*	
Mentha arrensis		Sweet William	6.0–7.5
Myrtle, crape	5.0–6.0	*Dianthus barbatus*	
Lagerstroemia indica		Tamarack	5.0–6.5
Ninebark	6.0–7.5	*Larix laricina*	
Physocarpus opulifolius		Tree-of-Heaven	6.0–7.0
Oak, bur	5.0–6.0	*Ailanthus altissima*	
Quercus macrocarpa		*Verbena hybrida*	6.0–8.0
Oak, English	6.0–8.0	Violet, sweet	6.0–7.5
Quercus robur		*Viola odorata*	
Oak, pin	5.0–6.5	Walnut, black	6.0–8.0
Quercus palustris		*Juglans nigra*	
Oak, red	4.5–6.0	Willow, pussy	6.5–8.0
Quercus borealis		*Salix discolor*	
Pansy, tricolor	5.5–6.5	Yarrow	6.5–8.0
Viola tricolor		*Achillea atrata*	
Peony	6.0–7.5	Yellowwood	6.0–8.0
Paeonia albiflora		*Cladrastis lutea*	
Periwinkle, perennial	6.0–7.5	Yew, Japanese	6.0–7.0
Vinca minor		*Taxus cuspidata*	
Phlox paniculata	6.0–8.0	*Zinnia elegans*	5.5–7.5

Effect of pH on Nutrient Availability

Availability of most nutrients is affected by pH changes. Charts have been constructed to show this relationship (Fig. 9.2). On these charts the pH at which most nutrients are readily available is from 6 to 7. At extremes of pH, availability of nutrients to plants often is reduced considerably. Some micronutrients such as copper or manganese, are soluble at low pH and have concentrations high enough to become toxic to plants. Many micronutrients at high pH form insoluble oxides and hydroxides that plants cannot use, so some micronutrient deficiencies may become evident.

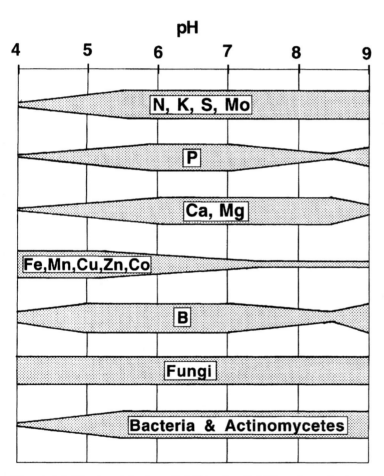

Figure 9.2 Plant nutrient availability. Availability of nutrients for plants and activity of soil microbes is indicated by the width of the bar at several pH levels.

FACTORS THAT CAUSE ACIDS
TO FORM IN SOILS

Soils form acids by the processes of aluminum hydrolysis, organic matter decomposition, leaching or irrigation, applying acid-forming fertilizers, and plant roots growing in a soil.

Aluminum Hydrolysis

Soils contain large amounts of aluminum (Al) that may chemically react with water (hydrolysis). During Al hydrolysis the water molecule is split apart and the hydroxyl part reacts with the Al^{3+} ion present.

During hydrolysis, the water molecule breaks apart into its two components—hydrogen ion (H^+) and hydroxyl ion (OH^-):

$$H_2O \rightarrow H^+ + OH^-$$

Either one or both parts of the water, that is, H^+ or OH^-, may combine with other entities in the solution. For Al hydrolysis, the OH^- combines with the Al^{3+} to form new entities. The newly created aluminum hydroxy-compounds can also hydrolyze in a stepwise fashion as pH rises:

(At low pH)
$$Al^{+3} + H\text{-}OH \leftrightarrows Al^{+2}(OH) + H^+$$
$$\updownarrow$$
$$Al^{+2}(OH) + H\text{-}OH \leftrightarrows Al^{+1}(OH)_2 + H^+$$
$$\updownarrow$$
$$Al^{+1}(OH)_2 + H\text{-}OH \leftrightarrows Al(OH)_3 + H^+$$
(At high pH)

The net result of Al hydrolysis is one $Al^{+3} \rightarrow 3\ H^+$.

The Al hydrolysis is an equilibrium reaction that can go in either direction depending on the pH of the solution.

Organic Matter Decomposition

During the decomposition process several kinds of acids are formed:

plant remains + $O_2 \rightarrow H_2O + CO_2 + \ldots$ + other strong acids $\rightarrow H+$
Also, $H_2O + CO_2 \rightarrow H_2CO_3 \rightarrow H^+ + HCO_3^-$ (a weak acid)

The strong acids include nitric acid, hydrochloric acid, and sulfuric acid. All of these acids, either strong or weak, make soils more acid by decomposition.

Leaching or Irrigation

Leaching is the removal of bases (positively charged ions) when a soil is drained (Fig. 9.3). As water is passed through a soil, ei-

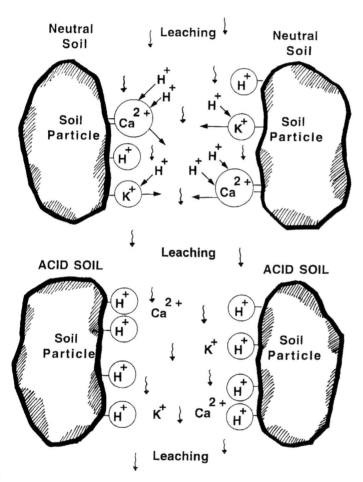

Figure 9.3 How soils can become acidic. When water leaches through soils, positively charged bases of neutral soils are replaced by hydrogen ions. On further leaching, the bases are removed and lost from soils with the soil becoming acid.

ther naturally during rainfall or by irrigation, any H^+ ion present replaces bases (i.e., Ca^{++}, Mg^{++}, K^+, Na^+, etc.) on the soil particles. The bases then are free in the soil solution and can be leached from the soil. Each time a H^+ ion becomes attached to a soil particle, the soil becomes more acid than before.

Acid-Forming Fertilizers

When acid-forming fertilizers are mixed in a soil, they are oxidized as a source of energy by special microbes producing H^+ (acid) as a by-product (explained in Chapter 11). The H^+ formed is attracted to soil particles replacing the bases making the soil more acid.

Plant Roots Growing in a Soil

Any plant root growing in a soil is constantly exchanging H^+ for positively charged bases (Fig. 9.4). The bases are nutrients that the plant requires for proper growth. Thus, the H^+ produced by the plant during metabolism exchanges for the bases needed by the

Plant Root Hair

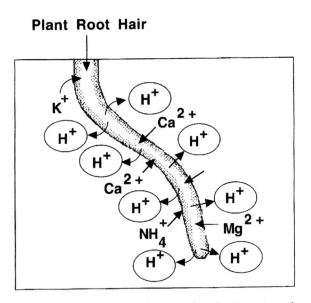

Figure 9.4 Growing plants produce acid soils. Growing plant roots absorb positively charged cations in exchange for exuded hydrogen ions that create acid conditions.

plant. When H$^+$ is released into the soil solution, it can replace positively charged bases on the soil particle which then becomes more acid.

CORRECTING SOIL ACIDITY

In order to understand how acidity in soils is corrected, one needs to know how acidity reacts in a soil. Changes of acidity in a soil are related to buffering.

Buffering

A buffer is a *material in a soil that resists a change in soil pH.* The action of a buffer is called "buffering." Buffers in soils are clays and organic matter. The amount of buffering is regulated by the kind and amounts of clays and organic matter present. The order of buffering, from most to least, is:

Organic matter > Smectite clays (2:1) > Illitic clays (2:1) >
Kaolinitic clays (1:1) > Hydrous Oxide clays (tropics).

Buffering of organic matter is very high, whereas hydrous oxides have a very low buffering ability.

Buffering is important in soils as it *prevents a drastic change in pH (acidity) that could be detrimental to plants and microbes.* This could be by the direct effect of H$^+$ concentration or by the indirect effect through change in availability of nutrients (Fig. 9.2).

Factors Affecting Extent of Buffering

Buffering is determined by four main factors:

1. Amount of clay present,
2. Type of clay present,
3. Amount of organic matter present, and
4. Type of organic matter present.

An example of how buffering is affected by amount of clay present can be represented by examining the amount of limestone needed to change the soil pH from 6.0 to 6.5.

Soil Type	Amount of Lime (tons/acre) Needed to Change pH from 6.0 to 6.5
Sandy loam	0.5
Silt loam	0.9
Silty clay loam	1.25

The amount of clay present above is reflected in the texture of the soil, progressing from the coarsest (sandy loam) to the finest (silty clay loam). The sandy loam soil has only a small amount of clay, whereas the silty clay loam has a large amount of clay (Fig. 4.2).

Creating Acidity for Acid-Loving Plants

Soil acid conditions are desirable for some plants, including *Abelia, Azalea, Camellia, Catalpa, Citrus, Dichondra, Fragaria, Gardenia, Gladiolus, Hibicus, Hydrangea, Ilex, Juniper, Ligustrum, Liquidambar, Lonicera, Magnolia, Photinia, Pyracantha, Quercus, Rubus, Rhododenron, Spirea, Vaccinium, Verbena, Vinca, Salix*, and *Wisteria.* Sometimes the soil may not be acid enough for these plants to grow well, especially if the soil has been limed to create conditions favorable for grasses or other vegetation to grow. Therefore, one may need to change the soil reaction by making the soil more acid. This can be done by adding organic matter and certain chemicals or fertilizers.

Organic matter, especially naturally acidic materials such as mulches of pine needles, fir bark, or corncobs, cause the soil to become acid during the decomposition process. You will recall that any time plant or animal remains are decomposed acids are formed. Therefore, any kind of organic material added to the soil will make it more acid.

Certain Chemicals or Fertilizers

Chemicals or fertilizers that can be added to soils to create acidity are:

Sulfur. Sulfur (S) in nature is a yellow powder (flowers of sulfur). This is the elemental form and all of this becomes sulfuric acid upon combining with water. Sulfur is probably the best material to add for quick results to landscape plantings.

Iron Sulfate. Iron sulfate could be added, but its acidifying effects are somewhat limited.

Aluminum Sulfate. Aluminum sulfate is acid forming, but highly undesirable as the Al is toxic to plants; probably better not to use this source.

Sulfuric Acid. Sulfuric acid is fast acting in soil, but must be used with caution to prevent acid burns to either skin or leaves.

Ammonium (NH_4^+)-containing or Ammonium-forming Fertilizer. Any ammonium fertilizer or one that forms ammonium, such as urea, will create acidity. Upon breakdown in soils, these fertilizers produce relatively large amounts of H^+ as a by-product.

BASE-FORMING FACTORS

In the humid areas, soils generally become more acid by natural processes already mentioned. Many plants grow better in soils with a slightly acid or neutral soil reaction. Therefore, one may need to alter the soil reaction by making it more basic. Soils can be made more basic by adding lime, weathering of rocks or clays, or irrigation.

Adding Lime

When a source of lime, containing Ca and/or Mg, is added to soils, the soil acids are neutralized, which raises the pH, making the soil more basic (Fig. 9.5).

Weathering of Rocks and Clays

When rocks (primary minerals) or clays (secondary minerals) undergo weathering (physical, chemical, and biological breakdown), soil bases (positively charged ions called "cations") are released to the soil solution (Fig. 2.5). These bases can exchange for the H^+ on the soil particles creating more basic conditions similar to the reaction of limestone in acid soils (Fig. 9.5). Also, in dry areas where rainfall is limited, bases are not leached and can accumulate in soils. Hot and dry conditions often cause the soil moisture to evaporate from the soil surface. As water moves upward it carries the bases (dissolved salts) with it (Fig. 9.6). However, the salts cannot evaporate, so they often collect on the surface. In some soils so much salt accumulates that a white salty deposit becomes evident. This may occur in potted plants if they

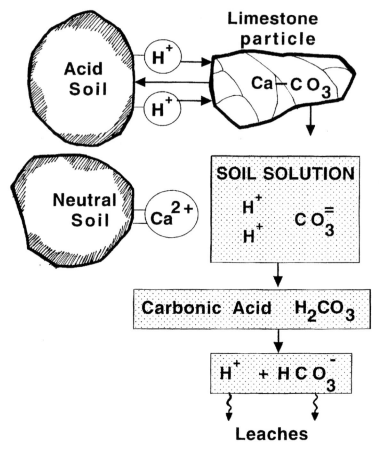

Figure 9.5 Neutralization of acid soil by liming. Limestone applied to acid soils reacts with the hydrogen ions, resulting in a neutral soil as hydrogen ions are leached.

are not watered with sufficient water to carry the salts out by leaching.

Irrigation

In some cases irrigation may also create basic conditions. If the water that is used for irrigating contains salts and it is applied to dry land, the bases may accumulate in the soil or on the soil surface. Contrast this reaction with irrigation that produces acid conditions by leaching of bases from a soil as described previously in this chapter.

Water Evaporates

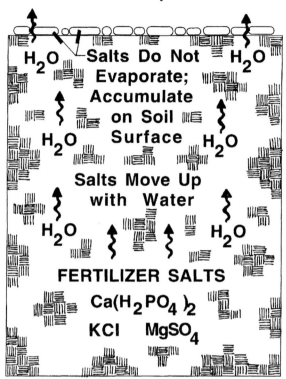

Figure 9.6 Accumulation of salts on soil surfaces. During dry conditions, water containing dissolved salts moves upward in soils. The water changes from a liquid to a gas evaporating into the atmosphere, but salts do not become gaseous and accumulate on the surface as white deposits.

CORRECTING ALKALINITY IN ARID REGIONS

In arid regions salts often accumulate in soils as there is insufficient rain to wash out the salts. Sometimes these high concentrations of salts interfere with plant growth and may cause wilting (Fig. 8.1) from high salt concentration. Alkaline soils can be made more acid by several techniques, depending on the type of alkalinity present. For correction of alkalinity for either saline or sodic soils, the timing of irrigation is important, especially at planting. Young plants are very sensitive to salts, whereas older plants can tolerate some salts. Vigorous, healthy plants also can tolerate more salts than those lacking in sufficient nutrients.

Saline Soils

Saline soils have an accumulation of salts present. These soils are low in sodium (less than 15%) with a pH between 7.0 and 8.5. This condition can exist in potted plants unless care is taken to keep the salt content low. This will be covered in the section on "Plant Disorders" under Salts (Chemical Injuries, chapter 17). The alkalinity of saline soils can be reduced by leaching with large amounts of water to wash out the salts; however, adequate drainage is essential. The large amount of water needed to flush out the salts must be removed from the field or pots for this to be effective. Tolerance to salinity varies widely among varieties in a genus. The genera of some plants that will tolerate high salt concentrations are *Araucaria, Bougainvillea, Callistemon, Carissa, Cortaderia, Delasperma, Drosanthemum, Hibicus, Hymenocyclus, Lagunaria, Morea, Nerium, Phoenix, Platycladus, Rhagodia, Rosmarinus,* and *Westringia.* On the other hand, some plants that are very sensitive to excess salts are *Adiantum, Antirrhinum, Begonia, Berberis, Camellia, Cotoneaster, Cymbidium, Dahlia, Euonymus, Fushia, Gardenia, Iberis, Ilex, Lilium, Picea, Podocarpus, Primula, Pseudotsuga, Rhododendron, Rosa, Rubus, Saintpaulia, Salix, Spirea, Tilia, Verbena,* and *Viola.*

Sodic Soils

Sodic soils are high in sodium (more than 15%), with a pH of up to 10, and are very difficult and expensive to reclaim. The high amounts of sodium generally cause puddling of the soil surface with a very undesirable soil structure, thereby making addition of amendments difficult (Fig. 9.7). The poor soil physical condition results in very low permeability and difficulty in draining out the saline water. Correcting alkalinity of these sodic soils requires working gypsum ($CaSO_4$) or sulfur (S) into the soil, and then leaching with water low in sodium. The gypsum does add some salt to the soil, but it is necessary to replace the sodium (Na^+) with calcium (Ca^{2+}) that will produce a more desirable soil structure. Sulfur, added to soils, requires time for the microbes to convert it to sulfuric acid. To speed up the process, sulfuric acid can be used, but this material is hazardous to use as it will react with metals and burn the skin.

Non-Sodic Soil

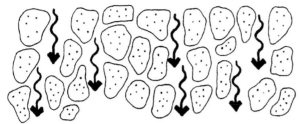

**Fast Infiltration;
good structure**

Sodic Soil

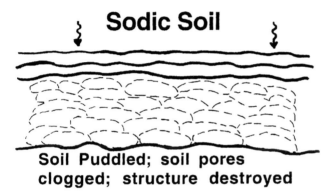

**Soil Puddled; soil pores
clogged; structure destroyed**

Figure 9.7 Sodic soils have poor tilth. Soils with low amounts of
sodium salts have good structure, allowing water and gases to
infiltrate easily, whereas in sodic soils (high in sodium) the
structure is destroyed, particles run together, and pores are
clogged (puddling), preventing passage of water and air.

SUMMARY

Acidity/alkalinity of a soil can be expressed as pH, which is a
convenient way of evaluating hydrogen ion concentration in a
soil. Most plants thrive in a pH between 6 and 7. Soil acidity
develops from aluminum hydrolysis, organic matter decomposition, leaching of cations, use of acid-forming fertilizers, and
growth of plant roots.

A buffer is any substance in a soil that prevents a rapid change
in pH. Buffers are important to keep growing conditions stable

for plants and microbes. Four main factors affecting buffering are amount of clay, type of clay, amount of organic matter, and type of organic matter.

Soils can be acidified by adding sulfur or ammonium-containing fertilizers. Soils can be made more basic by liming, weathering, or irrigating with salty water. Alkaline soils can be reclaimed by flushing salts out with water. Sodic soils (high in Na^+) require treatment with gypsum to replace Na^+ with Ca^{2+} and then flushing with water.

REVIEW

What is pH and why is it used?
What is the optimum pH range for most plants?
What are the five main ways soils become more acid?
What is a buffer and how is this important in soils?
Four factors determine extent of buffering in soils. Do you know what they are?

10

Soil Nutrients
(Soil Fertility)

Under the section on "Soil Aeration" (Chapter 4), it was explained that all living plants respire (Fig. 10.1). This is the process where oxygen is used to burn food into carbon dioxide and
water. Now we will consider another process used by green plants
to manufacture their own food called "photosynthesis." In photosynthesis, carbon dioxide and water are used along with light
energy in the plant cell chloroplasts (containing chlorophyll) to
produce their own food (carbohydrates) with oxygen produced
as a by-product (Fig. 10.1):

$$CO_2 + H_2O \xrightarrow[\text{chlorophyll}]{\text{light energy}} \text{Food (carbohydrates CHO)} + O_2$$

Although this seems to be the opposite process from respiration,
yet there are differences. Note that light energy and chlorophyll
are required in photosynthesis. Chlorophyll is the green coloring
matter in plants.

ELEMENTS REQUIRED BY PLANTS
(ESSENTIAL NUTRIENTS)

There are, at present, seventeen (17) elements that plants need
to grow and complete their life cycle. These are called "essential elements" or "nutrients." Usually an essential element can-

Respiration vs. Photosynthesis

All Living Organisms Respire:

$$O_2 + \begin{array}{c} \textbf{Energy Source} \\ \textbf{(carbohydrates)} \end{array} \longrightarrow CO_2 + H_2O$$

Only Green Plant Photosynthesize:

$$CO_2 + H_2O \xrightarrow[\textbf{Chlorophyll}]{\textbf{Light}} \begin{array}{c} \textbf{Carbo-} \\ \textbf{hydrates} \end{array} + O_2$$

Figure 10.1 Respiration versus photosynthesis. All living organisms respire using oxygen, giving off carbon dioxide and water, but only green plants (containing chlorophyll) can use light energy with carbon dioxide and water to produce food (carbohydrates) and give off oxygen as a byproduct.

not be completely replaced by any other element. There are also four (4) other elements, although not essential, that help plants to grow better. These are called "functional" or "metabolic." To remember all of these elements a memory aid, a mnemonic (the first letter is silent) has been devised. The 21 elements used by plants, carbon (C), hydrogen (H), oxygen (O), phosphorus (P), potassium (K), nitrogen (N), sulfur (S), calcium (Ca), magnesium (Mg), copper (Cu), zinc (Zn), nickel (Ni), cobalt (Co), manganese (Mn), molybdenum (Mo), vanadium (V), boron (B), silicon (Si), chlorine (Cl), and sodium (Na), can be listed in their chemical abbreavtions with the mnemonic below (Fig. 10.2):

C H OP K   N S   Ca Fe   Mg
[C. H o p k (i) n s   CaFe   M(ighty) g(ood)] ·

Cu Zn Ni   Co Mn Mo V   B Si Cl   Na

CouZin Ni,   CoM 'n' Mo V(e) B(Si)Cl(e) Na(ow).

Note: No "I"; iodine is not required by plants.

"Mighty good" uses the first letter of each word for Mg. "Cousin" appears as CuZn; "come 'n'" stands for Co and Mn.

Figure 10.2 Required nutrients. C Hopkns Cafe mnemonic to aid in remembering all elements needed by plants.

"Move" for Mo and V. B(I)SiCl(e) [bicycle] for B, Si, and Cl; but notice B for boron, not Bi (bismuth). Na(ow) for Na.

Nonmineral Elements (C, H, O)

The elements carbon, hydrogen, and oxygen can be considered nonmineral elements, as these are obtained by plants from air and water (O_2, CO_2, and H_2O) and not from the soil. Plants use these three elements to form simple carbohydrates from which large amounts of more complex plant compounds (about 95% of plant tissue) are formed. There is little control of these elements by man, except for water. Supplemental CO_2 has been provided to plants to increase photosynthesis by using solid CO_2 (dry ice), but this has not proved economical. All of the remaining elements are usually absorbed by plants from the soil.

Macronutrients—Used in
Large Amounts

The elements N, P, and K are called the "fertilizer elements" as they are found in complete fertilizers that are commonly used (Fig. 10.3).

The elements Ca and Mg are considered the "lime elements" as they are usually provided to plants in the form of lime or limestone (Fig. 10.3).

Macro-nutrients

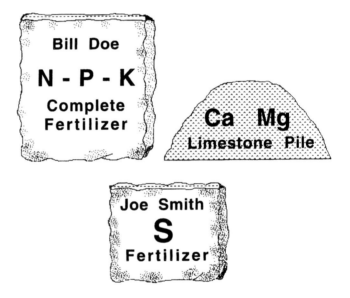

Micro-nutrients

Fe,Cu,Zn,Ni,Co,Mn,Mo,V,B,
Si,Cl,Na

Figure 10.3 Amount of nutrients needed. Contrast between plant macronutrients (N, P, K, Ca, Mg, and S) used in large amounts and micronutrients used in small amounts.

Sulfur is another element that is used by plants in relatively large amounts (Fig. 10.3).

Micronutrients—Used in Small Amounts

All of the remaining elements, after considering the nonmineral elements and macronutrients, are called "micronutrients" (Fig. 10.3) because they are used in small amounts. These are sometimes called "trace" or minor elements, but minor is an improper word to use as these elements are just as important for plant growth as the macroelements already considered. The functional or metabolic elements are Co, V, Si, and Na. Interestingly, bromine (Br) can replace chlorine (Cl); and Na can replace some of the required K.

Forms of Elements Absorbed by Plants

Each element needed by plants is absorbed in one or more forms:

Element	Forms in Which Absorbed
C	CO_2 (gas)
H	H_2O
O	O_2 (gas), H_2O (water)
P	$H_2PO_4^-$, HPO_4^{2-}
K	K^+
N	NO_3^- (nitrate), NH_4^+ (ammonium), urea
S	SO_4^{2-} (sulfate), SO_2 (gas)
Ca	Ca^{2+}
Fe	Fe^{2+}, organic iron
Mg	Mg^{2+}
Cu	Cu^{2+}, organic copper
Zn	Zn^{2+}, organic zinc
Ni	Ni^{2+}
Co	? probably Co^{2+}
Mn	Mn^{2+}, organic manganese
Mo	MoO_4^{2-} (molybdate)
V	? probably VO_3^- (vanadate)
B	$H_2BO_3^-$, HBO_3^{2-}, BO_3^{3-}, $B_4O_7^{2-}$
Si	? probably $Si(OH)4$
Cl	Cl- (chloride)
Na	Na^+

SUMMARY

The 21 elements that plants need to prosper are C, H, O, P, K, N, S, Ca, Fe, Mg, Cu, Zn, Ni, Co, Mn, Mo, V, B, Si, Cl, Na. They can be remembered by a mnemonic, namely, C. Hopkns CaFe Mighty good, CouZn Ni, CoM(e)n MoV(e) BsiCl Na(ow). Plants obtain the nonmineral elements, C, H, and O, from oxygen, carbon dioxide, and water. All of the other nutrients needed by plants are usually obtained from the soil. Those elements needed in large amounts are called macronutrients and include C, H, O, N, P, K, Ca, Mg, and S; all the remaining required nutrients are used in small amounts—the micronutrients—and include Fe, Cu, Zn, Ni, Co, Mn, Mo, V, B, Si, Cl, and Na. All 21 elements are important for plant growth and reproduction; there is no one element that is more important than any other—if any nutrient is deficient, then growth will be restricted and the plant will die prematurely. The fertilizer elements are N, P, and K as these are usually supplied to plants in complete fertilizers. Lime elements are Ca and Mg and are most often supplied to plants as liming material. The remaining micronutrients are usually provided by the soil.

REVIEW

Can you name the 21 elements needed by plants?

What is an easy way to remember all nutrients required by plants?

From where do plants obtain the nonmineral elements?

From what source do plants obtain all of the other nutrients?

Distinguish between macronutrients and micronutrients.

Which element is most important?

Which elements are considered fertilizer elements?

Can you name the lime elements?

It is important to know the forms in which each nutrient is absorbed by plants. Do you know them?

11

Macronutrients

Nitrogen

NITROGEN IN PLANTS

Important considerations concerning nitrogen in plants include the amount of nitrogen required, the forms of nitrogen (inorganic and organic) present in plant tissue, the ways that nitrogen is used in plants and affected by fertilization, and symptoms plants show when nitrogen is deficient.

Amounts of N in Plants

After the nonmineral elements, N is found in the next largest amount. More N is needed by plants than all the other nonmineral elements combined, except for K. The range of N concentrations in plants is from 0.5 to 6.0%, with most plants having 1.5 to 3.0%.

Forms of N in Plants

Inorganic forms of N in plants are NO_3^- (nitrate) and NH_4^+ (ammonium). These forms are usually present in relatively small amounts. Other inorganic forms of N do not accumulate without injury to the plants.

Organic forms of N predominate in plants, mainly as amino acids (Fig. 11.1) and proteins. During and after absorption, N often follows this pathway:

N → simple amino acids → complex proteins → protoplasm → growth and
    (move in plants)   (formed in place,   reproduction
                    that is, not
                    translocated)

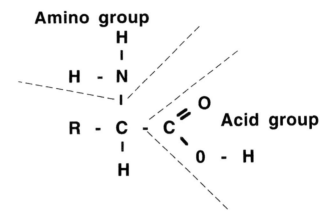

An Amino Acid

**Relatively small molecule--
moves in plant easily**

Figure 11.1 Amino acid structure. Small amino acid molecules move readily in plants.

Proteins consist of a number of amino acids linked together into a large molecular structure (Fig. 11.2). Once the proteins are formed in plants, N moves to other parts of the plant only if the proteins are split apart by hydrolysis into amino acids (Fig. 11.3). The amino acids then flow freely to other parts of the plant where they can recombine into proteins again. Proteins consist of 12 to 19% nitrogen.

Other complex proteins formed from amino acids are enzymes that act as catalysts in biochemical reactions. Proteins also act as reserve food in the seeds that is released during germination for early seedling growth. Another type of N-containing material is chlorophyll (the green coloring matter in leaves necessary for photosynthesis). In the center of a chlorophyll molecule is a Mg atom surrounded by four N atoms (Fig. 11.4). Therefore, N is a part of the chlorophyll molecule and if N is deficient, then plants become yellow since there is insufficient chlorophyll produced.

Other important N-complexes are purine and pyrimidine bases that can form adenosine triphosphate (ATP) (Fig. 11.5) during the respiration process as an energy carrier.

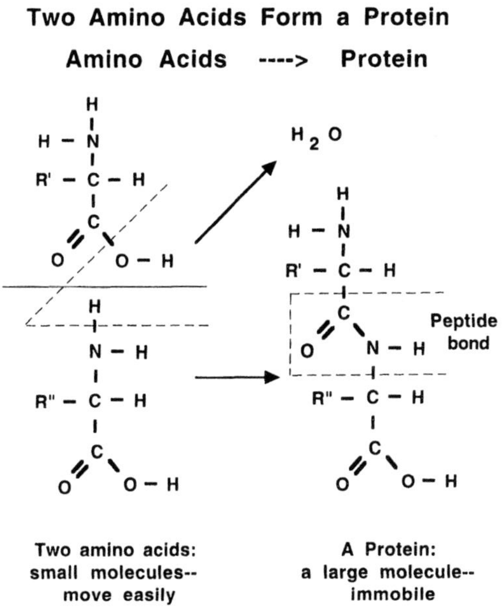

Two Amino Acids Form a Protein
Amino Acids ----> Protein

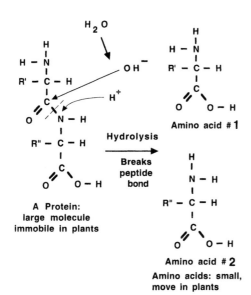

Figure 11.2 Protein formation from amino acids. A large protein molecule forms when two amino acids combine through a peptide bond releasing a water molecule. The protein is too large to move in plants and is immobile.

A Protein Hydrolyzed to 2 Amino Acids

Figure 11.3 Hydrolysis of proteins. To move in plants, proteins must be broken apart into two smaller amino acids by hydrolysis and breaking of the peptide bonds.

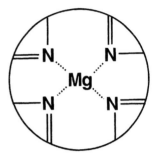

Figure 11.4 Internal structure of chlorophyll. The chemical structure of a chlorophyll molecule shows 4 N atoms surrounding a Mg atom.

Effects of N on Plants

Nitrogen in plants encourages vegetative growth, green color, and succulence. Application of N to plants often shows the quickest and most pronounced effect of all fertilizers.

An excess of N in the soil can weaken plants as they tend to have more vegetative growth, do not mature properly, and are more susceptible to diseases and attack by insects. Ex-

Adenosine Triphosphate (ATP)

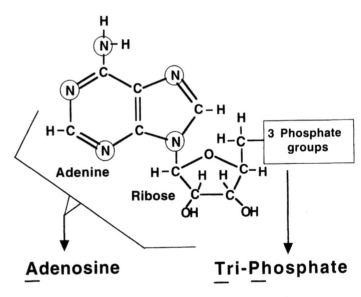

Figure 11.5 ATP molecule. Five N atoms are present in one adenosine triphosphate (ATP) molecule in plants.

cess N in the soil is evident in grain fields after a wind storm, as some of the plants are lodged, that is, knocked down and remain flat.

Nitrogen Deficiency Symptoms

Plants deficient in N generally show symptoms on the leaves of distinct yellowing, small leaves, and the leaves may drop prematurely. Older leaves are affected first. On conifers the needles become yellow, short, close together, and may drop. The lower parts of conifers become yellow and the upper crown remains green. Lack of N also causes restriction of root growth.

NITROGEN IN SOILS

Amounts of N in Soils

Most mineral soils have from 1 to 10% N, with the usual amount around 3,000 pounds per acre or 7 pounds per 100 square feet.

Forms of N in Soils

Inorganic nitrogen is present in soils as NO_3^- (nitrate), NH_4^+ (ammonium), NO_2^- (nitrite), gases, such as N_2O, NO, NO_2, N_2 NH_3, and NH_4^+-fixed between clay crystals. All of these forms only amount to about 2 to 3% of the total N in soils.

From 97 to 98% of the total soil N exists in organic forms as complexes.

Amino Acids and Proteins.   Amino acids or proteins may be adsorbed or combined with clays, lignins, and other compounds forming *complexes*. This is the reason why organic matter is resistant to decomposition, since these complexes are much more difficult to degrade by microbes. Most of the organic N (about 24 to 37%) is in these forms.

Nucleic Acids.   Nucleic acids and their derivatives (compounds formed from nucleic acids that are slightly different) are present usually from about 3 to 10% of organic N in soils. Nucleic acids are very large, complex molecules.

Amino Sugars.   Only about 5 to 10% of organic soil N is in the amino sugar form. An amino sugar is a saccharide (sugar) with an amino group (NH_2) attached.

Other Unidentified Compounds.   About 50% or more of organic N in soils has not been identified. These organic N substances could be complexes formed from (a) reaction of lignin with ammonia; (b) polymerization of quinones with N; or (c) condensation of sugars with amines. All these types of complexes are generally strongly adsorbed and highly resistant to decomposition.

TRANSFORMATIONS OF NITROGEN IN SOILS

Mineralization vs. Immobilization

Two processes in soils alter availability of N—mineralization and immobilization. Mineralization is the conversion of complex organic N to simple inorganic forms. This process proceeds whenever organic substances are in the final stages of decomposition and is usually beneficial as it releases N so that it becomes available for plant growth. Immobilization is the reverse of mineralization, for example, changing of simple organic N compounds into complex organic compounds. This process occurs as N goes into a temporarily unavailable form in the bodies of microorganisms during the decomposition process. Generally, this process is undesirable for immediate plant use of N; however, in the long run this process benefits plants.

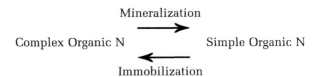

$$\text{Complex Organic N} \quad \underset{\text{Immobilization}}{\overset{\text{Mineralization}}{\rightleftarrows}} \quad \text{Simple Organic N}$$

DECOMPOSITION (MINERALIZATION) PROCESSES

Aminization = Formation of Amines

In this process complex proteins are digested by microbes into simpler amino compounds with the by-product of carbon dioxide. Thus:

$$\text{Proteins} \xrightarrow{\text{microbes}} \text{amino compounds } (\text{-NH}_2) + \text{CO}_2 + \text{energy} + \ldots$$

Ammonification = Formation
of Ammonia

amino compounds   microbes
(-NH₂) + H₂O   →   NH₃ + R-OH + energy
                          hydrolysis

The ammonia (NH_3) formed in this process can combine with soil moisture forming ammonium hydroxide, or with carbonic acid to form ammonium (NH_4+) and carbonate:

$$NH_3 + H_2O \quad \rightarrow \quad NH_4OH \quad \rightarrow \quad NH_4^+ + H_2O$$
$$2\,NH_3 + H_2CO_3 \quad \rightarrow \quad (NH_4)_2CO_3 \quad \rightarrow \quad 2\,NH_4^+ + CO_3^{2-}$$

Fate of NH_4+ Formed

1. Adsorbed onto soil particles and available for plants;
2. Used by soil microbes;
3. Used by higher plants, especially young plants, and acid-loving plants (azaleas, hollies, rhododendrons) in acid soils;
4. Fixed between clay crystals in Illitic soils—temporarily not available to plants, but is slowly released with time;
5. Volatilized as a gas (NH_3) and lost to the atmosphere;
6. Used in the process of nitrification.

NITRIFICATION = FORMATION OF NITRATES

Nitrification is a two-step process involving microbial enzymatic oxidation. Specific microorganisms (*Nitrosomonas, Nitrosococcus*) derive energy by oxidizing ammonium (NH_4^+). In the first step, nitrite (NO_2^-) is formed along with water and H^+. In the second step, nitrite is oxidized by a different and only one specific microbe only *Nitrobacter* into nitrate (NO_3^-).

Step 1.   *Nitrosomonas* or *Nitrosococcus*
   $2NH_4^+ + 3O_2 \quad \rightarrow \quad 2NO_2^- + 2H_2O + 4H^+ + energy$
Step 2.   *Nitrobacter*
         $2\,NO_2^- + O_2 \quad \rightarrow \quad 2NO_3^- + energy$

Important Items of Nitrification to Consider

1. The initial reactant in nitrification is the ammonium ion (NH_4^+). Anything that produces ammonium will start this reaction if conditions are conducive to the specific microbes involved.

2. Molecular oxygen (O_2) is needed—soil aeration is important. Anytime the soil is disturbed, that is, by spading, plowing, cultivating, etc., oxygen can enter and stimulate this process.

3. Only specific bacteria are involved in nitrification. Other microbes, besides *Nitrosomonas* and *Nitrosococcus*, can operate for step one, but *Nitrobacter* is the only bacteria that can oxidize nitrite in soils. All of these special bacteria are extremely sensitive to their environment, and the extent of their activity depends on the environmental conditions that are suitable to them.

4. Nitrite (NO_2^-) is toxic to plants. Fortunately, this product does not accumulate in slightly acid, well-drained soils because the second step in nitrification is very rapid, occurring as soon as the NO_2^- is formed. However, if these conditions are not met, then plant growth may be less than desired.

Factors Affecting Nitrification

The degree and speed that nitrification occurs in soils are directly affected by the amount of ammonium ion (NH_4^+), the C/N ratio of material present in the soil, the soil reaction (pH), the amount of soil aeration, the amount of moisture present in the soil, and the prevailing soil temperature. A disporportional change of one of these factors can override any other, thereby increasing or decreasing the extent that nitrification occurs.

Ammonium ion is the substrate used for nitrification. Conditions must favor release of NH_3 from organic decomposition or NH_4^+ from some other source, such as ammonium fertilizer. However, too much NH_3 or urea can be toxic, especially to *Nitrobacter*.

The C/N ratio must not be too wide as this reduces the amount of NH_4^+ available for nitrification. The C/N ratio varies when the following are present:

	C/N Ratio
Bodies of microorganisms	9/1
Undisturbed topsoil in equilibrium and organic matter in mineral soils	12/1
Legumes	20/1
Straw	100/1
Sawdust	400/1

The practical importance of this ratio can be illustrated. If one uses large amounts of sawdust, the N may be temporarily immobilized in the bodies of microbes during the decomposition process, and plants growing nearby may suffer N deficiency. To prevent this from happening, one can add N fertilizer whenever sawdust or other carbonaceous material, such as wood chips, is used for mulching. Another alternative would be to allow at least six to eight weeks after adding the carbonaceous material to the soil for the microbes to complete the decomposition process, at which time N would once again become available for plants.

Soil pH

The optimum pH for nitrification is 8.3, but this pH is not practical to have in most humid region soils. Nitrification processes slow considerably in very acid soils. Therefore, acid soils in the humid regions should be limed to stimulate nitrification.

Soil Aeration

Nitrification is an oxidation process. So any manner of getting oxygen into soils, such as plowing, cultivation, stirring the soil, will improve aeration for this process. Desirable soil structure also helps move the oxygen to the area where nitrification is proceeding.

Soil Moisture

Nitrifying bacteria have specific moisture requirements. Nitrification is retarded when moisture becomes very low, as in drought, or very high, as when flooded. Some nitrification can occur at low soil moisture, even below the wilting point; however, nitrification is more reduced when too much water is present, that is, flooding. Nitrification is encouraged when the soil is alternately wetted and dried, as this stimulates more rapid oxidation of organic matter providing greater amounts of the substrate NH_4^+.

Soil Temperature

Nitrification has an optimum temperature of about 85° F, but stops completely at 32° F and 125° F. Nitrification is similar to a large locomotive—it is difficult to get it started (e.g., in early spring), but once nitrification has started and the temperature drops, it takes a long time for nitrification to slow down (as in the fall of the year). This means that sometimes extra N fertilizer is needed for plant growth in the early spring but not in the fall.

NITROGEN FIXATION IN SOILS

Nitrogen fixation is the process in soils where nitrogen gas (N_2) from the air is converted into a form that is available for plants. Do not confuse this N-fixation with nitrification. When fixation is mentioned in relation to soils, the element has usually been converted into a form that is no longer available for plants. However, N-fixation is just the reverse of this since the N is released and available for plants. Therefore, N-fixation is the only type of fixation in which the element becomes more available for plants.

There are four different types of N-fixation: (1) symbiotic bacteria in legume nodules; (2) symbiotic actinomycetes or blue-green algae in nodules of nonlegumes; (3) symbiotic blue-green algae or bacteria not in nodules; and (4) nonsymbiotic by free-living bacteria or blue-green algae.

Symbiotic N-Fixation by Bacteria in Nodules of Legume Roots

Rhizobium

Bacteria of the genus *Rhizobium* live in swellings (nodules) that form on the roots of legumes, have the ability to use nitrogen gas (N_2) from the soil air (in equilibrium with the atmosphere), and convert it to a plant-available form that the legume plant can use. This relationship is *symbiotic* in that these two species live together for the mutual benefit of both. The bacteria provides available N for the plant while the plant provides a food supply (carbohydrates) for the bacteria.

The species of this *Rhizobium* genus are *specific* for the legume host that they infect (Fig. 11.6). Some examples, alfalfa (*Medicago sativa*) plants only fix N when they become infected by *Rhizobium meliloti*, and white clover (*Trifolium pratense*) plants only fix N when they become infected by *Rhizobium trifolium*. Each of these two legumes may fix as much as 250 pounds of N/acre/year, which is more N fixed than by other legume species.

The practical importance of this is that if grasses in lawns are grown with properly inoculated white clover legumes, the bacteria will fix N from the air that both the legumes and grasses

Symbiotic N-Fixation:
Nodules on Legumes with Rhizobium bacteria

Alfalfa Plant Roots

Clover Plant Roots

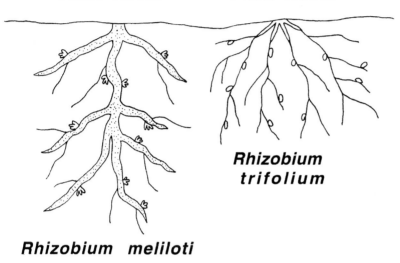

Rhizobium trifolium

Rhizobium meliloti

Figure 11.6 N-Fixation by *Rhizobium*. Nodules on legume roots contain specific *Rhizobium* bacteria that can fix N (make N available for plants from N_2 gas). Alfalfa root nodules appear as finger-like projections, whereas clover root nodules are round or oval shaped.

growing together can use; therefore, less expensive N fertilizer is needed.

Requirements for Rhizobium bacteria.   Conditions that are optimum for growth of the legumes that fix N will also be optimum for growth of the *Rhizobium* bacteria. These include adequate aeration, optimum temperature of 85° F, pH 5.5 to 7.0, adequate molybdenum (Mo), and avoiding high concentrations of Mn (toxic). Also, one must avoid large applications of N fertilizer as this will discourage these bacteria from fixing N (they become lazy if you provide N in a fertilizer form).

In order to assure that these specific bacteria are present in the soil, one should inoculate the legume seed with the specific bacteria prior to seeding. This is accomplished by buying the inoculant of the appropriate bacteria that are adsorbed onto fine charcoal, mixing the inoculant with slightly moistened seed, and planting the inoculated seed. The bacteria infect the legume root as the seed germinates; in about three weeks the nodules form and can fix N.

One can tell if the bacteria are effective in fixing N by removing a nodule and cutting it in two. If the inside is red or pink, the bacteria are fixing N; if the inside is black, brown, or gray, no N is being fixed. In the latter case, nodules may be present but are not fixing N, probably as the legume root has been infected with a strain of bacteria that is ineffective in fixing N. Some of these *Rhizobium* bacteria will inhabit the soil by the nodules being sloughed off when they become old or when the legume plant dies. The bacteria can remain viable in the soil up to 10 years. One does not have to inoculate the legume seed if the area has been inoculated recently; however, the inoculant is so inexpensive in relation to the N which is fixed that it is wise to inoculate all seed (from plants that fix N) whenever planted.

The N that is fixed by the bacteria is (a) used by the legume host plant for better growth and higher protein; (b) passed into the soil by excretion or root or nodule sloughage; or (c) used by nonlegume grasses growing adjacent or even in succeeding years.

Symbiotic N-Fixation by Nodulated Nonlegumes

Actinomycetes (Frankia)

Nitrogen can be fixed by the actinomycete genus *Frankia* in nodules on the roots of Alder trees (*Alnus*). This actinomycete can fix as much as 150 pounds/acre/year. There are only about 160 species of nonlegumes that can fix N compared with 13,000 legumes species. A blue-green algae can also fix N in nodules of *Gunneria* (an aquatic plant) but only in very small amounts.

Symbiotic N-Fixation by Nonlegumes (No Nodules)

The blue-green algae genus *Anabaena* fixes up to 300 pounds/acre/year when associated with *Azolla* (floating fern plants) in tropical and semi-tropical rice paddies.

Nonsymbiotic N-Fixation

Free-living bacteria and blue-green algae in soil can fix N but only in very small amounts. These bacteria include *Azotobacter* (aerobic), *Clostridium* (anaerobic), and photosynthetic bacteria.

NITROGEN ADDED TO SOILS
FROM THE ATMOSPHERE

Significant amounts of N can be added to soils by air contamination from industry as fallout or from acid rain. Much lesser amounts are added to soils as N becomes fixed (available) when lightning occurs in thunderstorms. The rain or snow that falls contains only small amounts (5 pounds/acre/year) of N.

LOSSES OF NITROGEN FROM SOILS

Nitrogen can be lost from soils during leaching, erosion of organic matter, volatilization, and ammonium-fixation within clays.

Leaching of Nitrate

Leaching of nitrate occurs in the drainage water because nitrate is negatively charged and is repelled from the negative charges on the soil particles.

Erosion of Organic Matter

Soil organic matter contains appreciable amounts of N. Whenever soil is eroded, organic matter associated with the clays is also eroded.

Volatilization

Nitrogen can change into a vapor form that may be lost to the atmosphere. Considerable N can be lost by volatilization that especially occurs when conditions become anaerobic, that is, flooded or compacted soils. More N is lost in this way if the soil has an abundance of nitrate (NO_3^-) instead of ammonium (NH_4^+).

N Gases.   At low pH, nitrate can change into gases that can be lost to the atmosphere:

$$NO_3^- \rightarrow NO_2^- \rightarrow NO \text{ (gas)} \rightarrow N_2O \text{ (gas)} \rightarrow N_2 \text{ (gas)}$$

Ammonia.   At pH above 7, ammonium in soils can be converted to the ammonia gas that can be lost to the atmosphere.

$$NH_4^+ + H_2O + OH^- \rightarrow 2H_2O + NH_3 \text{ (gas)}$$

Much N is lost at high temperatures from surface-applied manure, urea, or ammonium fertilizers. Losses can be held to a minimum by working these materials into the soil or by applying them on top of a mulch.

Ammonium-Fixation Within Clays (Temporary)

Ammonium can be held so tightly between illite clay crystals that it is no longer available for plants. The clay-fixed ammonium is only temporarily lost, as it can be released slowly by wetting and drying or freezing and thawing cycles.

SUMMARY

In plants, N is present as inorganic NO_3^- and NH_4^+ ions and as organic molecules that include amino acids, proteins, ATP, and chlorophyll. The organic forms predominate. Nitrogen fertilization shows effects very fast as it stimulates formation of green color; it also encourages vegetative growth and succulence. An excess of N will cause rapid top growth that is weak, plants may fall over, and plants often are more susceptible to attack by diseases and insects. Deficiency of N will cause older leaves to become yellow and drop prematurely.

In soils, N exists as small amounts of inorganic forms (NO_3^-, NO_2^-, NH_4^+, and gases—N_2, NO_2, NO, N_2O, NH_3) and very large amounts (about 98%) of organic forms, including amino acids, proteins, nucleic acids and derivatives, amino sugars, and many other unidentified compounds.

Mineralization in the soil is the change from complex organic compounds into simple forms that are available to plants and microbes. The reverse of mineralization is immobilization, in which the simple N forms are converted into complex organic forms by microbes. Two processes involving N that occur during decomposition are aminization (formation of amines) and ammonification (formation of ammonia). Aminization involves microbial breakdown of proteins or other complex N compounds for energy into intermediate amino-compounds with by-products of carbon dioxide. The amino-compounds are further attacked by microbes for energy during hydrolysis to form alcohols and ammonia. The ammonia gas (NH_3) formed will react with water to form an ammonium ion (NH_4^+). This ammonium can be adsorbed onto soil particles, used by microbes and plants, fixed into clays, volatilized as a gas, or used in the nitrification process.

Nitrification is a two-step process where, in the first step, ammonium is oxidized for energy by special bacteria *Nitrosomonas* or *Nitrosococcus* into water, H^+, and the intermediate product nitrite (NO_2^-); in the second step, the nitrite is further oxidized for energy only by specific bacteria *Nitrobacter* into nitrate (NO_3^-). Nitrification requires an abundance of NH_4^+, a low C/N ratio, near neutral pH, adequate aeration, sufficient moisture, and warm temperatures.

Nitrogen fixation is the process whereby inorganic N gas is converted into plant-available N. This process often involves a symbiotic relationship between bacteria (*Rhizobium* spp.) in root nodules with the legume host plant. Nitrogen fixation can occur as symbiotic relationships of (a) bacteria in legume root nodules, (b) blue-green algae or bacteria in nodules of nonlegumes, or (c) blue-green algae or bacteria not in nodules, or (d) nonsymbiotic free-living bacteria or blue-green algae. *Rhizobium* bacteria, specific for each legume species and present in root nodules, fix large amounts of N. The bacteria are inoculated (placed onto the legume seed) and infect the plant as the seedling grows. As the *Rhizobium* multiply a symbiotic relationship occurs. The legume root reacts by forming a nodule in which the bacteria uses root carbohydrates and transforms gaseous N_2 to a form that the legume can use. *Rhizobium* bacteria require the same conditions as their legume host plants, but will stop fixing N if large amounts of N fertilizer is present. If the color inside of nodules is red or pink, N is being fixed; however, if it is white, brown or black, N is not being fixed. Nitrogen that is fixed by *Rhizobium* can be used by the legume host plant, passed into the soil by excretion or root or nodule sloughage, or used by nonlegumes growing adjacent or even in succeeding years.

Other kinds of symbiotic N fixation can occur in large amounts by actinomycetes (*Frankia*) in nodules of alder trees and by blue-green algae (*Anabaena*) associated with floating fern plants in the tropics. Much smaller amounts of N are fixed by the free-living bacteria, *Azotobacter* or *Clostridium*.

Small amounts of N are fixed every year by lightning in thunderstorms coming to earth as rain.

Nitrogen can be lost from soils during leaching, erosion, or by gases. Much N is lost by volatilization as N gases, especially at low pH under anaerobic conditions, and at high pH as ammonia gas (NH_3). Some N may be temporarily lost when ammonium is held between illite clay crystals.

REVIEW

Which forms of N are present in plants?
Of the N forms found in plants, which are
    present in very large amounts? Can you
    name the forms?
How does N react in plants? Is a large amount
    of N detrimental to plant growth?
How would one describe symptoms that
    plants show when N is deficient?
In what forms is N present in soils? Which
    predominate?
Differentiate between mineralization and
    immobilization.
Can you name and describe the two N pro-
    cesses that occur during decomposition?
Does the ammonia produced remain in that
    form in soil or change into some other
    form?
What becomes of the ammonium in soils?
Describe the nitrification process in detail.
What is critical for nitrification to proceed in
    soils?
Differentiate between nitrification and
    nitrogen fixation.
What are the different kinds of nitrogen
    fixation in soils?
Describe how N is fixed by bacteria in nod-
    ules of legume roots.
What are the requirements of *Rhizobium*
    bacteria?
How can one determine if N is being fixed by
    these *Rhizobium* bacteria?
How can the N that is fixed by legume roots
    be used by plants?

(*continued*) ➥

REVIEW (*continued*)

Describe the other kinds of N fixation that
  occur and how much N is fixed by each?
By what natural process is a small amount of
  N added to soils each year?
Describe the conditions under which N is lost
  from soils?

12

Macronutrients

Phosphorus and Potassium

Plants have a P concentration between 0.03 and 0.70%, but the usual amount is between 0.1 and 0.4%. Phosphorus is found in every living cell of a plant and is involved in genetic transfer and energy relationships. The actively growing parts, that is, stem tips, new leaves, and new roots, need much P. Seeds, especially at maturity, also have a rich supply of P acting as reserve food. Phosphorus is used in plants for (a) root development—especially the lateral and fibrous roots; (b) cell division—energy for metabolism; (c) reproduction—flowering, fruiting, seed formation all controlled by nucleic acids; (d) maturation—counteracts the ill effects of excessive N fertilization; and (e) disease resistance—especially important in root rots of seedlings.

Forms of Phosphorus in Plants

Plant P is a major constituent of chromosomes present as DNA (deoxyribonucleic acid) used in reproduction and RNA (ribonucleic acid) used in growth processes. Plant P is also a constituent of adenosine triphosphate (ATP) (Fig. 12.1) that stores energy for plant use, along with many other phosphate compounds, such as phytin (inositol hexaphosphate) (Fig. 12.2) stored in seeds, phospholipids in the chloroplasts, and complexes of sugars, sugar amines, aldehydes, amides, and acids—all involved in plant metabolism.

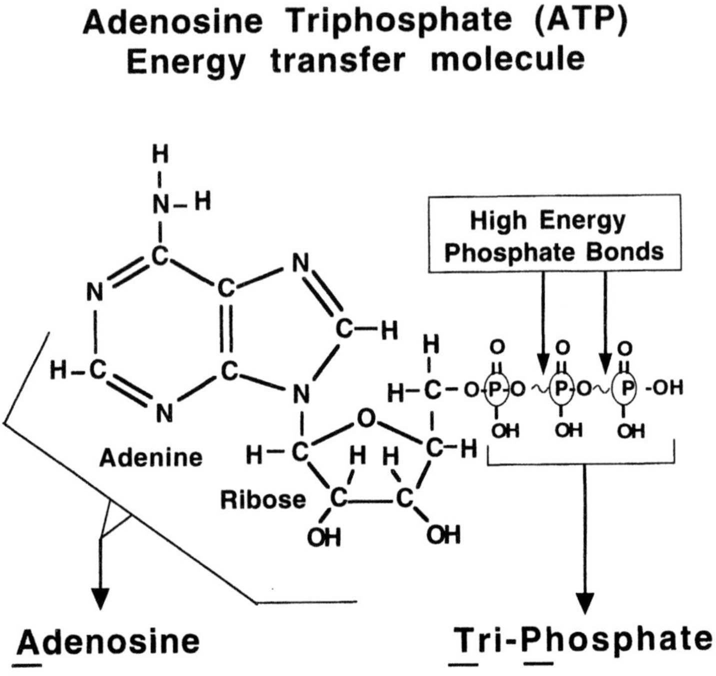

Adenosine Triphosphate (ATP)
Energy transfer molecule

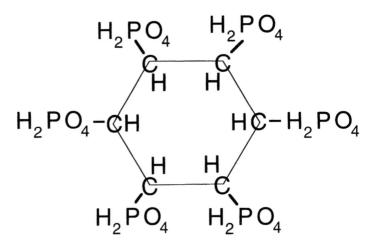

Figure 12.1 Structure of an ATP molecule. Three P atoms are present in each adenosine triphosphate (ATP) molecule in plants. Two of the P atoms are linked by a high energy phosphate bond that gives energy for plant processes during metabolism.

Figure 12.2 Phytin. Each phytin (inositol hexaphosphate) molecule contains six phosphate groups.

Phosphorus Deficiency Symptoms

Deficiency of P is not striking or characteristic and is difficult to diagnose. The older leaves may be dark bluish-green, bronze, or purple. The stalks are thin, leaves small, limited lateral growth, delayed maturity, and defoliate prematurely. Probably the most obvious symptom would be the purple coloration, but this is exhibited by only a limited number of plants. The best way to determine if a plant is deficient in P would be to conduct a plant tissue test. If the P level is lower than 0.2% P, then P probably is deficient and the soil in which the plant is growing would benefit from P fertilization.

Phosphorus Toxicity?

Phosphorus toxicity has not been observed in the field and has only been evident in greenhouse culture solutions when P was present at extremely high concentrations. The leaves had an unusually high P concentration of 0.9% P resulting in necrotic (dead) spots.

PHOSPHORUS IN SOILS

The amount of P in soil is very low and varies from 0.02 to 0.22% depending on the parent material (rocks). The main problem of P in soils is due to three situations: (1) low amounts present in most soils, (2) most of the P that is present is not readily available to plants, and (3) much of the P added in fertilizer is fixed into an unavailable form. Although the low amounts in soils may be detrimental to most crops, the amounts are usually sufficient for many trees and large shrubs.

Mycorrhizae

Mycorrhizae are fungi that attach themselves to the roots of plants, especially young trees, and grow in symbiotic relationship with the host plant. The finger-like extension of *Mychorrhizae* provide a larger surface for absorbing P and pass it on to the plant on which they are growing (Fig. 12.3). *Mycorrhizae* are sometimes added to the nursery soil in which tree seedlings are started. Generally, *Mycorrhizae* are only helpful to plants on soils that are extremely low in P. On soils heavily fertilized with P, the fungi do not provide sufficient P to the plants growing thereon to be effective.

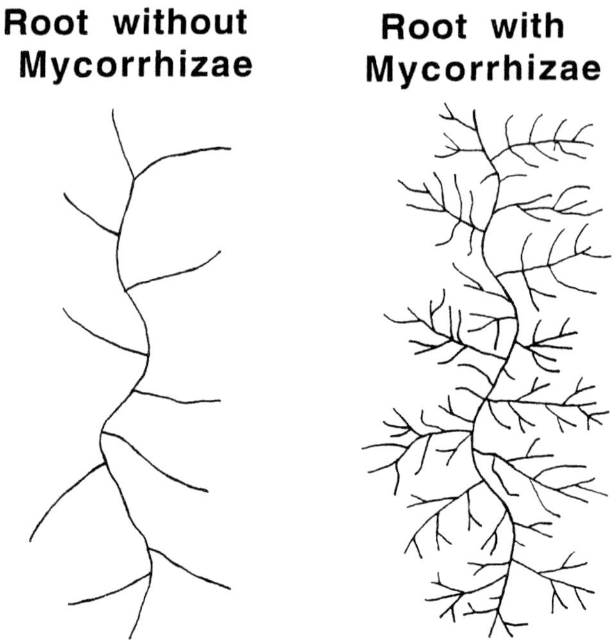

Root without Mycorrhizae

Root with Mycorrhizae

Figure 12.3 Mycorrhizal fungi on plant roots. Mycorrhizae act as root extensions providing greater area for root absorption, especially when P is present in very small amounts in soils.

Forms of Phosphorus in Soils

Phosphorus is present in soils in organic (25 to 80%) and inorganic (20 to 75%) forms. Inorganic forms are present as phosphates ($H_2PO_4^-$ and HPO_4^{2-}) of Ca, Fe, or Al. More is known about the calcium phosphates than those of Fe or Al.

Calcium Phospates ($H_2PO_4^-$ and HPO_4^{2-})

Solubility of Ca-phosphates varies with the different forms:

$Ca(H_2PO_4)_2$	mono-Ca phospate	most soluble
$CaHPO_4$	di-Ca phosphate	↑
$Ca_3(PO_4)_2$	tri-Ca phosphate	↕
$Ca_3(PO_4)_2$-X	apatite minerals	least soluble

$$X = CaF_2; \ CaCO_3; \ Ca(OH)_2; \ \text{and CaO}$$

Iron, Manganese,
and Aluminum Phosphates

Phosphates of Fe, Mn, and Al are probably present as hydroxy-phosphates. They are very insoluble and stable in acid soils. After P fertilizer is added to a soil, Al-phosphates form first and with time change to Fe-phosphates.

Organic Phosphorus

Organic forms of P are present in a number of forms. They vary from 40 to 80% with most of the organic P present as phytin.
  Phytin. Phytin is inositol hexaphosphate, a six-membered saturated carbon ring structure that has six phosphate groups (Fig. 12.2). Each phosphate group ($-H_2PO_4$) is attached to one of the C atoms. Phytin can be hydrolyzed in soil by the phytase enzyme secreted by microbes, resulting in phytin derivatives (compounds similar to the original compound). Phosphate groups are removed one at a time leaving a derivative consisting of 5, 4, 3, 2, or 1 phosphate groups. Therefore, a total of six phosphate anions can be formed from one phytin molecule. The phosphate anion ($H_2PO_4^-$) is released into the soil solution and can be used by plants or microbes or enter into fixation reactions.
  Complex Nucleic acids, nucleoproteins, and phospholipids. These are present only in small amounts in soils.
  Other Unidentified P forms. There are many other P forms in soils that have not been identified.

FACTORS AFFECTING AVAILABILITY OF PHOSPHORUS IN SOILS

The availability of phosphorus in soils is related to (a) soil physical properties of aeration, compaction, moisture, texture, and temperature; (b) soil chemical properties of soil pH, presence of soluble and hydrous oxides of aluminum, iron, and manganese at low pH, presence of calcium at high pH, presence of hydroxyaluminum polymers, and reaction with kaolinite clay; and (c) biological properties of organic matter decomposition, presence of microbial organic acids, and reactions with phytin.

Soil Physical Properties

Soil physical properties that influence P availability in soils are
(a) aeration, (b) compaction, (c) moisture, (d) texture, and (e)
temperature.

Aeration.   In well-aerated soils decomposition can proceed
rapidly, resulting in mineralization of organic P to the inorganic form that plants can use. Oxygen is necessary for
metabolic processes of many microorganisms.

Compaction.   A decrease in pore size from compaction
results in less root penetration. Since P does not move much
in soils, the soil P becomes positionally unavailable.

Moisture.   The optimum moisture for plant growth is the
optimum for P availability.

Texture.   As soil particle size decreases, there is a greater
area for the P to become fixed in soils and made unavailable.

Temperature.   Temperature affects mineralization rate of
organic P and thus affects available P present. Also, very
high or very low temperatures affect metabolic processes
in plants so that less P is absorbed.

Soil Chemical Properties

Soil chemical properties that directly affect forms of phosphorus present in soils are (a) soil pH; (b) soluble Al, Fe, and Mn; (c)
hydrous oxides of Al, Fe, and Mn; (d) presence of Ca at high pH;
(e) fixation by hydroxyaluminum polymers; and (e) reaction with
kaolinitic silicate clays.

Soil pH

Changes in soil pH, even in solution, affect availability of P present.

$$\text{very low pH} \quad \longleftrightarrow \quad \text{very high pH}$$
$$H_3PO_4 \quad \leftrightarrows \quad H_2PO_4^- \ HPO_4^{2-} \quad \leftrightarrows \quad PO_4^{3-}$$
$$\text{most available} \quad \text{least available}$$

Soluble Al, Fe, and Mn (Fixation by Precipitation)

Iron, Mn, or Al are soluble at low soil pH and can react with
soluble phosphate, resulting in the phospate becoming insoluble
and unavailable for plants (Fig. 12.4).

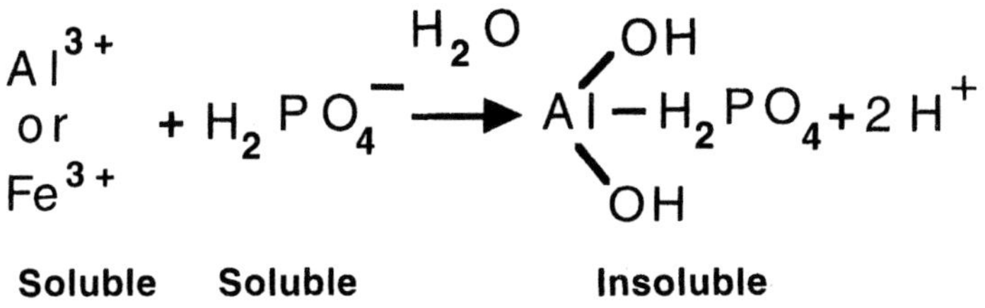

$$\begin{array}{c} Al^{3+} \\ or \\ Fe^{3+} \end{array} + H_2PO_4^- \xrightarrow{H_2O} Al\underset{OH}{\overset{OH}{-}}H_2PO_4 + 2H^+$$

Soluble   Soluble   Insoluble

Figure 12.4 P-Fixation by soluble Al or Fe. Soluble P can become fixed in an unavailable form for plants by reacting with soluble Al or Fe at low pH.

Hydrous Oxides of Al, Fe, and Mn
(Fixation by Precipitation)

When hydrous oxides of Fe, Al, or Mn are present in soils, they can react with soluble phosphate similar to the soluble forms (Fig. 12.5). The only difference is the initial form in which the Fe, Al, or Mn is present.

Presence of Calcium at High pH

Presence of insoluble $CaCO_3$ or Ca adsorbed as Ca^{++} can react with soluble $Ca(H_2PO_4)_2$ to form insoluble tri-Ca-phosphate $[Ca_3(PO_4)_2]$, a relatively insoluble P that cannot be used by plants (Fig. 12.6).

Fixation by
Hydroxy-Aluminum Polymers

Hydrous oxides of Al can form long chain polymers that complex with soluble phosphate making it unavailable. These polymers can occur at any pH.

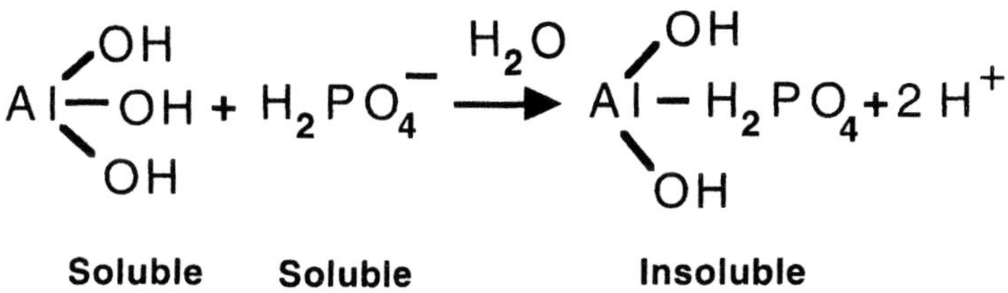

$$Al\underset{OH}{\overset{OH}{-}}OH + H_2PO_4^- \xrightarrow{H_2O} Al\underset{OH}{\overset{OH}{-}}H_2PO_4 + 2H^+$$

Soluble   Soluble   Insoluble

Figure 12.5 P-Fixation by oxides of Al, Fe, or Mn. Soluble P can become fixed in an unavailable form for plants by reacting with hydrous oxides of Al, Fe, or Mn at low pH.

$$Ca(H_2PO_4)_2 + Ca^{2+} \longrightarrow Ca_3(PO_4)_2 + 4H^+$$

Soluble　　　**Adsorbed**　　　**Insoluble**

$$Ca(H_2PO_4)_2 + CaCO_3 \longrightarrow Ca_3(PO_4)_2 \begin{array}{l} +CO_2 \\ +2H_2O \end{array}$$

Soluble　　　**Insoluble**　　　**Insoluble**

Figure 12.6. P-Fixation with Ca. Soluble P can become fixed in an unavailable form for plants by reacting with Ca at high pH.

Reaction with Kaolinite Silicate Clay

Kaolinte clay (1:1) in soil can react with soluble phosphate producing an unstable material that breaks the clay apart into an aluminum hydroxy-phosphate precipitate (insoluble and unavailable for plants) along with sand (SiO_2) (Fig. 12.7). Thus, part of the kaolinite clay is destroyed.

Soil Biological Properties

Availability of soil phosphorus is affected by soil biological properties of (a) speed of decomposition of soil organic matter; (b) the presence of microbially derived organic acids; and (c) reactions or organic phytin in soils with Fe, Al, or Mn present.

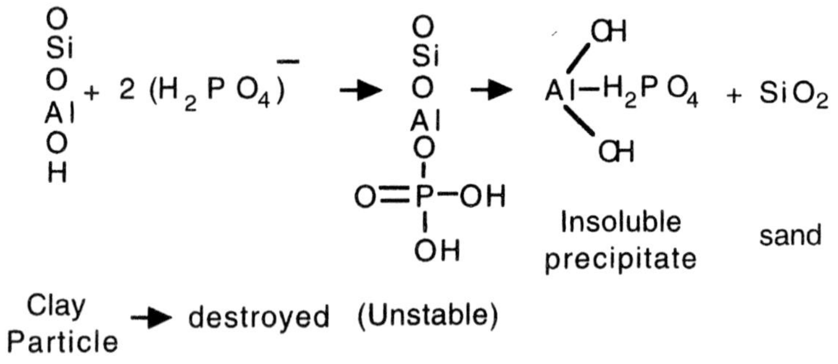

Figure 12.7 P-Fixation by reaction with kaolinite. Soluble P can become fixed in an unavailable form for plants by reacting with kaolinite clay particles, resulting in the clay's destruction.

Rapid Decomposition
of Organic Matter

When organic matter is rapidly decomposed, P is tied up in the bodies of microbes, similar to N, making it temporarily unavailable for plants. After about six to eight weeks, the P is released and available for plant use.

Organic Acids

Some microbes produce certain organic acids that will solubilize the P-containing mineral apatite, thereby releasing the P for plant use. Other microbes produce 2-keto-gluconic acid that can complex with Cu, Fe, Al, Mn, Ni, or Ca and may release P from salts of these elements.

Reactions with Phytin

Phytin or its derivatives can combine with Fe, Al, or Mn to form insoluble phytates that are not available for plants.

PRACTICAL CONTROL
OF PHOSPHORUS AVAILABILITY

Availability of phosphorus in soils can be adjusted by practical means of (a) liming the soil, (b) proper placement of P fertilizer in the soil, and (c) maintaining as much organic matter as possible in the soil.

Liming

By adjusting the pH by liming to between 6 and 7, phosphorus is kept in the most available form for plant use. This reduces the amount of P fixed when P fertilizers are added. Some can be released from insoluble fixed-forms to plant-available forms after liming.

Placement of Fertilizer P

Phosphorus moves very little in soils, therefore, it is important to place the P where the plants can use it. Broadcasting of P on the surface and working it into the soil is fine for building up the level of P in the soil; however, much of the fertilizer P that is applied will not be used immediately and will become fixed as mentioned previously in this chapter. For more efficient use, P fertilizer should be placed in concentrated areas in the soil, such as below or adjacent to the transplant. Since P does not move much in soils, it would be wise to place the P fertilizer in the planting hole for a continual supply of this element. Phosphorus fertilizer will not burn the plant roots as other fertilizers do; therefore, P fertilizer can safely be concentrated close to the roots without harm to the plant.

Maintenance of Soil Organic Matter

By keeping relatively large amounts of organic matter in soils, whether in the form of composts, manure, peat, sphagnum peat moss, or sawdust, a reserve of P will be present and the P can become available during decomposition. Much of the organic P does not combine with Fe, Al, Mn, or Ca, and therefore, organic matter increases the availability of P present.

POTASSIUM IN PLANTS

Potassium (K) is important in maintaining the general tone and vigor of a plant. Potassium is important for root growth, helping the plants to resist the effects of drought by maintaining turgor that reduces water loss and wilting. Potassium is also important in increasing the ability of a plant to (a) resist diseases, such as rusts and mildews, (b) resist attack by insects, such as aphids, (c) be more winter hardy, and (d) be more efficient in using CO_2 for photosynthesis.

Potassium is used in many plant processes—chlorophyll formation, starch formation and translocation, cellulose and lignin formation, protein formation—and aids in many enzyme reactions as catalysts for energy reactions.

Forms of Potassium in Plants

K^+

Potassium is present in plants only as the K^+ ion. There are no organic forms of K present. The potassium as a cation is very mobile and moves freely from one plant part to another.

Amounts of Potassium in Plants

Potassium is present in plants in very large amounts (similar to N). The range in plants is aobut 0.04 to 11.0% with the usual range of between 1 and 3%. Sometimes more K is absorbed by plants than is needed for growth; this is called "luxury consumption." Although the concentration of K increases, there is no additional growth from this extra K.

Potassium Deficiency Symptoms

Potassium deficiency is easily recognized in plants. Most plants deficient in K show *yellow or brown edges of the leaves* (scorching or "firing"). These edges eventually become dry and necrotic (dead). Since K can move easily throughout the plant and the plants try to continue to grow when any element becomes deficient, the K is moved from the older leaves to the new younger leaves, resulting in the older leaves being affected first. The younger leaves tend to remain green until the deficiency becomes very severe. Deficiency of K may also cause premature leaf drop.

Deficiency symptoms of K on some legumes may also have irregular spots on the outer third of the leaf that may be white, yellow, brown, or drop out.

POTASSIUM IN SOILS

Most U.S. soils have large amounts of K present; in fact, usually this nutrient element is the most abundant of the major and secondary elements in soils (up to 25 tons/acre); however, most of the original soil K is not readily available for plant use.

Origin of Soil Potassium

Potassium is present in soils as rocks (primary minerals) or clays (secondary minerals). The primary minerals containing K are potassium feldspars and micas—biotite and muscovite. All these primary minerals are not readily available to plants.

Potassium in secondary minerals is mainly present in illites, vermiculites, or chlorites or mixtures of these clays. Illite is particularly high in K; a soil K content in a soil low in illite may be 0.1%, but one high in illite could have 3.6% or more K.

Potassium Problems in Soils

Soils have three types of potassium problems—availability, loss of K by leaching, and plant removal.

Availability of Potassium in Soils

Although the total K in most mineral soils is very high, the amount of K available for plants is usually very small. Therefore, it is important to provide the soil with supplemental K through fertilizers or plant remains. Plants must also compete with microbes for K. Microbes are more efficient in using K than plants and when decomposition occurs, microbes use the K first and plants can use only what remains.

Moderate amounts of K are also lost by leaching from soils, depending on the kind of soil and rainfall. In high rainfall areas, coarse sandy soils lose more K than the finer silty or clayey soils. Loss of K can be retarded by liming a soil to maintain a more favorable pH for plant growth.

Plants remove large amounts of K from soils—even to the extent of luxury consumption. Since fertilizers would be only a small part of the total cost related to landscaping an area, some K fertilizer should be mixed with soil that goes into the planting hole without regard to the extra cost. Some additional K fertilizer could be added at any time since most is water soluble and will eventually reach the plant roots.

Potassium Equilibrium in Soils

There is an equilibrium of K in soils, that is, K can be shifted from one form to another. If there is an abundance of one kind, with time the K shifts toward another kind that is lower in amount.

K^+ solution $\rightarrow$	K adsorbed $\rightarrow$	K-fixed $\rightarrow$	K in Primary
(water $\leftarrow$	on soil $\leftarrow$	within clays $\leftarrow$	Minerals
soluble)	particles	(illites)	(rocks)
1 part	9 parts		
----------------------		-----------	-------------
1–2%		1–10%	90–98%
readily available to plants		slowly available to plants	
and microbes		and microbes	

The readily available forms of K are water soluble or adsorbed onto the soil particles and may be leached from the soil. The amount leached depends on the soil pH—going from about 16%

leached at pH of 7.0 to 70% leached at pH of 4.8. The K-fixed within clays is only slowly available with time, is not subject to leaching, but is important in conservation of K in soils. The fixed-K can be released by alternate freezing and thawing; many soils are high in water soluble K in the spring of the year. The K in primary minerals of feldspars and micas is resistant to weathering, with only a very gradual release to more available forms by action of acids in soils.

Practical Application To K Problems in Soils

Potassium fertilization is related to frequency of fertilizer application, leaching losses, fixation to an unavailable form, labor costs in applying the fertilizer, K-supplying power of a soil, and soil pH.

Light, frequent application of K fertilizer would avoid the problems of luxury consumption, leaching losses, and fixation to an unavailable form; however, the cost of labor to do this may be more than the cost of fertilizer K absorbed or lost. Therefore, one must balance the cost of labor for fertilizer application with the cost of fertilizer losses as indicated above. Usually landscape architects avoid K problems by applying generous amounts of K fertilizer (often as a complete fertilizer) at planting to prevent adding more K later.

The idea of replacing each pound of K removed by an equivalent amount may not be correct for those soils that have a large reserve of K available. Therefore, the kind of clay and rocks present in a soil has a definite bearing on how much K should be applied to that soil.

Liming a soil to near neutral will also affect the ability of a plant to absorb K and also retard the extent of K that is leached.

SUMMARY

Phosphorus in plants exists mainly as DNA, RNA, ATP, phytin, and phospholipids, which are important in metabolic processes, stored energy, and used in root growth, flower, fruiting, seed formation, and maturation. Phosphorus deficiency in plants is difficult to detect—some plants may show purple coloration of leaves. There is no known toxicity of excess P in soils. Supply of soil P is limited due to (a) the low amount present in most soils, (b) the large amount of P that is already fixed in soils in unavailable forms, and (c) the fact that much of the fertilizer P becomes fixed rather quickly and is not available for plant use. The fungus *Mycorrhiza* can be helpful in providing P to tree seedlings when grown on beds where the P is present in very low amounts. Phosphorus exists in soils as inorganic phosphates of Fe, Al, Mn, and Ca and organic forms of phytin, complex nucleic acids, nucleoproteins, and phospholipids. The only readily available P forms present in soils are the orthophosphate ions, that is, $H_2PO_4^-$ and HPO_4^{2-}. Some organic P becomes available during microbial decomposition of plant and animal remains.

Availability of P in soils to plants is related to (a) soil physical properties of aeration, compaction, moisture, texture, and temperature; (b) soil chemical properties of pH, presence of Al, Fe, Mn, and Ca, and presence of kaolinitic (1:1) clays; and (c) soil biological properties of organic matter decomposition and reactions with phytin. Much of the soil P is fixed in unavailable complexes with Al, Fe, Mn, and Ca. Practical ways to help control P availability include liming, proper placement of fertilizer P, and maintaining organic matter in the soil.

Potassium is found in plants only as K^+ but is present in very large amounts and is required for many metabolic processes of water relations, resistance to diseases and attack by insects, winter hardiness, and efficiency in photosynthesis. Potassium deficiency symptoms appear as yellowing and browning of older leaf edges. There is no known toxicity due to K fertilization, but excess K in plants is called "luxury consumption," in which the K is not used for extra plant growth.

In soils, large amounts of K are present in rocks (primary minerals) and clays (secondary minerals), but most of this is only slowly available for plant use. Plants have limited access to soil K since much is not available, and considerable amounts of K are lost by leaching and plant removal. Forms of soil K exist in an equilibrium of available soluble K^+, adsorbed as available K onto clays, unavailable fixed-K within clays, and unavailable K in rocks.

REVIEW

In what ways is phosphorus (P) used by
   plants?
In what forms does P exist in plants?

(continued) ➤→

REVIEW (*continued*)

Can you describe P deficiency symptoms?
  Toxicity symptoms?
Why is P a problem in soils?
How can mycorrhizae help in P relations in
  some soils? Which ones?
Name the forms of P that exist in soils.
What P forms are readily available for plants?
Which P forms can be made available during
  decomposition?
Can you describe the chemical, physical, and
  biological factors that affect availability of P
  in soils?
Which elements fix large amounts of P in
  soils?
In what forms is potassium (K) found in
  plants and how is it used?
How much K is needed by plants?
Describe the usual K deficiency symptoms.
Can K become toxic to plants?
What is the name for excess K in plants and
  how does it affect the plants?
How much and what kinds of K exist in soils?
Are these available for plants?
Do you know the three types of K problems in
  soils?
Describe how availability of K in soils can be
  represented by an equilibrium.

13

Macronutrients

Calcium, Magnesium, and Sulfur

CALCIUM AND MAGNESIUM IN SOIL
IS RELATED TO LIMING

Application of limestone to a soil changes the (a) soil physical properties by encouraging granulation and improving tilth; (b) soil chemical properties by decreasing soil acidity, increasing availability of a number of essential plant nutrients, and decreasing levels of aluminum, iron, and manganese that potentially may be toxic; and (c) soil biological properties by improving conditions for micriobial organic matter decomposition with release of nitrogen, phosphorus, and sulfur for plant use, and by stimulating root development.

Physical Properties Changed
by Liming

Granulation Encouraged. Applying lime to soils improves soil physical conditions by encouraging granulation and crumb formation (Fig. 7.1) and aggregation (Fig. 6.3).

Tilth Improved. Tilth is the ability to work or cultivate a soil. By improving physical conditions with more granulation and crumb formation, soil tilth is improved.

Chemical Properties Changed
by Liming

Lowering H⁺ Concentration (Acidity). When lime is applied to a soil, acidity is reduced and pH is raised. This is especially important in the humid regions where rainfall and other factors constantly make a soil more acid (explained in Chapter 9).

Plant Nutrient Availability Increased. Liming a soil will increase availability of plant nutrients by (a) increasing Ca and Mg in the soil from added liming material; (b) adjusting soil to a higher pH so that N, P, K, S, and Mo are solubilized; and (c) reducing solubility of potentially toxic levels of Fe, Al, or Mn.

Lowering of Potentially Toxic Levels of Al, Fe, and Mn. At very low soil pH, Al, Fe, and Mn are soluble and may be present in a high enough concentration to be toxic to plant growth. When lime is applied, the pH increases and these three elements become less soluble and less available for plants.

Biological Properties Changed
by Liming

Microbial Decomposition Enhanced. Soils that are limed provide conditions for active microbial decomposition of organic materials in soils, resulting in mineralization and release of N, P, and S in forms that plants can use. Liming also increases the amount of humus formed, thereby improving water infiltration and water-holding capacity. Furthermore, liming soils stimulates other types of biological transformations, such as nitrification, N-fixation, and S-oxidation, that improve plant growth.

Deep Rooting Stimulated. Use of lime on soils produces more vigorous plants by stimulating deeper rooting, especially legumes. The vigorous root systems of these plants help resist disease and insect attack.

AMOUNT OF LIMESTONE TO APPLY

The best way to determine the amount of limestone to apply to a soil is to have the soil tested for lime requirement. This particular test evaluates the buffering ability of a soil. The pH itself can be determined, but this only measures the active acidity in the soil solution and does not consider the H⁺ present on the soil particles. The H⁺ present on the soil particles is considered "reserve acidity" or "buffering capacity."

A common "rule of thumb," to be used only as a last resort, is to use annually 550 pounds of limestone per acre or 12 pounds of limestone per 1,000 square feet of area.

KINDS OF LIME

There are many different kinds of lime (or liming materials). Common ones are calcite, dolomite, calcium oxide, hydrated lime, and wood ashes.

Calcite

Ground agricultural limestone, calcite, calcic lime, or calcium carbonate ($CaCO_3$) is probably the best general type of lime to apply. Calcite usually neutralizes acids for a long time, but after applying, some time is required for this lime to begin to neutralize soil acids.

Dolomite

Dolomitic limestone, dolomite, or $CaMg(CO_3)_2$ contains magnesium (Mg) needed by plants. It is especially important to apply this type of lime if the soils are deficient in Mg, which can be determined by a soil test. This lime is somewhat slower to react than $CaCO_3$.

Calcium Oxide

Calcium oxide (CaO), oxide of lime, quicklime, or burned lime is produced by burning $CaCO_3$. This lime is caustic and difficult to handle as it will burn your hands. However, it does have a great ability to neutralize soil acids and is fast acting, but it is also more expensive.

Hydrated Lime

Calcium hydroxide [$Ca(OH)_2$], hydrated lime, or slaked lime is produced by treating burned lime with water. This slightly decreases its ability to neutralize soil acids, but it is still more effective than calcite. This lime is also caustic, fast acting, and expensive.

Wood Ashes

Although wood ashes are not sold commercially, they can be applied to soils to provide some neutralization of soil acidity. Generally, wood ashes have from 30 to 50% equivalency to $CaCO_3$ with more Ca^{++} being present in hardwood ashes. Wood ashes are better composted if they are to be used on alkaline soils. Wood ashes also contain 8 to 30%K and about 2% P.

NETURALIZING POWER
OF LIMING MATERIALS

Neutralizing power of a liming material indicates the ability of the material to neutralize or overcome the effects of soil acids. This measurement is based on the $CaCO_3$ equivalent set at 100. If a liming material has neutralizing power more than 100, it is more efficient in neutralizing acids; if less than 100, more of the liming material would be needed to have the same neutralizing effect.

Forms of Lime	Neutralizing Power
CaO	179
$Ca(OH)_2$	136
$CaMg(CO_3)_2$	109
$CaCO_3$	100
$CaSiO_3$ (slag)	86

FINENESS OF A LIMESTONE

The finer the lime particles, the more contact they would provide with the soil particles and the more rapidly the acidity would be neutralized. Fineness of a limestone, or the size of the individual lime particles, is measured by that amount passing through a series of sieves. Each sieve would have a different number of openings called the mesh or the number of openings per linear inch. A 10-mesh sieve has 10 openings per linear inch or 100 openings per square inch, and all lime passing through this sieve would be considered coarse. A 400-mesh sieve has 400 openings per linear inch or 160,000 openings per square inch, and lime passing through this sieve would be very fine. Thus, the finer the limestone the higher the mesh number (Fig. 13.1).

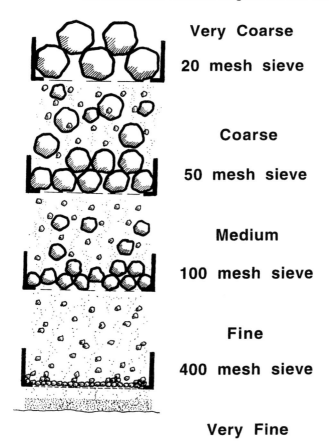

Very Coarse

20 mesh sieve

Coarse

50 mesh sieve

Medium

100 mesh sieve

Fine

400 mesh sieve

Very Fine

Figure 13.1 Limestone particle sizes by sieves. Liming particles are separated by size by passing through a series of sieves. The sieve mesh is the number of holes per linear inch with the coarse material being held on the low mesh–size screen and the very fine material passing through the high mesh–size screen.

WHEN AND HOW TO APPLY LIME?

The most desirable time to apply lime is before applying fertilizers and only when the soil is not excessively wet to avoid compaction, which destroys soil structure and impedes plant root growth. The methods used to apply lime include placing the lime where needed for plant root growth and thorough mixing of the lime with the surface soil particles for neutralizing soil acidity.

Before Applying Fertilizers

If lime is needed by a soil, it should be applied at least six months, preferably, one year prior to applying any fertilizer. This would allow sufficient time for the lime to neutralize some of the acid on the soil particles.

Any Time Soils Are Not Wet

Lime can be applied to a soil any time you can safely get onto the soil, but not when soils are wet. Wet soils will compact, resulting in poor growth of plants grown thereon.

Placement of Lime Is Related
to Reaction of Lime in a Soil

Limestone particles move very little in soils, therefore, it is important to place the lime *where needed.*

Lime applied to a soil must be thoroughly mixed for maximum effectiveness, as this will provide more individual contact of the limestone particles with the soil particles and thereby neutralize the acidity. During seeding of a lawn, lime should be applied first, if needed, and worked into the soil for best results. However, once a lawn is established, "lime topdressing" is satisfactory for maintenance. Limestone particles neither move nor leach from a soil. Once the lime reacts with the soil acids, Ca^{++} and/or Mg^{++} present in the lime is released into the soil solution and can be exchanged for H^+ ions on the soil particles neutralizing the soil. This was explained in Chapter 9 (Fig. 9.5). The Ca^{++} and Mg^{++} cations released from the dissolved limestone can move in soil by leaching in soluble forms (Fig. 9.3).

SOIL CALCIUM AND MAGNESIUM
PER SE

Both Ca and Mg are present in combined forms in certain minerals and are released by weathering. Calcium is present in calcite, dolomite, apatite, feldspars, and hornblende. Magnesium in present in dolomite, micas, hornblende, serpentine, and clays. Soluble Ca^{++} and Mg^{++} are present in soil solution and can be held onto soil particles. The total amounts in soils range from 0.07 to 3.6% for Ca (usually about 1–2%), and from 0.12 to 1.5% for Mg (mostly 0.3 to 0.6%). If the concentration of Ca is more than 0.5%, the soil will fizz when treated with drops of dilute acid (1:5 HCl:water). Both Ca and Mg are usually added to soils in the form of lime or fertilizers. Some Ca is provided in gypsum ($CaSO_4$) when reclaiming sodic soils.

Calcium and Mg in soils can be (a) absorbed by microbes, (b) absorbed by plants, (c) adsorbed on soil particles—clays and organic matter, (d) complexed with organic matter, (e) eroded and lost, (f) leached and lost in the drainage water, and/or (g) reprecipitated as secondary Ca or Mg compounds, especially in arid regions.

PLANT CALCIUM AND MAGNESIUM

Calcium

Concentrations of Ca in plants range up to 8%, but in most plants it is about 1%. Calcium is present in the middle lamella of all plant cells providing strength. *Calcium in plants is relatively immobile* once absorbed and placed where needed, except for western white pine. Plants need Ca for (a) protein formation, (b) enzyme systems, (c) carbohydrate translocation, (d) cell division, (e) growth of meristematic tissue, especially root and stem tips, (f) germination and growth of the pollen tube, and (g) keeping the root cell membranes functional and protected from leaking.

Calcium pectate and Ca-oxalate help the plant to detoxify undesirable elements.

Although Ca is not a part of the chlorophyll molecule, much Ca is found in the chloroplasts that contain chlorophyll.

Magnesium

Magnesium concentrations in plants range up to 5%, but usually it is about 0.3%. Seeds generally have a high concentration of Mg. *Magnesium in plants is highly mobile* and can be easily translocated throughout the plant as needed. Plants need Mg for (a) protein synthesis, (b) enzyme activation, (c) P metabolism (absorption and movement), (d) carbohydrate metabolism, (e) citric acid cycle, (f) N metabolism, and (g) oil synthesis.

Magnesium is an integral part of the chlorophyll molecule and is in the center surrounded by four N atoms (Fig. 11.4).

Magnesium is associated with organic acids in plant tissue.

Deficiency Symptoms of Calcium
and Magnesium

Deficiency of Ca results in *damage to* the *growing points* of a plant, that is, stem and root tips. An example is blossom end rot of tomatoes. This results from the immobility of Ca in the plant. If insufficient Ca is available for the plant to complete its life cycle, the growing points shut down and growth stops. However, Ca deficiency symptoms are usually not observed in the field.

Deficiency of Mg results in chlorosis (*yellowing* from lack of chlorophyll) in *older leaves* with reduced growth. When Mg becomes deficient, insufficient Mg will be available for the growing points. Due to the high mobility of Mg in plants, Mg is translocated from the older leaves to the younger plant parts. Thus, the older leaves become spotted with yellow and the younger plant parts remain green.

SULFUR IN PLANTS

Plants use about as much S as P. Sulfur is usually absorbed by plants from soils as sulfate (SO_4^{2-}), but some can enter the plant from the atmosphere as SO_2 gas through the leaf stomates. In areas where S-containing fossil fuels are burned, enough SO_2 is absorbed from the atmosphere by plants through their leaves that S does not become deficient. *Sulfur in plants is highly mobile.*

Amino Acids—Cystine, Cysteine,
and Methionine

Sulfur is found in plants as three amino acids—cystine, cysteine, and methionine. Some of these amino acids are constituents of S-containing proteins.

Deficiency Symptoms of Sulfur

Deficiency of S in plants exhibits a *general yellowing* (chlorosis) *over the whole plant.* In conifers, older needles are affected the most with the tips becoming red, yellow, or mottled (speckled), and may eventually become dead and drop off. Sulfur deficiency does not occur in areas where high S-containing coal has been burned in electrical power generating plants. However, with the recent government restrictions on burning of S-containing coal, S deficiencies will become more common.

SULFUR IN SOILS

Sulfur in soils is present as metallic sulfides, sulfate salts, elemental S, and in the organic forms of proteins or sulfate esters of organic acids.

Soil Organic Matter

Soil organic matter is high in S. During the latter stages of decomposition of organic matter by microbes, S is mineralized and becomes available for plants or microbes. Sulfur can also be immobilized by microbes and made unavailable to plants during the initial stages of decomposition. Many soil S reactions are enhanced by microbial action. Sulfur can be added to soils by SO_2, combining with water in the atmosphere and falling as rain or snow. Some soil S comes from sea salt spray near beaches and from hydrogen sulfide (H_2S) gas in marshes.

Sulfur can also be added to soils in (a) crop residues, (b) green manure, (c) animal manures, (d) composts, (e) commercial fertilizers, and/or (f) adsorption of SO_2 onto soil particles.

SUMMARY

Liming improves soils physically, by enhancing granulation, resulting in desirable tilth; chemically, by lowering acidity, making plant nutrients more readily available, and reducing effects of toxic Al, Fe, and Mn; and biologically, by improving microbial decomposition and deeper rooting. Amounts of lime to apply can best be determined by soil testing.

Lime usually is available as ground agricultural limestone, dolomite, and oxide and hydroxide of lime. The best lime for general use is ground agricultural limestone as it has a mixture of sizes, some of which react fast and others slow. When Mg is needed, dolomite should be used. The oxides and hydroxides of lime are very fast acting, but are expensive and caustic to plants and man.

Liming materials are evaluated by their ability to neutralize soil acids and by their fineness, with the finer lime reacting faster than coarser particles. Lime can be applied any time one can get on the soil without causing damage (i.e., not when wet), but preferably prior to fertilizing. To be effective in neutralizing soil acids, lime must be thoroughly mixed with the soil—the more mixing the better.

Calcium and Mg exist in soils as minerals and as Ca^{2+} and Mg^{2+} adsorbed onto soil particles and free in the soil solution. In plants these elements react differently—Ca is immobile and Mg is highly mobile. Ca is present as Ca-pectate, Ca-oxalate, chloroplasts, and in cell walls; whereas Mg is present as part of the chlorophyll molecule and associated with organic acids. Deficiency symptoms of Mg are often seen as yellowing of older leaves, but deficiencies of Ca appear as death of the growing points and are not seen in the field.

Sulfur in plants is present as some proteins and three amino acids which are highly mobile, resulting in deficiencies by complete yellowing of older leaves. Sulfur is present in soils mostly as organic forms in soil organic matter. Sulfur can be added to soils in crop residues, green manure, animal manure, composts, rain, and commercial fertilizers. Some S can be absorbed as SO_2 gas through the leaves.

REVIEW

How does liming affect soils physically? Chemically? Biologically?

How does one determine how much lime to apply?

Can you name the different kinds of lime available and when each would be used?

What ways are used to evaluate liming materials?

When and in what manner should lime be applied to a soil?

In what forms do Calcium (Ca) and Magnesium (Mg) exist in soils?

Contrast Ca and Mg forms, uses, and mobility in plants.

How do deficiency symptoms of Ca and Mg differ?

In what forms is sulfur (S) present in plants and how can one distinguish S deficiency symptoms?

In what forms does S exist in soils?

In what forms can S be added to soils?

14

Micronutrients

Micronutrients needed by plants are Cu, Fe, Mn, Zn, B, Mo, Cl, Ni, Co, V, Si, and Na. The required amounts of each of these elements is very small but still essential for desirable plant growth and reproduction. These elements must be applied to soils cautiously for the *range between deficient and toxic is very small.* It is unwise to use a fertilizer containing all of these micronutrients. Any one of them may already be high enough in soils to cause toxicity from that particular element. If a micronutrient is suspected of being deficient, it would be wise to get soil tests and plant tissue tests to corroborate your suspicions. If a micronutrient is deficient, one should apply only the amount recommended but no more. Sometimes a toxicity of an element is more difficult to correct than a deficiency.

FORMS OF MICRONUTRIENTS PRESENT IN SOILS

Copper, Iron, Manganese, Cobalt, and Zinc (Cations)

Copper, iron, manganese, cobalt, and zinc can be present in soils as (a) several types of precipitates, (b) adsorbed onto the surface of soil particles, (c) present in primary minerals (rocks) and secondary minerals (clays), and (d) present as complex ring compounds. These forms may or may not be available to plants.

Precipitates

Precipitates of Cu, Fe, Mn, or Zn often form in soils at high pH (after liming Fig. 14.1). This may occur in soils near buildings

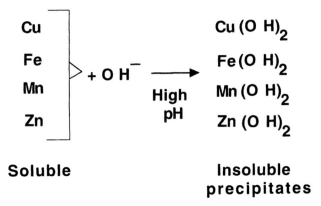

Soluble   **Insoluble precipitates**

Figure 14.1 Micronutrients become unavailable at High pH. Micronutrient cations (Cu, Fe, Mn, and Zn) become insoluble and unavailable hydroxides precipitate at high pH.

from the lime used in the mortar. Soil acids dissolve the lime into Ca^{++} or Mg^{++} that migrate into the soil raising the pH and cause these micronutrients to precipitate. Often an Fe deficiency is evident, particularly on acid-loving plants, such as azaleas, rhododendrons, or hollies. If this is extensive, the soil near the buildings may need to be replaced. With limited areas, the soil can be acidified by adding elemental S near the plants affected.

The elements Cu, Fe, Mn, and Zn can exist as soluble forms or precipitates, depending on the pH of the soil. The soluble forms as cations are present when soils have poor internal drainage (poorly drained soils), whereas the oxides of these elements are present where the soil is well aerated. This oxidation-reduction is related to the color of subsoils. In soils of poor internal drainage, Fe is reduced and present as Fe^{2+}, which shows as dull colors of blue or gray. However, in soils with good internal drainage, the Fe is oxidized and present as Fe^{3+}, giving bright colors of red, yellow, or brown.

Surface Adsorption Onto Soil Particles

Cations of Cu, Fe, Mn, Co, and Zn can be held onto soil particles for future plant use (Fig. 14.2). Copper, cobalt, and zinc are held very strongly in soils. These elements also react with soil organic matter. In black organic soils, Cu is held so strongly by the organic matter that it may be deficient for plant use. These soils

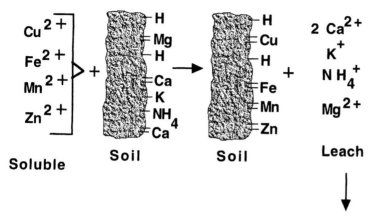

Figure 14.2 Micronutrient cations (Cu, Fe, Mn, and Zn) can be adsorbed onto soil particles in an available form for plant use.

may require Cu fertilizer for adequate plant growth! The organic matter in mineral soils is often the most important part in providing Cu, Zn, B, and Mo to plants.

Primary Minerals (Rocks) and Secondary Minerals (Clays)

Some micronutrients are present in complexed forms in rocks and as part of the internal structure of clays. These forms can be released on weathering of the rocks or clays (Fig. 14.3). Those associated with clays are Fe, Mn, Zn, and Co.

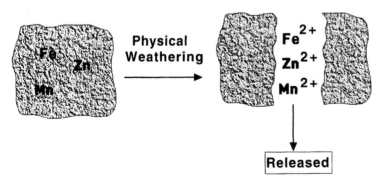

Figure 14.3 Micronutrient release from rocks. During weathering of rocks and clays, some micronutrients can be released for plant use.

Chelates (Complex Organic
Ring Structures)

Chelates are natural or synthetic organic compounds that can complex with metal cations (Fig. 14.4). Once in this form the elements do not enter into chemical reactions in soils, but they are *available for plants* and are *easily absorbed by plants.* "Chelate" means "claw," referring to the ends of the complex organic compound wrapping around a metal. Some examples of organic compounds that form chelates with metals are EDTA (Ethylene

Formation of a Chelate Structure

Ethylene $CH_2=CH_2$
Ethylene diamine
$$H_2 N\text{-}CH_2\text{-}CH_2\text{-}NH_2$$

Ethylene diamine tetra acetic acid

$$HOOC\text{-}CH_2 \diagdown \atop HOOC\text{-}CH_2 \diagup N\text{-}CH_2\text{-}CH_2\text{-}N \diagup^{CH_2\text{-}COOH} \atop \diagdown CH_2\text{-}COOH$$

**Zn-EDTA (Ethylene diamine tetra acetic acid)
[A Chelate]**

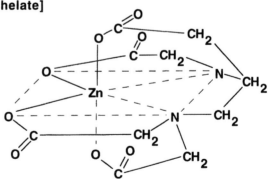

Figure 14.4 Formation of a chelate structure. Complex organic ring structures (chelates) can form and wrap around basic cations (e.g., Zn), making the cation unreactive to usual soil reactions, but the cation is available for plant use.

diamine tetra acetic acid), EDDHA [Ethylene diamine di(o-hydroxy phenyl acetic acid)], and DTPA (Diethylene triamine penta acetic acid).

There are many different kinds of chelates, usually consisting of long complex chain structures combined with metals. The extent that these chelates operate in soils depends on their stability. Chelate stability is related to (a) pH, (b) the kind of chelate present, (c) the amount of chelate present, (d) kind of ions present, and (e) concentration of carbon dioxide (CO_2). A common order of stability of metals associated with chelates is: $Cu^{2+}>Ni^{2+}>Fe^{3+}>Zn^{2+}>Cd^{2+}>Fe^{2+}>Mn^{2+}$. An example of how stability operates is as follows:

If a soil requires Zn and one adds Zn-chelate to an alkaline soil, the Zn may be replaced by the large amount of Fe^{3+} present in the soil, becoming an Fe^{3+} chelate that is more stable than the original Zn^{2+} chelate. The Zn that is released can form $Zn(OH)_2$ that is insoluble and not available. Thus, the Zn-chelate that was added to the soil was changed to an Fe-chelate, and the Zn forms an insoluble compound that is not available for plant use.

$$Zn\text{-chelate} + Fe^{3+} \rightarrow Fe\text{-chelate} + Zn^{2+}$$
$$Zn^{2+} + OH\text{-} \rightarrow Zn(OH)_2 \text{ (insoluble)}$$

This problem can be avoided by spraying the Zn-chelate onto the leaves of the Zn-deficient plants. The Zn-chelate can be absorbed directly by the leaves. Although chelates are generally more expensive than nutrients in other forms, usually less of the chelate is needed than the other forms—so they are almost economically equivalent.

FACTORS AFFECTING AVAILABILITY OF MICRONUTRIENTS

Availability of micronutrients depends on (a) soil pH, (b) oxidation potential, (c) other inorganic soil reactions, (d) weathering, (e) leaching, (f) presence of organic matter and microbiological activity, and (g) activities in the Rhizosphere.

Soil pH

Soil pH is probably *the most important factor* in altering availability of micronutrients. Generally, at low pH all micronutrients are more soluble, except for Mo. In fact, some micronutrients, for example, Fe and Mn, may be present in such large amounts that they become toxic to plants. This is one of the reasons for liming an acid soil, that is, to reduce the effects of potentially toxic ions present (this includes Al, even though it is not required by plants). As pH is raised above 7 into the alkaline range, the micronutrients form oxides or hydroxides, which are insoluble precipitates that are not available for plants. Thus, liming must be regulated carefully on those soils with low buffering ability, such as coarse-textured sands. It is very important to maintain the pH between 6 and 7 for availability of most micronutrients. The stability of chelates is also influenced by pH as already indicated.

Oxidation Potential

Some micronutrients, such as Cu, Fe, and Mn, have more than one oxidation state. For instance, we have Cu^+ and Cu^{2+}; Fe^{2+} and Fe^{3+}, and Mn^{2+}, Mn^{3+}, and Mn^{4+}. We have already learned that oxidation depends on the presence of oxygen—which is abundant in well-drained soils. On poorly drained soils, as in swamps, these micronutrients are in the lower oxidation state that is more soluble and could be toxic to plant growth.

Other Inorganic Reactions

When soils are fertilized with very large amounts of P, soil Zn or Fe can react with the P creating a deficiency of either of these nutrient elements. Also, the presence of 2:1 clays can result in fixation of Fe, Mn, or Zn making these nutrients deficient. This is a minor problem for Fe or Mn as these are present in rather high concentrations in soils originally; however, only limited amounts of Zn are usually present in soils and this then may create a Zn deficiency. Furthermore, interactions can occur between different kinds of soluble nutrient elements or nonnutrient elements that could be either antagonistic or synergistic to plant absorption.

Weathering

During weathering of rocks or clay minerals that contain micronutrients, some micronutrients may be released (Fig. 14.3). The micronutrients released are soluble and can be used by plants.

Leaching

Micronutrients can be lost from soils as water passes through a soil by leaching. This is especially critical on coarse-textured sandy soils in regions of high rainfall.

Organic Matter and Microbial Action

During decomposition of organic substances in soils, some micronutrients are temporarily immobilized in the bodies of the microbes and with time they are released in an available form. Also, chelates usually consist of metals combined with organic molecules that are often present in organic matter. We have already seen how these are important in plant growth by keeping some of the nutrients in an available form for plant absorption.

Rhizosphere

The rhizosphere is the area in the soil that is affected by activities of the roots growing therein (Fig. 14.5). It differs from the nonrhizosphere area in that the soil microbes are usually more

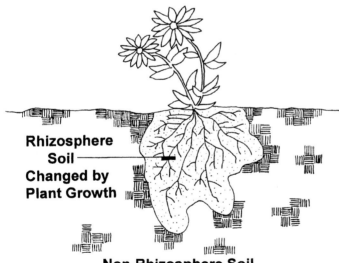

Figure 14.5 Rhizosphere. The soil zone around a plant root has been changed by that plant and is called the "rhizosphere." The soil are beyond plant root influence is the nonrhizosphere zone.

active in the rhizosphere and sometimes plant roots exude substances that can solubilize some nutrients.

ANIONS—BORON, CHLORINE, AND MOLYBDENUM

Boron

Boron is present in soils as the mineral tourmaline which is extremely resistant to weathering. The amount of B that is available for plant use depends on (a) pH, (b) leaching, (c) organic combinations, and (d) dry weather.

Soil B decreases in availability at extremes of soil pH. Boron in soils is readily leached in most humid region soils, except clays. Boron in soils is often in the form of an organic complex with sugars. Dry weather can cause a soil that is seemingly abundant in B to be B deficient. The reason for this is that the topsoil, in which most of the absorbing roots grow, also contains organic matter complexed with the B. During dry weather, the roots extend into the subsoil for water, but the B is in only very low amounts there, creating a B deficiency in the plants (Fig. 14.6). If the soil is deep enough for the kind of plants grown, this B deficiency should not be a problem. Otherwise, additional organic material can be added to a landscaped area to combat this B problem.

Boron is relatively immobile in plants, resulting in deficiency symptoms showing first in the growing parts (young leaves). The leaves may be small, brittle, distorted, red, bronzed, or scorched. The shoots show rosetting (stunting or die-back), discoloring, and appearing with no or few flowers. On shrubs, conifers, and hardwood trees, the terminal buds die. Foliar application of B is effective, even after a B deficiency shows, because the leaves can absorb the B directly.

Care must be taken not to overapply B as it can also become toxic. Woody perennials are generally more sensitive to excess B than most annuals. Toxicity symptoms show brown (necrotic) spots between veins on the leaves. The leaf margins and tips become yellow and turn brown or black. Shoots often die back and become gummy. On conifers, shoots die back, may curl, and dry with a flow of resin.

Alfalfa and a few other plants tolerate high concentrations of B in soils.

Boron Deficiency -- No new flowers

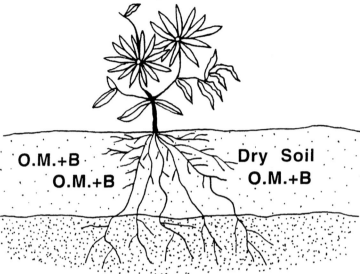

O.M.+B
O.M.+B

Dry Soil
O.M.+B

Moisture but
No Organic Matter -- No Boron

Figure 14.6 Boron deficiency during drought. During dry weather, plant roots extend to depths below the A horizon seeking water. Boron is complexed with organic matter in the topsoil (A horizon); however, when the roots extend below this layer, there is no organic matter and little B, creating a B deficiency in the plant.

Chlorine

Much Cl is added to soils in rain. There are often impurities of Cl in commonly used fertilizers. However, Cl leaches easily. Deficiencies of Cl in woody plants has not been reported.

Large amounts of chlorine can become toxic in soils from salt in irrigated areas, along seacoasts, and from salt applied to roads in the winter. The best way to correct this is to leach the soil to remove the excess Cl. Toxicity symptoms include small leaves, yellowing of leaf margins and tips, and scorch resulting in leaf drop.

Molybdenum

Molybdenum, absorbed onto clays as molybdate (MoO_4^{2-}), is usually available for plants. Molybdenum is also present in soils as water soluble molybdates and as organic complexes. The pH affects this element opposite of other micronutrients, that is, Mo is less available at low pH and more available at high pH (Fig. 9.2). Whenever a soil is limed, Mo present becomes more available for plants. Molybdenum in soils and plants is similar to phosphate reactions. Deficiencies of Mo are rare in woody plants.

SOIL MANAGEMENT AND MICRONUTRIENT NEEDS

Problems of Micronutrient Deficiencies or Toxicities

Deficiencies or toxicities of micronutrients in plants often develop under certain conditions, such as soils with very low pH, soils with very high pH, sandy soils, soils heavily fertilized with macronutrients, poorly drained soils, and soils high in organic matter.

Soils with very low pH may result in toxicities from excess soluble Al, Fe, or Mn, or a deficiency of Mo. On the other hand, in soils with very high pH, solubilities of Cu, Fe, Mn, or Zn are reduced, and these become insoluble hydroxide precipitates, resulting in Cu, Fe, Mn, or Zn deficiencies. Generally, toxicity of Mo does not occur in soils.

Sandy soils, in areas of high rainfall, or when used in potting mixtures, are readily leached, thereby removing soluble nutrients including micronutrients. Some provision may be necessary to restore the nutrients that are removed. The same precaution mentioned previously in this chapter holds that a general mixture of micronutrients should not be applied to a soil for plant growth. If a micronutrient deficiency is suspected, the tissues of the plants growing thereon should be analyzed and treated accordingly.

Correction of Micronutrient Problems

The problem of improper pH can be overcome by liming very acid soils or adding S or other acid-forming fertilizers to alkaline soils (high pH). Alkaline soils so treated may require leaching to reduce salt concentrations (explained in chapter 9).

If a soil is very sandy, organic material such as muck, peat, composts, or well-rotted manure, can be incorporated to help hold the nutrients and retard leaching. For potted plants, having a mix of correct proportions of sand, muck, lime, phosphate fertilizer, and filler will usually prevent deficiencies from occurring for some time. With time and watering, nutrients will be removed by plant growth and leaching and will need to be replenished. The best way to do this is to use a slow-release complete fertilizer.

Poorly drained soils may have high concentrations of Fe and Mn. The solubility of Fe and Mn can be reduced by making sure the soils have adequate drainage. Liming may also help, but only after the drainage problem is corrected.

Any soil or soil mix very high in organic matter may have the Cu held so tightly that plant Cu deficiencies develop. If a Cu deficiency is suspected, the plant tissue should be analyzed in a laboratory. If Cu concentration is low, follow the recommendations of the lab for amending the soil or use a Cu spray applied to the leaves.

If any micronutrient is deficient in a soil, corrections can be made by adding the deficient chemical to the soil or by spraying the nutrient needed onto the leaves of plants where they can be absorbed directly. Either inorganic or chelated forms may be used, but be sure the particular deficiency is present before acting to avoid creating a problem of toxicity.

SUMMARY

Micronutrients must be applied to a soil *with caution* as there is only a very narrow range between deficiency and toxicity. Micronutrients are present in rocks and in soils as insoluble precipitates, soluble ions, or adsorbed onto soil particles. They can also exist as chelates, that is, complex compounds in which metals are bound in a form that plants can use, but the metals do not enter into the usual chemical reactions. Soil conditions altering micronutrient availability to plants are soil pH, oxidation reactions, inorganic soil reactions, weathering, leaching, amount of organic matter present, and microbial activities.

Availability of B for plant use depends on pH, amount of leaching and organic matter, and dry weather. Deficiency of B shows as small red, distorted young leaves and dieback of terminal buds. Toxicities show as yellow or brown leaf margins with brown spots between leaf veins. Deficiencies of Cl or Mo have not been observed on woody plants.

Micronutrient problems occur on soils that have either very low or very high pH, sandy soils, poorly drained soils, muck soils (high in organic matter), and heavily fertilized soils. These problems can be corrected by careful use of lime or acid-forming fertilizers, organic matter additions, proper drainage, testing soil and plants, and using only the recommended amounts of fertilizers.

REVIEW

Why must caution be used in fertilization with micronutrients?

In what forms are micronutrients present in soils?

What soil conditions determine availability of micronutrients?

What soil factors determine availability of B for plant use?

What are symptoms of B deficiency? B toxicity?

Under what soil conditions do micronutrient deficiencies or toxicities occur?

15

Fertilizers

Fertilizers for soil on which plants grow come in a variety of forms, such as organic, inorganic, single nutrient, double nutrient, complete fertilizer (contains N, P, and K in that order), speciality fertilizers, composts, and manures. Information about each of these forms follows.

NITROGEN FERTILIZERS

Most of the N used in fertilizers is derived from a synthetic process developed by Europeans called the "Claude-Haber process." This process uses nitrogen gas (N_2) from the atmosphere along with hydrogen gas (H_2) from natural gas in a device where pressure can be increased and temperature can be raised. The reaction is accelerated using an iron catalyst and removing the product (NH_3) as it is formed. The Fe catalyst is subject to poisoning from impurities, such as As, Co, P, or S.

$$
\begin{array}{lllll}
& & & \text{Fe catalyst} & \\
N_2 & + & 3H_2 & \rightarrow & 2\,NH_3 \\
\text{air} & & \text{natural} & 500^\circ\,C & \text{removed} \\
& & \text{gas} & 200^- & \text{as formed} \\
& & & 1000\ \text{atmos.} & \\
& & & \text{pressure} & \\
\end{array}
$$

Anhydrous Ammonia (82% N)

Anhydrous ammonia has the highest percentage of N and the cheapest per unit of N since no processing is involved. Anhy-

169

drous (without water) ammonia is a gas but when compressed changes to a liquid. For application to soils a pressurized tank is required with a device to inject the liquid ammonia into the soil. Upon release of pressure, the liquid changes back to a gas; however, the ammonia gas reacts with the moisture in the soil to form NH_4^+ that is available for plants. One problem with ammonia is that NH_3 gas is toxic to seedlings and growing plants, so must be applied prior to planting. This limits its use for landscape projects.

Aqua Ammonia and Other Salt Solutions (30–45% N)

Salt solutions of aqua ammonia are obtained by dissolving ammonia gas, ammonium nitrate, or urea in water. The amount dissolved will vary the concentration of N in the final product. This can be used in landscape projects, but care must be used as this material can salt out and plug up orifices when sprayed onto a soil. There is no real difference between liquid or solid fertilizers, provided the percentage of N is the same.

Ammonia Derivatives

Ammonia Nitrate [NH_4NO_3] (33.5% N)

Ammonium nitrate is formed by ammonia gas reacting with nitric acid:

$$NH_3 + HNO_3 \rightarrow NH_4NO_3$$

This material is hygroscopic (absorbs water from the air) and requires moisture-proof bags for storage. Sometimes this material is coated with clay to prevent caking. This material is also used for explosives.

ANL = Ammonium Nitrate with Lime (20.5% N)

Sufficient lime is added to the ammonium nitrate to neutralize the acidifying effects caused by nitrification.

Ammonium Nitrate-Sulfate (30% N) (5% S)

Ammonium Sulfate [$(NH_4)_2SO_4$] (21% N) (23% S)

Ammonium sulfate is formed by treating ammonia with sulfuric acid:

$$2\,NH_3 + H_2SO_4 \rightarrow (NH_4)_2SO_4$$

Soil acidity is increased with continual use of this fertilizer.

Urea [(NH$_2$)$_2$CO] (45% N)

Fertilizer urea exists as noncaking, free-flowing prills (compressed particles about 1-2mm in diameter) that are water soluble and can be absorbed directly by plants. It is excellent for landscape use. Urea is formed by ammonia gas reacting with carbon dioxide:

$$2\,NH_3 + CO_2 \rightarrow (NH_2)_2-CO + H_2O$$

Urea Derivatives (35 to 38% N)

Urea-Formaldehyde (about 38% N). Urea can be combined synthetically with other products, usually formaldehyde. These fertilizers are often excellent slow-release materials—contain much insoluble N that solubilizes with time. However, these products are expensive. But their use can be justified where frequent fertilizer applications are inconvenient or where it is desirable to apply large amounts of N in a single application.

Calcium Nitrate [Ca(NO$_3$)$_2$] (15.5% N)

Calcium nitrate fertilizer is formed by mixing calcium carbonate (limetstone) with nitric acid:

$$CaCO_3 + 2\,HNO_3 \rightarrow Ca(NO_3)_2 + CO_2 + H_2O + heat$$

Calcium nitrate is so hygroscopic that even when kept on the laboratory shelf in a bottle, sufficient water is absorbed by the Ca(NO$_3$)$_2$ to liquefy it. This fertilizer is not used much in the United States but is popular in Europe.

Calcium Cyanamide [CaCN$_2$] (22% N)

Calcium cyanamide is not used much as a fertilizer as it is costly per unit of N.

Sodium Nitrate [NaNO$_3$] (16% N)

Sodium nitrate is mined in Chile; however, some refining is necessary. It has a high cost per unit of N due to the low concentration of N present. It is undesirable for most soil applications because it has so much sodium that can cause soils to puddle, creating an undesirable soil structure with poor tilth (Fig. 9.7).

Other Inorganic N Sources
(various % N)

A number of other N sources have been formulated. Many of these are not readily available and are expensive. These include ammonium chloride, ammoniated superphosphate, mono-ammonium phosphate, di-ammonium phosphate, ammonium polyphosphates, magnesium-ammonium phosphates, and po-tassium nitrate.

Sulfur-Coated Urea (SCU) (various % N)

Sulfur-coated urea was developed as a slow-release N fertilizer, but it is expensive for the amount of N it carries.

Slow-Release Fertilizers (various % N)

Many slow-release fertilizers provide N, and often P and K also, in a slowly available form. They exist either as a mixture of coarse particles or as prills. These are very popular for use in green-houses or potted plants for landscape use. Instructions indicate how they can be added to potting soil and last for three to four months before another application is needed.

Natural Organic N Fertilizers
(various % N)

Many organic fertilizers have been developed for fertilizer use. Currently, very few of these are sold because they are expensive compared to the common fertilizers already discussed. However, they are fine for landscaping as they release nutrients slowly and do provide additional needed organic matter.

	% N		% N
Dried blood	13.0	Castor pumice	6.0
Bat guano	13.0	Digested sewage sludge	2.0
Fish meal	10.4	Winery pumice (dried)	1–2
Tankage	7.0	Cotton gin trash	0.7
Cottonseed meal	6.5	Seaweed (kelp)	0.2
		Activated sewage sludge	6.5

N Fertilizers for Woody Plants

Usually woody plants are planted without N fertilizer.

PHOSPHORUS FERTILIZERS

The main P fertilizers are the superphosphates. Other types are used, but they are generally less easily obtained and are more expensive per unit of P. All superphosphate fertilizers use phosphate rock mined from the ground as the initial reactant. Phosphate rock deposits are present in Florida, Tennessee, North Carolina, Idaho, Montana, Utah, and Wyoming. Phosphate rock itself can be used as a fertilizer, but it is insoluble in neutral or alkaline soils, and therefore only used where the soil is very acid. The soil acids dissolve the rock phosphate releasing the phosphate similar to the reaction used to make superphosphates:

Phosphate Rock (Apatite mineral) (6 to 17% P)

Ordinary Superphosphate (7 to 9% P)

$$\underset{\text{(rock phosphate)}}{[Ca_3(PO_4)_2]_3 . CaF_2} + \underset{\substack{\text{(sufuric}\\\text{acid)}}}{7H_2SO_4} \xrightarrow{H_2O} \underset{\substack{\text{(soluble}\\\text{mono-calcium}\\\text{phosphate)}}}{3\,Ca(H_2PO_4)_2} + \underset{\substack{\text{(gypsum)}\\\underline{\hphantom{xxxxxxxxxxx}}\\\text{(byproducts)}}}{7CaSO_4} + \underset{\text{(gas)}}{2\,H\,F}$$

Concentrated or Triple Superphosphate (10 to 22% P)

$$\underset{\substack{\text{Rock}\\\text{Phosphate}}}{\text{Rock}} + \underset{\substack{\text{Phosphoric}\\\text{Acid}}}{H_3PO_4} \rightarrow \underset{\text{Phosphate}}{\text{mono-Ca-}} + HF \text{ (no gypsum)}$$

Double Superphosphate (10 to 15% P)

Double superphosphate is made by combining ordinary superphosphate and triple superphosphate to produce a fertilizer intermediate in P.

Basic Slag $[(CaO)_5 . P_2O_5 . SiO_2]$ (0.6 to 11% P)

Ammonium Phosphates (21% P)

$$\begin{array}{ccc} NH_3 + H_3PO_4 & & NH_4H_2PO_4 \\ \text{or} & \rightarrow & \text{or} \\ NH_3 + \text{mixtures of } H_3PO_4 \text{ \& } H_2SO & & (NH_4)_2HPO_4 \end{array}$$

Nitric Phosphates (up to 70% P)

$$\text{Rock phosphate} + HNO_3 \rightarrow \text{Nitric Phsophates}$$

Polyphosphates (26 to 28% P)
(rather insoluble)

Bone Meal (5 to 7% P)

Guano (0.9% P) (13% N)

Excreta of Waterfowl from Peru

Phosphate Fertilizers
for Landscape Plantings

For landscaping with tree plantings, two methods can be used:

1. Mix 5g of superphosphate to each 10 liters of soil backfill (0.3 oz. per cubic foot); or
2. Dig the planting hole four inches deeper and place the P in a ring at the bottom of the hole (20 inches dia.) with 0.2 ounce of P fertilzer. Cover the fertilizer with soil before planting the tree.

POTASSIUM FERTILIZERS

The most common K fertilizer used is muriate of potash (potassium chloride, KCl). This material is mined from the ground, needs to be dissolved, and is recrystallized by the flotation process, but does not require treatment with heat or strong acids. Extensive K desposits are found in Oklahoma, New Mexico, Texas, Utah, and western Canada.

Potassium Chloride [KCl] (50% K)

Potassium Salts (up to 15% K)

Potassium Sulfate [K_2SO_4] (42 to 44% K)

$$2KCl + H_2SO_4 \rightarrow K_2SO_4 + 2HCl$$

Potassium Magnesium Sulfate (18% K); Potassium magnesium sulfate is also sold as Sul-Po-Mag and contains Mg and S.

Potassium Nitrate [KNO_3] (39% K) (14% N); Potassium nitrate; also called "saltpeter" (a salt substitute).

Tobacco Stems and Leaf Ribs (4 to 8% K) (2 to 4% N)

Kelp (Seaweed) from Pacific Coast (25% K in ash)

Wood Ashes (8 to 30% K)

Also contain 15 to 25% Ca and less than 2% P.)

Seawater

One cubic mile of seawater = 1,600,000 tons of K

SULFUR FERTILIZERS

Sulfur fertilizers exist as elemental sulfur (flowers of sulfur), ammonium sulfate, or ordinary superphosphate. Additionally, some S is added to soils in acid rain.

Elemental Sulfur [S] (100% S)

Ammonium Sulfate (24% S) (21% N)

Ordinary Superphosphate (4% S); Ordinary superphosphate fertilizer contains gypsum ($CaSO_4$) as an impurity. Triple superphosphate does not contain gypsum.

Rain: usually deposits about 5 pounds/acre/yr; however, as much as 100 pounds of S/acre/year is deposited in industrial areas.

MICRONUTRIENT FERTILIZERS

Copper [$CuSO_4$] (25 to 35% Cu)

Iron [$FeSO_4$] (20% Fe)

Chelates: FeEDTA or FeEDDHA

Manganese [$MnSO_4$] (23% Mn)

Chelate [MnEDTA]

Zinc [$ZnSO_4$] (23 to 35% Zn)

Chelate [Zn EDTA]

Boron [$Na_2B_4O_7 \cdot 10$ H2O](sodium borate) (18% B)

Molybdenum [$Na_2MoO_4 \cdot 2$ H_2O] (sodium molybdate) (37 to 39% Mo)

MIXED FERTILIZERS

Complete Fertilizers

Complete fertilizers are those that contain all three fertilizer elements (N P K in that order). The *percentage* of each of these present in a bag of fertilizer *must be specified.* These are some of the best kinds of fertilizers to use at planting of seeds or perennials. It is better not to apply to transplanted shrubs or trees as the N may cause too much top growth.

Fertilizer Guarantee

On each bag of fertilizer the manufacturer must show the guaranteed minimum amounts of % N, % P, and % K. This allows one to compare fertilizer price based on each of these elements present.

Elemental versus Oxide Forms

For many years, fertilizer phosphorus and potassium have been indicated as oxides—P_2O_5 and K_2O. Within the last 10 to 15 years, there has been a trend to indicate the kinds of nutrients present in an elemental form, that is, N, P, and K. An example of the conversion is:

A 10-10-10 fertilizer indicates 10% N, 10% P_2O_5, and 10% K_2O Fig. 15.1). The actual amount of N, P, and K would be 10% N, 4.4% P, and 8.3% K, or 10 pounds of N, 4.4 pounds of P, and 8.3 pounds of K present in a 100-pound bag.

FARMYARD MANURES

In Europe farmyard manure is considered a fertilizer, whereas in the United States it is a soil organic amendment. Farmyard manures can be from any of the farm animals such as cattle, sheep, hogs, horses, or other livestock. Almost all of these ma-

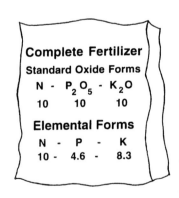

Figure 15.1 Oxide versus elemental forms. Fertilizer elements (N, P, and K) can be designated in either the oxide or elemental form.

Complete Fertilizer
Standard Oxide Forms
N - P_2O_5 - K_2O
10   10   10

Elemental Forms
N - P - K
10 - 4.6 - 8.3

nures have much moisture, making them heavy and difficult to move. Usually manures are spread on the farms where the manure is produced, as the hauling costs become too expensive to transport very far.

Chemical Composition

A ton of average farmyard manure provides about as much N, P, and K nutrients as 100 pounds of 10-5-10 fertilizer. However, manure is frequently applied to fields at the rate of 20 tons or more per acre. Notice the elements provided are not in balance. Manures are usually low in P, so farmers reinforce them with superphosphate, sometimes spreading the fertilizer right on top of the manure wagon.

Nutrients in manures are not all immediately available. Usually, availability of nutrients in the first season is about half of the total N, one-sixth of the available P, and half of available K. There are considerable residual effects from manure. After the first year, less nutrients are available than the first year, but the overall effects of manure have been measured in experiments to be still apparent after 40 years or more.

Manure needs to be handled properly to avoid losses during storage, fermentation, and decay, especially under aerobic conditions. For landscape use, well-rotted manure would be preferable to avoid the undesirable odors of fresh manure.

METHODS OF FERTILIZER APPLICATION

A number of techniques have been used to apply fertilizers for plant growth. Among these are (a) broadcasting and mixing into the soil, (b) topdressing (applying to the surface) of an established planting, (c) applying in the irrigation water, and (d) applying as a foliar spray, especially for micronutrients.

Broadcasting and Mixing into Soil

For general landscape use, broadcasting fertilizer and mixing with soil works fine; however, if limestone is needed it should be applied first and worked into the ground prior to fertilizing. Be sure not to apply superphosphate and lime together as they could react to form insoluble and unavailable tricalcium phosphate [$Ca_3(PO_4)_2$]. For shrubs or small trees, broadcast the fertilizer around the planting area and thoroughly work the fertilizer into the ground, preferably to a depth of six inches and soak the soil with water. If a soil mix is to be used in the planting hole for shrubs or trees, the mix should have at least 5% organic material. Many plantings do well with slow-release fertilizers. A compressed peg of nutrient material can be driven below the surface and will decompose with time providing nutrients over time. It is best to apply micronutrients only when a deficiency is diagnosed because indiscriminate fertilizing with micronutrients could result in plant toxicities.

Topdressing Established Plantings

Trees and shrubs are usually fertilized annually in late winter or early spring. This enhances new root and shoot growth for the following season. Most landscape plants should not be fertilized in the hot summer as this will stimulate late fall growth and retard winter hardening, making the plants susceptible to winter injury.

For established trees, apply the fertilizer by drilling holes with a small auger about one yard apart all around the tree at the drip line. The drip line is the area containing most of the feeder roots of the trees and is located by looking at the tree and determining where the outer leaves would drip onto the ground; that would be the area to fertilize. Be sure not to use fertilizer-herbicide combinations in this manner as the trees may be killed.

Irrigation Water

Soluble fertilizers can be dissolved in water used for irrigation. This system is often used in greenhouses where the fertilizer is used only periodically and can be adjusted to plant growth. Care must be taken to adjust the amount added to avoid too high a concentration of fertilizer salts. If the concentration is very high, it could be detrimental for plant growth. Furthermore, the high concentrations of fertilizer may salt out and plug the irrigation equipment.

Foliar Sprays

Micronutrients can be applied to leaves of plants where a deficiency is found. The nutrients are absorbed directly by the leaves. This type of fertilization is *not* effective for macronutrients, as too large amounts are needed by plants to be absorbed in this manner. If very large amounts of macronutrients are sprayed on the leaves, the leaves will die from salt effects. Some success has been found with foliar N application on strawberries at bud-formation time, but care must be used.

MOVEMENT OF FERTILIZERS IN SOILS

Negatively charged ions (anions), especially NO_3^-, move the most in soils. Phosphorus is an exception. Although it is present in two anionic forms, $H_2PO_4^-$ and HPO_4^{2-}, P moves very little in soils. This is probably due to the many fixation-type reactions that occur between P and inorganic elements in soils as explained previously (Chapter 12). Positively charged ions (cations) can also move in soils or leach through soils, especially Ca^{2+}, Mg^{2+}, and K^+.

The amount of moisture in soils is often critical to fertilizer placement. By having concentrated fertilizers in soils, there is a distinct chance for fertilizer burn of seedlings and plant roots, especially in dry conditions. When rainfall is abundant, the fertilizer salts are diluted and make conditions desirable for fertilizer use. Nitrogen and potassium are particularly troublesome in causing fertilizer burn. These kinds of fertilizers (N and K) are better applied often or in small amounts. Also, fertilizer burn can be reduced or eliminated altogether by using slow-release fertilizers.

Liquid fertilizers are just as good as solid forms for the same quantity of fertilizer nutrient. Liquid or solid forms can be mixed with water and applied in the irrigation system with equal success.

There are some residual effects from fertilizers, especially manures, composts, and other organic fertilizers.

SUMMARY

Most N fertilizers are derived from ammonia produced commercially by combining N_2 gas with H_2 gas. Nitrogen fertilizers commonly used include anhydrous ammonia, ammonium nitrate, ANL, and urea. Some specialty N fertilizers are the organics and some other slow-release fertilizer pellets.

Common P fertilizers are ordinary superphosphate and triple superphosphate. Ordinary superphosphate has gypsum ($CaSO_4$) as an impurity, whereas triple superphosphate has a higher level of P and does not have any gypsum. Most K fertilizer is sold as muriate of potash (KCl); however, a few plants can be damaged by chlorine in this fertilizer. Potassium sulfate is used in those cases.

Sulfur fertilizer is available as elemental S, ammonium sulfate, or gypsum present in ordinary superphosphate. Micronutrient fertilizers are usually sold as borates, molybdates, sulfate salts, or chelates.

A mixed fertilizer must contain N, P, and K and are shown on the fertilizer bag in that order. Elemental forms of these elements are shown as N, P, and K, whereas the old system of oxides were shown as N, P_2O_5, and K_2O.

Animal manures are useful in providing a source of organic material along with both readily available and slow-release nutrients. They generally have much moisture, are very heavy to transport, and often have undesirable odors. Some of these disadvantages can be overcome by having the manure dried, but this results in higher cost.

Methods used to apply fertilizer to soils include broadcasting and mixing with the soil, applying to the soil surface and mixing in, dissolving in the irrigation water, and spraying solutions on the leaves. Fertilizer anions, for example, NO_3^-, SO_4^{2-}, Cl^-, and MoO_4^{2-}, usually move readily in soils, but phosphates ($H_2PO_4^-$ and HPO_4^{2-}) do not. The fertilizer cations, for example, NH_4^+, Ca^{2+}, Mg^{2+}, and K^+, also move, but they can be adsorbed onto the soil particles and leach readily. Fertilizer burn often results when large amounts of certain fertilizers, usually N and K, are placed very close to the seeds or plant roots; this is aggravated by dry conditions where the fertilizer salts are concentrated. Another technique used by landscape architects is to use slow-release fertilizer that will not harm sensitive plant parts.

REVIEW

Most N fertilizers are derived from what material?

Can you name the common N fertilizers?

What specialty N fertilizers are used in greenhouses and landscaping?

What are the commonly used P fertilizers? How do they differ?

In what form is most K fertilizer sold?

(continued) ➡

REVIEW (*continued*)

What are the three different forms of S
  fertilizer that are used?
How is a mixed fertilizer represented on a
  fertilizer bag?
Can you explain the difference between
  elemental forms and oxide forms of the
  fertilizer elements?
What are the advantages and disadvantages of
  using animal manures?
What are the different ways to apply fertilizers to soils?
Can you describe how fertilizer nutrients
  move in soils?
Which moisture conditions may cause
  fertilizer burn?

16

Soil Organic Matter

IMPORTANCE OF SOIL ORGANIC MATTER

Soil organic matter (SOM) is probably the most important constituent of soils. The effect of SOM on soil properties far exceeds the relative percentage of this material in soils. The small amount of organic matter in soils, usually from 1 to 5%, is very important in providing a reserve food source for microorganisms and higher plants. Almost all properties of SOM are beneficial for plant growth.

DEFINITION OF SOIL ORGANIC MATTER

Soil organic matter can be defined as a complex, heterogeneous mixture of plant and animal remains in various stages of decay, microbial cells—both living and dead—microbially synthesized compounds, and derivatives of all of the above through microbial activity. Soil organic matter is probably the most complex of all naturally occurring substances. Some compounds in SOM are distinctive to soil and are not present in plants or animals.

COMPOSITION OF SOIL ORGANIC MATTER

By examining the composition of SOM, one can see why it is such a complex material. The following compounds have been isolated from chemical SOM extracts:

1. Carbohydrates (sugars, polysaccharides)—about 75% of dry weight
2. Lignin (a plant polymer of phenyl propane units)
3. Proteins (combinations of amino acids)
4. Hydrocarbons—fats, waxes, resins, and oils
5. Tannins (phenolic substances)
6. Pigments (chlorophyll)
7. Organic acids (many in the biochemical Krebs cycle)
8. Miscellaneous compounds—includes organic P, organic S, polynuclear hydrocarbons, nucleic acid derivatives, alcohols, aldehydes, esters, etc.

SOIL CHANGES WHEN ORGANIC MATTER IS ADDED

Whenever organic materials are added to a soil the physical properties of soil structure, water-holding capacity, and soil color are changed. The extent of change in these properties depends on the amount and type of organic material added, the soil microorganisms present in the soil, and the speed at which decomposition occurs.

Physical Properties Changed

Aggregation and granulation (crumb formation) is increased by polysaccharides produced by microorganisms during decomposition. This improves soil tilth (ability to work the soil) and helps stabilize the soil crumbs.

The ability of a soil to hold water is greatly increased by addition of SOM. This results in greater infiltration (water moving into the soil) and adsorption of water by the SOM, with consequently less erosion and loss of soil particles and fertility.

Usually when SOM is added to a soil, the color of the soil darkens, but it is not necessarily black. A dark soil warms up sooner in the spring than a light soil, particularly if the soil is well drained. If the soil is poorly drained, it may take longer to warm up, since raising the water temperature takes much energy.

Chemical Properties Changed

Addition of organic materials to a soil results in changes in the chemical properties: (a) cation exchange capacity is increased,

(b) buffering capacity is increased, (c) the amount and availability of plant nutrients are increased, (d) the amount of growth-stimulating substances is increased, and (e) there is a possible increase in a toxic substance. The extent of change in these properties also depends on the amount and kinds of organic material added, the soil microbial activity, and how quickly decomposition occurs.

Cation exchange capacity (CEC) is the *ability of a soil to hold onto positively charged nutrient ions*. Compared to mineral soils, organic matter has from two to thirty times more CEC per unit of weight. The SOM accounts for 30 to 90% of the adsorbing power of mineral soils. The CEC of SOM depends on the extent of decomposition (humification). The more humified the SOM, the greater the CEC. Humification is reduced at low pH.

Buffering capacity is related to CEC. The higher the CEC, the greater the buffering. Organic matter has a great buffering effect in soils.

Organic matter contains much unavailable N, P, and S in organic form that can be released to plant-available inorganic forms during decomposition. Also, nutrient cations (e.g., Ca^{2+}, Mg^{2+}, K^+, Na^+, NH_4^+) are adsorbed onto organic matter surfaces that can be used by plants. Furthermore, organic groups on SOM can chelate some micronutrients that are available for plant absorption.

Soil organic matter acts as a source of many plant growth stimulators such as vitamins (especially B vitamins), hormones, auxins (giberellins), IAA (indole acetic acid). Experiments using humic substances in culture solution have shown improved plant growth, possibly from Fe or some unknown catalyst.

Chemical analysis by soil chemists in the early 1900s showed that a substance that is toxic to plants, that is, dihydroxystearic acid, is present in SOM extracts. Usually, this substance is not a problem in well-drained, acidic soils that have been limed and fertilized. However, this dihydroxystearic acid may contribute to poor growth of plants in very poorly drained and very acid soils. Overall, this detrimental affect of SOM is minor compared to the much greater beneficial effects listed above.

DECOMPOSITION OF SOIL
ORGANIC MATTER

Decomposition of SOM is a very important process in healthy soils. This process of oxidizing plant and animal remains for energy by microbes to carbon dioxide, water, inorganic elements, microbial synthates, and humus can be illustrated by an equation:

$$\text{Plant and animal remains} + O_2 + \text{soil microbes} \rightarrow$$
$$CO_2 + H_2O + \text{inorganic elements (N, P, S, acids)}$$
$$+ \text{HUMUS} + \text{microbial synthates} + \text{energy}$$

Humus

Humus is the "more or less" end-product in the decomposition process. The phrase "more or less" is used because humus itself can also decay, but it does so at a very reduced rate. So the first-formed humic material can be considered "humus," but when this material undergoes further decomposition and before everything has been decomposed to CO_2 and H_2O, the remaining humic material is also called "humus" (Fig. 16.1).

Experiments have shown that greater decomposition occurs when organic substances are added to soils at low rates than at high rates. Decomposition is accelerated by a number of factors.

Factors Affecting Rapid Decomposition

a. Low lignin and hydrocarbons (fats, waxes, resins, oils)
b. Much soluble material (green material and proteins)
c. Adequate supply of N
d. Favorable pH (slightly acid to neutral)
e. Favorable aeration (oxygen required)
f. Favorable moisture (very dry or very wet conditions result in slow decomposition)
g. Favorable temperature (85–90° F desirable)
h. Finely subdivided material disintegrates quickly
i. Mixtures of organic materials decompose faster than only a single type

Decomposition in soils is reduced by the presence of certain metals, especially Cu or Fe. Some reduction in decomposition can also occur with the presence of Al or Zn, but these only cause slight decrease.

Decomposition Process in Soil

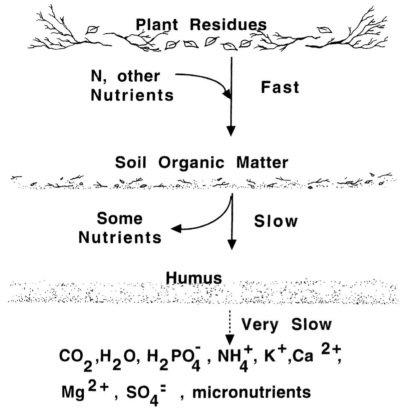

Figure 16.1 Decomposition in soil. Plant or animal remains in soils decompose breaking down into organic matter with eventual formation of humus and release of many plant nutrients.

Decomposition is also decreased under two conditions: (a) Inactivation of enzymes by being adsorbed onto SOM, which prevents the enzyme from reaching the substrate, and (b) Inaccessibility of substrate that enzymes attack by the substrate itself being adsorbed onto the SOM. This protective action, which can also occur with certain 2:1 type of clays, is important in helping to conserve organic matter in soils and may be one of the reasons that most of the organic material remains in many soils.

SOURCES OF ORGANIC MATTER

Organic matter can be added to soils in the form of (a) green manure, (b) animal manures, (c) composts, (d) plant root and top residues, (e) mulches, and (f) sewage sludges. Furthermore, any management practice that improves plant growth, such as liming, fertilizing, or drainage, will increase the amount of plant remains (leaves, stems, roots) which in turn will decompose adding to the SOM.

Green Manure

Green manure consists of plants that are grown to be plowed or worked into the ground. The advantage of these green plants is they have a narrow C/N ratio, permitting fast decay yielding much HUMUS. However, not any plant remain will do—it must be green (i.e., not mature) or the effect is lost.

Animal Manures

Animal manures also provide an important source of organic matter besides adding many plant nutrients. The main disadvantages of manures are the undesirable odor and heavy wet condition. These can be somewhat overcome by using well-rotted manure or dried manure. These products are useful for landscaping projects, but the additional handling raises the price.

Composts

Composts are organic products that are frequently used in greenhouses, nurseries, and gardens. Composts are formed by mixing carbonaceous material with green material along with some moisture, lime, and small amounts of soil, providing the microbes needed in the process as discussed in Chapter 7 (Fig. 7.3). However, they are too expensive and time-consuming to be created by farmers. For landscaping, they are very satisfactory in supplying organic matter.

Plant Root and Top Residues

Plant tissues, both roots and tops, are constantly being added to soils as the plants die. The microorganisms attack these substances making more SOM.

Mulches

Mulches have already been discussed in the section on "Covering Soil with Mulch" (Chapter 7).

Sewage Sludges

Municipal sewage sludges are being used for potting mixes. These sludges are an excellent source for organic matter, N, and P, and all the benefits received from organic matter. On the other hand, problems may arise from sewage sludge in mixes from odors, high concentrations of salts and/or heavy metals, low amounts of K, and the presence of viruses and noxious organic compounds. Usually, sludges have been subjected to high heat that kills most parasites and diseases, but little is known about the many viruses and undesirable organic compounds that can be present. The presence of heavy metals used to be a problem with sludges, but the sewage plants have generally restricted metal-plating industries from using the municipal systems.

SUMMARY

Even small amounts of organic matter added to mineral soils can provide significant improvement in the soil both physically and chemically. The highly complex soil organic matter (SOM) includes plant and animal remains, microbes, microbial synthates, and similar compounds to these. Chemical compounds present in SOM are carbohydrates, lignin, proteins, hydrocarbons, tannins, pigments, organic acids, and many more other compounds.

Adding organic matter to soils changes the soil physically by improving soil crumb formation and stabilizing the aggregates formed, increasing the infiltration and water-holding capacity, and a change in the soil color may occur; and chemically by increasing the CEC, buffering capacity, supply of total and available nutrients, and adding growth-stimulating substances.

An equation of organic matter decomposition in soils begins with plant or animal remains that become oxidized for energy by soil microbes releasing CO_2, H_2O, inorganic elements, acids, microbial synthates, and humus. Decomposition can be increased by having material containing low amounts of lignin and hydrocarbons, large amounts of soluble material (green containing proteins), adequate N, finely ground material, mixtures of substances, favorable pH, and correct amounts of aeration, moisture, and temperature.

Organic matter can be added to soil as green manure, animal manure, composts, plant roots and tops, or mulches. Green manure is any plant that is grown to be worked into the soil while the plant is still green. This is very beneficial in improving humus and physical and chemical properties of the soil.

REVIEW

Why is soil organic matter (SOM) so important in mineral soils?

What are the components of "soil organic matter?"

Can you name the organic compounds present in SOM?

When soil organic matter is added to soils, how do the soils change physically? Chemically?

Can you show by an equation how organic matter decomposes?

What is meant by "humus?"

How can the rate of decomposition be increased?

In what forms can organic matter be added to soils?

What is green manure? How does it help soils?

17

Diagnosing
Plant Disorders

Tools to use for diagnosing plant disorders include overall plant appearance, plant tissue testing, total plant analysis, soil testing and analysis, and soil and root abnormalities. Plant appearance will show animal damage, weather-induced problems, chemical injuries, mechanical damage, biotic-associated problems, and plant nutrient deficiency and toxicity symptoms.

PLANT APPEARANCE

Many plant growth problems can be correctly diagnosed by skillfully examining the outward appearance of a plant. By knowing the appearance of a healthy plant, one can know what would be different to cause a plant disorder.

Animal Damage

Animals can damage plants in a variety of ways. Large animals, such as *deer*, squirrels, gophers, moles, mice, often graze on plant tops, may break off stems, or pull the plants out of the ground. These animals can be discouraged by electric or regular fencing or by placing some repellents close to the plants. Deer can be repelled by hanging small bars of odiferous deodorant soap on the plants; or by spraying the plants with a mixture of an egg in a bucket of water. They also do not like baler twine soaked in spent soil from automobiles. *Rodents* often live in mulch near trees and shrubs and feed on the roots or tender shoots sometimes killing the plants. Prevention of this kind of damage can be accomplished by placing a ring of gravel or hardware cloth around the shrubs or trees to discourage this feeding.

Birds also can be a problem. Woodpeckers and sapsuckers may dig holes in trees looking for insects. By keeping your trees healthy, these birds are discouraged. Other birds are often attracted to new seedings. If shrubs or small trees are damaged by birds, netting can be used to cover the plants as a final resort.

Dogs also can damage plantings, usually by urinating on them. There are repellants that can be used to discourage this.

Man-Made Damages

Man can cause damage to plants through accidents, neglect, or ignorance as to proper care. There are a number of ways that plants can be damaged mechanically, such as root damage, trunk damage, or leaf damage, usually resulting from accidents.

Accidents

Fires.   Fires started by nature or by man can cause much damage to plantings.

Automobiles or Lawnmowers.   Bark damage of trees or shrubs can also occur by being struck by automobiles or lawnmowers (Fig. 17.1). This type of damage is especially critical in the spring and early summer when the cambium layer is active and the bark "slips," but this type of damage can occur anytime. Trees particularly vulnerable are those near parking lots, curbs, and driveways. Once a tree or shrub is damaged close to the ground there is more chance for decay to occur rapidly. Sometimes vandals damage plants. It is best to try to repair the damage by wrapping it with tape or applying wound dressing.

Neglect

Potted Plants.   Potted plants are often neglected, for example, not providing them with adequate light or water. When roots become pot-bound they should be transplanted to larger containers or growth will be stunted. Potted plants through neglect may die from accumulation of salts due to improper watering. When insufficient water is added, evaporation from the soil surface results in salts, forming as a white crust. This can be avoided by always applying sufficient water to saturate the soil. When water starts running out the bottom of the pot, add about 10%

Lawnmower Damage
to Tree Trunk

Figure 17.1 Lawnmower damage. Tree trunks can be damaged by careless use of lawnmowers.

more water to wash away the undesirable salts. This results in nutrients being removed and therefore fertilizers need to be added to replace the salts removed. A slow-release fertilizer is ideal for potted plants, but should be applied at relatively low rates. Since more nutrients are released from slow-release fertilizers during hot weather, one must reduce the amount of fertilizer used at that time. Also, salts are more likely to form crusts when pots are irrigated from the bottom up.

Salinity can also be present in the potting mixes, often coming from sands, gypsum, composts, chicken manure, or sewage sludges. The fertilizer applied to potted plants needs to be adjusted to suit the salt tolerance of the specific plant.

Plants kept indoors need much less fertilizer, as little as 10% of that for those planted outside. Leaching efficiency is high if time is allowed for the soil mix in potted plants to dry somewhat between waterings; however, do not allow plants to become severely wilted, as they may not recover when watered.

Newly Seeded Lawns. New lawn seedings should be mulched with straw and provided with some form of water, usually by sprinkling, during the critical seedling stage. Fertilizers should not be applied to new lawn seedings until the grasses are well established. Care should be taken not to use fertilizers containing Na^+, Cl^-, or SO_4^{2-} in excess, as these salts are detrimental to plants. Even large amounts of N or K can be detrimental to germination of young seeds.

Landscape Plantings. In times of drought, supplemental water must be applied at the proper time to landscape plants if they are to survive. Trees and shrubs need to be checked periodically for damage from insects, diseases, and weeds.

Improper Care Through Ignorance

Root Damage. Whenever soils are cultivated or disturbed, care must be taken to avoid cutting off tree roots, especially the feeder roots located at the drip line around the tree. This often happens when trenches are dug for repairing or installing utilities (Fig. 17.2). When the roots are damaged, they could subject the shrub or tree to wind damage. When landscaping where soil must be removed from around a tree, some provision needs to be made

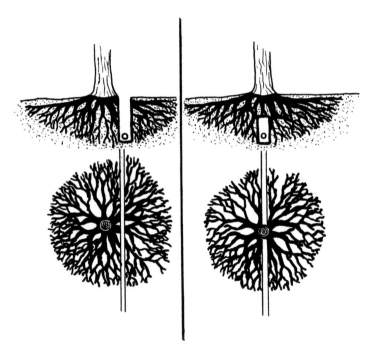

Figure 17.2 Utility damage to tree roots. Tree roots can be damaged when utility lines are dug near or under the trees.

to maintain the root system. This can be done by constructing a retaining wall with provision for water and air movement around the tree roots (Fig. 17.3). Sometimes new trees or shrubs need to be above the finished grade. A raised planter with appropriate tubes for irrigation and drainage (Fig. 17.4) can be constructed. Other types of raised planters in a stepwise fashion are sometimes used for strawberries or beds of flowers (Fig. 17.5). Also, existing tree roots must not be covered with soil as this excludes the needed oxygen for roots to survive. To avoid this problem a dry well can be constructed around the tree (Fig. 17.6) with gravel and pipes to allow oxygen to reach the roots. Retaining walls can be used when regrading around existing trees on a slope (Fig. 17.7).

Root Girdling. Sometimes roots can unknowingly become girdled (Fig. 17.8) below the soil line and not be noticeable. In a nursery roots may start to encircle the plant. It is important to straighten out the roots even in a large planting hole. If this is not done, the roots can grow in a circle and may cut off the lower roots

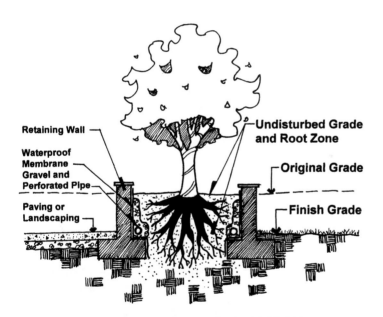

Retaining Wall

Waterproof Membrane
Gravel and Perforated Pipe

Paving or Landscaping

Undisturbed Grade and Root Zone

Original Grade

Finish Grade

EXISTING TREE PROTECTION DETAIL FOR CUT AREAS

Figure 17.3 Retaining wall construction. To prevent damage to tree roots when removing soil near them, a retaining wall can be constructed with appropriate pipes for air and drainage.

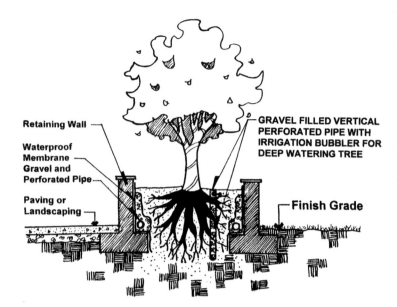

Retaining Wall

Waterproof Membrane

Gravel and Perforated Pipe

Paving or Landscaping

GRAVEL FILLED VERTICAL PERFORATED PIPE WITH IRRIGATION BUBBLER FOR DEEP WATERING TREE

Finish Grade

Raised Planter Detail for New Tree

Figure 17.4 Raised planter. New trees placed above finish grade can be kept alive by a raised planter with appropriate pipes for air and drainage.

Raised Planter for Strawberries

Figure 17.5 A step-wise raised planter can be used for strawberries or flowers for ease in harvesting or for aesthetics.

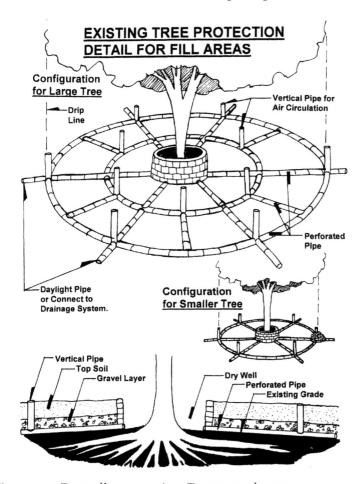

EXISTING TREE PROTECTION DETAIL FOR FILL AREAS

Configuration for Large Tree

Drip Line

Vertical Pipe for Air Circulation

Perforated Pipe

Daylight Pipe or Connect to Drainage System.

Configuration for Smaller Tree

Vertical Pipe
Top Soil
Gravel Layer

Dry Well
Perforated Pipe
Existing Grade

Figure 17.6 Dry well construction. To prevent damage to tree roots when soil is placed near them, a dry well can be constructed.

from their supply of water and nutrients. This may take years to develop and is often noticed as a gradual decline of the tree with the leaves beginning to color early and fall off prematurely. Once this has occurred a homeowner can dig down beside the tree and cut off the offending encircling root with chisel and mallet. Sometimes this develops because an auger used to drill the hole compacted the sides keeping roots from penetrating the surrounding soil. Try to keep the soil friable to prevent this from happening.

Improper Staking or Guying. Damage to shrubs or trees can occur from improper staking or guying for support of recently

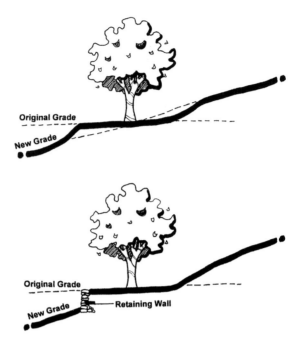

Figure 17.7 Retaining walls on slopes. When changing grade around a tree, the tree can be kept alive by use of a retaining wall on the downhill side.

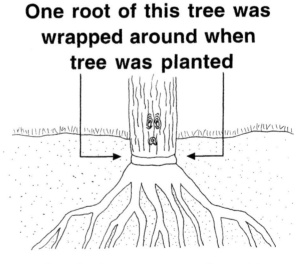

Figure 17.8 When planting trees, care must be used to prevent a root from encircling the main stem as the wrapped root can prevent growth later and may kill the tree.

planted trees or shrubs (Fig. 17.9). If only wire is used and stretched very tightly, the trees may become girdled when the bark on the tree trunk grows around the wire. It is best to use wire covered with rubber hose where it is next to the tree bark to allow the tree to grow unhindered. Plants braced with wires need regular inspection for damage, because the tree may grow around the guy wire and constrict the living vessels under the bark (Fig. 17.9).

Improper Fertilization.   Too little fertilizer can result in plant nutrient deficiencies, whereas too much fertilizer can sometimes result in burning of seeds or plants nearby. The timing of fertilization is also critical. During dry weather, fertilizer salts remain concentrated and can cause burning of plants.

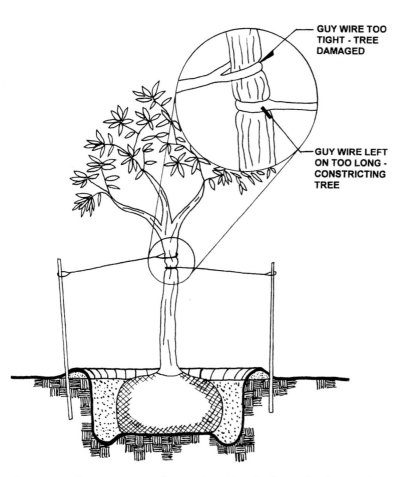

Figure 17.9 Improper use of guy wires. Tree bark can be damaged by improper guying of trees at planting.

Weather-Induced Problems

Weather-induced problems can be divided into two categories—environmental and pollution.

Environmental Problems

Low Temperatures. Plants suffer when temperatures are extreme, especially very low temperatures. Annuals are susceptible to frost damage if planted too early in the spring. Perennials likewise can be damaged from extremely cold conditions, especially if accompanied with wind. Often these plants can be protected by placing wire cages filled with leaf mulch prior to the very cold spells. Also one must avoid applying fertilizer, especially N, in the late summer and fall as this will encourage late fall growth that may not be winter-hardened and can become damaged.

Light and Water. The supply of light or water may limit plant growth. Plants should be placed where the light conditions are best for growth. Plants that require direct sunlight will grow poorly in shaded areas because their stems stretch trying to reach the light. Plants that grow better in shade will not thrive in direct sunlight and the leaves may become scalded. Water requirements for plants also differ. Some plants can survive with only limited amounts of water, whereas others require an abundance for proper growth. Growth habits must be considered. In arid areas or during drought, supplemental water often is required for plant growth. Too much water, as in flooding, can be as detrimental to plant growth as insufficient water.

Wind, Snow, and Ice. Branches of many shrubs and trees may split or break when subjected to wind or loads of snow or ice. Those most susceptible to damage of this sort are ash, catalpa, hemlock, hickory, horse chestnut, Siberian elm, yellowwood, red maple, tulip poplar, junipers, and yew.

Lightning. Lightning often strikes trees that are tall and have deep taproots, such as lombardy poplar. Trees of this nature should not be planted close to houses.

Pollution Problems

Dusts

Dusts consist of particulate matter that can be detrimental to leaves of plants. Dusts often arise from refuse burning or kiln dust from cement plants.

Automobile By-Products

In the past automobile exhaust has resulted in lead (Pb) deposits on plants. With the no-lead fuels of today, Pb is no longer being deposited. However, there may be effects of previously deposited Pb near heavily traveled highways. Also, spent oil from auto crankcases may not be disposed properly and can damage plants. Remedies include hosing down plants with detergent followed by water or just water alone.

Chemicals

Chemicals in the atmosphere can also be detrimental to plants (Table 17.1). Common air pollutants include *sulfur dioxide* (SO_2), *hydrogen fluoride* gas (HF), *ozone* (O_3), *peroxyacetyl nitrates* (PAN); less common air pollutants are ammonia (NH_3), HCl, Cl_2,

Table 17.1 Sources, toxic levels, and plant symptoms of four common air pollutants

| | Air Pollutant | | | |
	Sulfur Dioxide	Fluoride	Ozone	PAN*
Source	Atmospheric point S-containing coal and oil burning in industries	Atmospheric point F-containing catalysts and fluxes from industries	Atmosphere Auto exhaust and coal and oil combustion	Atmosphere Auto exhaust and coal and oil combustion
Toxic levels	0.7 ppm for 1 hour 0.18 ppm for 8 hours	1 ppb for 24 hours	0.05 ppm for 4 hours	10 ppb for 4 hours
Broadleaf plant symptoms	Light brown interveinal areas on both leaf surfaces	Marginal or tip yellowing or browning	Spotting or mottling on upper leaf surfaces	Silvering or glazing of lower leaf surfaces
Conifer plant symptoms	Needle tip browning and yellow banding	Needle tip death and yellowing	Needle tip death, yellowing of tips, banding, and mottling	White dead areas on needle portion most sensitive at exposure

*Pan = peroxyacetyl nitrates
ppm = parts per million
ppb = parts per billion

ethylene ($CH_2 = CH_2$), hydrogen sulfide (H_2S), and nitrogen oxides (NO_x). Sulfur dioxide issues forth from volcanoes or burning of coal, oil, or natural gas. Hydrogen fluoride gas is vented to the atmosphere from factories producing steel, aluminum, ceramics, glass, or P fertilizer. Ozone is derived from hydrocarbons and some photochemical reactions in the atmosphere. Burning of coal, oil, or gasoline in automobile exhaust can produce PAN. All these chemical pollutants can damage plants—some more than others. Plants that are under stress are sensitive to all these chemical pollutants. Some trees and shrubs are tolerant of pollutants. The chemical damage to plants often shows as brown spots (as if burnt) on any green plant part.

Chemical Injuries

Chemical injuries to plants can be caused either from pesticides, soil sterilants, salts, or toxic chemicals. Pesticides include herbicides, insecticides, and fungicides. Salt damage occurs from ocean spray, salts spread on roads or walkways, or improperly placed or excess fertilizers.

Herbicides

Of the pesticides, herbicides are probably most toxic. Application of herbicides is directed onto weeds; however, damage may occur to nontarget plants by too concentrated mixtures, too heavy application, careless application or drift, or movement in soil or water, especially in sands followed by root absorption.

Insecticides

Some insecticides may be harmful to plants if applied above temperatures of 80° F.

Fungicides

Some fungicides also may be detrimental to plants if applied above certain temperatures, usually 80° F.

Soil Sterilants

Soil sterilants are often used to kill weed seeds, soil insects, disease vectors, and nematodes; however, if not applied properly, they can damage adjacent plantings. Careful application will avoid damage. If contamination does occur, the soil can be removed or the chemicals can be absorbed by stirring in activated charcoal or finely divided compost or sawdust. The mix must be moistened for these products to react.

Salts

Ocean spray containing salts is most damaging to plants growing adjacent to salt water lakes and oceans, but salty water can also be carried inland by hurricanes. Salt damage to plants can occur near roads, walkways, or driveways when salt is used for deicing. Large amounts of salt can seep into the soil creating conditions that are detrimental for most plants. This problem can be avoided by limiting use of salt or keeping plantings away from areas needing salt. If this type of damage does occur, plants should be washed off with water from a hose or sprayer or injured parts can be pruned off. Well-drained soils can be leached of salts. If this is a recurring problem, one should only grow salt-tolerant species. Other remedies would be to install barriers to keep the road salt away, apply salt sparingly and only when needed, or use sand, limestone chips, or sawdust instead of salt.

Many *fertilizers* may cause salt problems on plants, especially if applied in very large amounts. The least-damaging fertilizer is P. Some of the most damaging fertilizers to plants are N, K, or B. If fertilizer salts are a problem, the soil can be thoroughly leached to remove the unwanted salts. Deficiencies or excesses of fertilizers was covered previously (Chapter 11, 12, 14, and 15).

Localized damage to plants can occur where there are toxic chemical spills. Correction of these is best left to experts.

Saline and Sodic Soils

Saline or sodic soils, discussed previously in Chapter 9 in the section on Correcting Alkalinity in Arid Regions, have inherently high concentrations of salts. Unless these are removed, most plant growth is defintely reduced.

Biotic-Associated Problems

When dealing with biological problems, distinction needs to be made between signs and symptoms. A *sign* is a visible causal organism that produces disease or plant stress, for example, rusts, powdery mildews, mistletoe. A *symptom* is an abnormality of

the host plant, for example, chlorosis (yellowing), necorsis (die-
back or browning), or wilting.

Insects

Look for insects themselves or eggs or frass (insect droppings) or
plant damage such as chewing spots. Some insects, such as grass-
hoppers or Japanese beetles, will damage any plant in their way.
Other insects only attack specific species of plants such as corn
earworm. Identification of insects may require an entomologist.

Diseases

Diseases of plants are often caused by fungi, bacteria, or viruses.
Each of these diseases has its own signs (causal agent) and symptoms (effect on plants).

Fungal Diseases.   Examples of fungal diseases are wilts,
root rots, Dutch elm disease, leaf spot, leaf blotch, anthrac-
nose, powdery mildew, blister, shot holes. Needles of conifers can exhibit spots, blight, or rust.

Bacterial Diseases.   Diseases caused by bacteria include
fire blight and crown gall.

Virus Diseases.   Examples of virus diseases are mosaics,
stem pitting, ringspot, scorch, and yellows. Disease identification and treatment is best left to a plant pathologist.

Infectious Diseases.   Infectious diseases can be character-
ized by (a) only one genus or species affected, (b) only one
plant in a group affected, (c) the same symptoms for all plant
parts, (d) plants only die slowly, or (e) the plant is weak-
ened from stress and is more susceptible to attack by other
diseases and insects.

Nematodes

Nematodes are found in abundance in all soils. There are many
different kinds—some are beneficial, but most are harmful to
plants. The damage is due to the nematode inserting a stylus
into the plant root and sucking the juices out, thereby weaken-
ing the plant and eventually killing it. The best technique in
controlling nematodes is prevention by using soil fumigants
prior to planting.

Plant Parasites

Other types of biotic problems are those in which another plant becomes a plant parasite on the host plant. Examples of this are mistletoe, dodder, and Spanish moss.

Plant Nutrient Deficiencies and Toxicities

Plant nutrient deficiencies and toxicities are not always easy to diagnose. Therefore, after all other suspected diagnostic problems have been eliminated, then one may suspect a deficiency or a toxicity of the plants affected. Some nutrient symptoms are specific for an individual plant species, are confused with other problems, such as insect or disease damage, or can be misleading when more than one element is involved. Deficiency symptoms only show when the supply of an element is too low for the plant to function properly. Symptoms are not always related to a deficiency of an element. Soil analysis may not be a good indicator of a nutrient deficiency.

Example 1:   A Cu deficiency could occur in plants growing on an organic soil having high concentrations of total Cu. The Cu is held so strongly by the soil organic matter that an insufficient amount of Cu is available for plant use.

Example 2:   An excess of K in a soil can result in antagonism of Mg absorption by plants, resulting in a Mg deficiency where soil Mg is present in high concentration.

Example 3:   An "Fe deficiency" in some plants results from a high soil pH, even though there may be a large amount of total Fe present in the soil, because the Fe is in an insoluble, unavailable form (oxide or hydroxide).

All of these examples how that the availability of a nutrient in a soil is more important than the total amount of that element present.

A generalized scheme has been devised to act as a guide in diagnosing plant nutrient deficiencies (Table 17.2). Some plants may not exactly fit into this key. Another approach is to summarize plant nutrient deficiencies according to the diagnosis of specific plant parts (Table 17.3). Much less is known about toxicity symptoms, but some, such as B, Na, Mn, or Al, can be generalized (Table 17.4).

Table 17.2 A Key to Nutrient Deficiency Symptoms in Plants

A	Symptoms general on whole plant or localized on **old lower leaves**	to B
A1	Symptoms localized on **young upper new leaves**	to F
B	Symptoms usually general on **whole plant**, although effect is often on older leaves as yellowing and browning.	to C
B1	Effect local on **older, lower leaves**	to E
C	**Foliage yellow**	to D
C1	**Foliage dark green**; lower leaves may be yellow between veins; more often **purple**, especially on **petioles**; growth delayed and **leaves drop prematurely**	PHOSPHORUS DEFICIENT
D	**Old leaves** more **yellow** than young ones; followed by a light tan color and drying; plant is stunted, stems slender, & a few breaks; little or **no dropping of leaves**	NITROGEN DEFICIENT
D1	**Uniform yellowing of all leaves**; some brown lesions may appear; little or no drying of older leaves	SULFUR DEFICIENT
E	**Lower leaves mottled; yellowing of tip** and **leaf margins** progressing toward the center, later **becoming brown** and margins curl under; old leaves drop; white spots on clovers	POTASSIUM DEFICIENT
E1	**Lower leaves yellow** in early stages, brown later; **yellow between leaf veins**, but **veins remain green; leaves may pucker** or leaf margins may curl up or down; chlorotic areas between veins become brown in 24 hours; leaf edges may become reddish-purple	MAGNESIUM DEFICIENT
F	**Terminal buds** remain **alive**	to G
F1	**Terminal buds** usually **die**	to K
G	**Veins remain green; interveinal yellowing**	to H
G1	**Whole leaf yellow**; old leaves die at tips	COPPER DEFICIENT
H	**Brown lesions absent**	to I
H1	**Brown lesions usually present** & scattered over entire leaf; **all veins remain green** (netting effect); blossoms (if any) are smaller than normal & color is faded	MANGANESE DEFICIENT
I	**All veins green**; only part of interveins are yellow; leaves abnormally small & show some yellow mottling; common on young plants	ZINC DEFICIENT
I1	Only **large veins remain green**	to J
J	**Young leaves wilt & die along margins**; leaves curl as expand	MOLYBDENUM DEFICIENT
J1	**Old veins remain green** longest; **all interveins become yellow**; new leaves show interveinal yellowing on entire leaf; eventually entire leaf becomes whitish-yellow; margins & tips may become brown; occurs mainly on alkaline soils	IRON DEFICIENT
K	**Young leaf base breaks down**; stems & petioles brittle	BORON DEFICIENT
K1	**Young leaves hook at tip** & breakdown at tip & margin; never observed naturally in the field	CALCIUM DEFICIENT

Table 17.3 Summary of Plant Nutrient Deficiency Symptoms

In most cases, but there are exceptions:					
Young terminals affected		Ca	B		
Young leaves affected	Cu	Fe	Mn	Zn	(S)
Old leaves; generalized symptoms	N	P	(Mo)		
Old leaves, localized symptoms		K	Mg	(Mo)	
Only large veins remain green		Fe			
All veins remain green		Mn			
Whole leaf yellow, even veins		S			

PLANT TISSUE TESTING AND ANALYSIS

Plant tissues for testing are *collected in the field and are analyzed there.* Special commercially available kits can diagnose certain nutrients in cell sap. The premise behind plant tissue testing is that the amount of an element in the plant is an indication of the supply of that element in the soil. However, a shortage of one element will limit growth, but other elements may be limiting or accumulate in the cell sap and show inaccurate tests regardless of the supply in the soil. Once a nutrient element is diagnosed as deficient, that element should be corrected by fertilizing the soils near the plant. After time is allowed for the fertilizer to react, plant tissues should be tested again to check if any other elements are deficient.

Reasons for Plant Tissue Testing

Plant tissues are tested to (a) determine how effective the fertilizer and soil are in supplying plant nutrient needs, (b) evaluate those nutrients where soil tests are not available (N), and (c) diagnose suspected nutrient deficiencies. Sometimes plants

Table 17.4 Symptoms of Specific Ion Toxicities

A. Yellowing of interveinal areas starting at leaf tip and extending inward from margins; followed by browning	BORON TOXICITY
B. Leaf tips and margins burnt (brown); not preceded by yellowing	SODIUM TOXICITY
C. Marginal leaf scorch (browning) and stunting of plants; often occurs under extremely acid conditions	MANGANESE TOXICITY or ALUMINUM TOXICITY

are deficient in a nutrient but do not show deficiency symptoms until the deficiency becomes severe. This is called "hidden hunger."

Techniques in Analyzing Plant Tissues

Testing of plant tissues can be performed rapidly, is simple to perform, and requires no elaborate equipment. The plant sap is squeezed out of the plant tissue onto a paper impregnated with special chemicals. The amount of an element present is determined by the extent of color formed. These tests only analyze for N, P, and K in the cell sap at the time of testing.

Limitations of Plant Tissue Testing

The actual amount of a nutrient that is needed by plants for normal growth is not known.

Plant tissue tests are only available for N, P, and K.

Plant tissue tests only give a qualitative analysis—that is, tests only show if an element tests very low, low, medium, or high at time of testing.

Care must be taken in selecting the plant part for testing—usually, the *most recently matured leaves* are sampled—not very young or old senescent leaves. The *stage of maturity* is critical—it is best to *test at bloom* or from bloom to early fruiting, when nutrient levels are at the maximum and when low levels are more easily detected.

Since individual plants vary in nutrition, one must test from *10 to 15 plants* and average the results.

Environmental conditions may affect tissue test results. For example, time of day is important—if a plant is tested late in the day, after the plant has been photosynthesizing all day, N will be used up and levels in the plant will be low compared with the beginning or middle of the day. Also, type of day, that is, whether sunny or overcast, will affect the level of nutrients in the plant sap.

The general vigor of the plant, level of other nutrients in the plant, presence of insects or diseases, and soil conditions such as aeration, moisture, etc. need to be noted. Consistency of testing is required for reliable results.

TOTAL PLANT ANALYSIS

Total plant analysis differs from plant tissue testing. Whole plants or parts of plants are collected in the field for total plant analysis, brought back to the laboratory, dried, ground, ashed, and *analyzed chemically*. Precise analytical techniques are used to determine the amount of an element present. Data can be quantified by a number. The total amount of all elements present in a plant can be determined. This technique also requires that the same plant parts are selected. A large number of the most recently matured leaves of plants should be sampled.

Limitations of Total Plant Analysis

Total plant analysis has a number of limitations including time for the laboratory analysis and interpretation of the tests themselves. Since there are no definite standards for the amount of an element that should be in a plant, interpretation of the results becomes difficult. One way around this is to compare data from a seemingly healthy plant with that of the plant in question.

SOIL SAMPLING AND ANALYSIS

Soil is sampled to determine the level of nutrients present and the results are used as a guide to apply lime or fertilizer needed for optimum plant growth. The most important aspect of soil sampling is getting a *representative sample*. This is accomplished by taking a large number of samples from the area under study, combining them into a composite sample, mixing thoroughly and then removing a subsample for analysis. Several different soil samples are necessary since soil varies considerably in appearance by slope, drainage, soil type, or past treatment.

Technique in Soil Sampling

Samples can be collected with a soil probe, soil auger, trowel, or spade and mixed in a clean bucket. Samples should be taken where roots are or will be, especially for shrubs or trees. For established trees, a number of samples should be taken to a depth of about six inches in a circle around the tree at the drip line (where the water would fall from the outer leaves). For lawns, soil samples are taken for the depth that the soil will be prepared for seeding. If lawns are established, only sample the top two to three inches where the roots are growing.

Time of Sampling Soil

Levels of pH, P, and K in soils only change slowly with time, therefore soil sampling is needed only every few years. If soil has been sampled lately, there is no need to sample again prior to seeding. Samples can be taken at any time of the year, so long as the ground is not wet or frozen.

Chemical Analysis of Soil

A chemical soil test is designed to estimate the amount of plant nutrients present. An ideal soil test involves (a) an extracting solution that will remove the total amount or a proportionate amount of the available form of a nutrient from soils with variable characteristics every time; (b) measuring the amount of nutrient in the extract with reasonable speed and accuracy; and (c) correlation of the amount of nutrient in the test with growth and response of each plant to that nutrient under various conditions.

Laboratory Procedure

A soil sample is analyzed by mixing a small measured amount of soil with a chemical extracting solution, removing the soil, and evaluating nutrients in the solution by instruments that can determine the amount of a specific nutrient present. Sometimes a color-enhancing chemical is added and the result is compared with a standard. Soils can be tested for almost all nutrients, but there are limitations. Usually, soil tests are routinely analyzed for P, K, Ca, Mg, pH, and lime requirement, and all these usually correlate well with plant growth. There is no desirable test for N as this element changes so rapidly in soils that what is tested today may be completely different from what happens tomorrow. Sulfur can be analyzed but is not needed in the humid eastern United States because much S has been deposited in the soils by burning of S-containing fossil fuel. Micronutrients are only tested in some laboratories or if requested for an additional charge, as they are more costly, require more elaborate tests, take more time, and are difficult to interpret. A test for soil pH determines only the active acidity, that is, H^+ in solution; whereas a lime requirement test considers the buffering ability (or the reserve acidity) of the soil particles. This type of test is necessary to be sure that the correct amount of lime is applied to a specific soil.

Commercial Soil Tests

Some companies selling lime or fertilizer will test soil samples free. Usually these laboratories use the same procedures as the state agricultural soil testing laboratories. However, testing by companies may be more costly than the state laboratories. Remember these companies are in business to sell lime and fertilizer.

Soil testing kits sold commercially must be used with caution. Limitations of these are (a) difficulty of keeping the glassware chemically clean (soap often contains P that may give false readings), (b) chemical reagents provided in the kits will deteriorate with time and may easily become contaminated (state labs make fresh solutions frequently to avoid these problems), (c) these kits are described as useful for all soils under all conditions (soils in Florida are completely different from those in Iowa, California, or elsewhere—this is the reason each state has its own soil testing lab), (d) evaluation of test results may be difficult for an amateur; test recommendations may be too high, just to be sure that a grower will apply some lime and fertilizer. It is best to have the soil samples analyzed and interpreted by well-qualified technicians at the state soil testing laboratory in your area, even though there may be a charge of a few dollars.

SOIL AND ROOT PROBLEMS

Drainage or Lack of Drainage

Poor internal drainage of a soil creates conditions of lack of air, water, and nutrients, resulting in root restriction. Fine clay soils are more likely to be compacted reducing movement of O_2 and water. The stem of many woody plants flares at or just below the soil surface. If there is no flare, the plant could have been placed too low in the planting hole and the fill soil may be covering the crown of the plant, eventually restricting plant growth. Plant roots require O_2 to absorb nutrients and water and will die if there is an excess of water for more than a few days. Flooding also encourages root rots. Healthy plants can withstand adverse conditions quite well for a few days. Water also can accumulate in depressions. Some means must be used to provide an outlet for the depressions to lower the water table so plants can grow. This method has been discussed previously in the section on "Soil Water" in physical properties of soils (Chapter 4).

Excess Drainage

Sloping areas often become very dry because water drains downhill. This can be remedied by construction of terraces (Chapter 7). Sandy soils also drain readily and are often droughty. This problem can be corrected somewhat by incorporating organic matter to help hold the moisture for plant growth.

Sometimes the media in pots is allowed to dry. Some organic materials, such as peat moss, bark, or sawdust, become water repellent when allowed to thoroughly dry. Any water applied to the pots will run down the sides with none of it available for plant use. This condition can be avoided by regular watering, mulching, adding a wetting agent during watering, or sometimes by including limestone as part of the growing medium.

ALTERATION OF THE ENVIRONMENT BY MAN

Unfortunately, people alter the environment in ways that are undesirable for plant growth. Some of these changes involve (a) improper placement of soil or fill during or after construction, especially around houses; (b) use of heavy equipment on soil that is wet, causing compaction that is difficult to correct; (c) underwatering or overwatering, and (d) natural gas leaks from underground pipelines.

Fill Soil

During planting or construction, plants may be damaged by having too much soil placed near them, especially if the fill soil is compacted during the smoothing process around houses.

Compaction

Compaction becomes a major problem whenever a soil is wet. This can even occur during construction when heavy equipment is used by workers that are unaware how detrimental their actions can be.

Improper Use of Water

Most plants require a certain amount of water. However, plants are not able to tolerate underwatering or overwatering for more than a few days.

Gas Line Leaks

Leaks of natural gas lines release gases, for example, CO_2 and methane, that are toxic to plants. Grasses around a gas leak become yellow and will die if this condition is not corrected. Also, under anaerobic conditions, sulfate turns to hydrogen sulfide gas (H_2S) that is detrimental to plant growth.

SUMMARY

Plants are diagnosed for disorders by physical appearance, plant tissue testing, total plant analysis, soil testing and analysis, and soil and root problems. Plants should be examined for animal damage, root girdling, weather-induced problems, chemical injuries, mechanical damage, and biotic-associated problems of insects, diseases, and nematodes. Weather problems of low temperatures, insufficient light, drought, flooding, wind, snow, or ice damage, lightning damage, pollution by particulate matter or chemicals can also cause plant disorders. Plants can be injured by chemicals such as herbicides, insecticides, fungicides, soil sterilants, or salts. Mechanical damage to plants can result in root damage when removing soil close to the roots, when digging close to plants, or as trunk or stem damage, especially from lawnmowers or automobiles or when staking or guying trees. Biotic factors that can cause plant disorders include insects chewing, sucking, or egg-laying, fungal diseases (such as wilts, rots, leaf spots, mildews), bacterial diseases, viruses, nematodes, and plant parasites.

Plant tissue testing consists of analyzing leaf tissue in the field. This type of testing helps to determine how much N, P, and K are present in the cell sap, so that alterations can be made to correct the problems before they become severe.

For total plant analysis, plant tissues are collected in the field, taken to the laboratory and dried, ashed, and analyzed chemically. Limitations of this technique include extra time for sample preparation and analysis and no definite plant standards for comparison.

Soil sampling and analysis can be used as a guide for applying lime or fertilizer, thereby improving conditions for plant growth and reproduction. The most important part of soil sampling is to get a "representative sample." Large number of samples should be taken, mixed thoroughly, and a composite subsample removed for chemical analysis. Care must be taken to only sample areas that are similar by appearance as to slope, drainage, soil type, and previous treatment. Soil is secured by a probe, auger, or spade to the depth of rooting in a large number of places any time the ground is not wet or frozen, transported to the lab, and dried for analysis. A known amount of soil is mixed with chemicals, shaken, and the resulting solution is filtered and analyzed by instruments for the desired elements. Commercial soil testing kits have limitations of contamination of glassware, deterioration and contamination of chemicals used, inability to test all soils under all conditions, and evaluation of results difficult for amateurs.

Improper soil drainage can cause flooding that is detrimental to plant growth; this disorder can be corrected by installing drains to lower the high water table. Dry slopes can be made more conducive to plant growth by construction of terraces and adding organic matter to hold moisture. Man can create plant disorders during planting, by compaction when a soil is wet, by improper use of water, and during construction, for example, gas line leaks.

REVIEW

Do you know how plant disorders can be diagnosed?

How are plants examined for a disorder?

How does weather create environmental and pollution problems for plants?

What kind of damage can result from use of chemicals applied to plants or soils?

Can you describe different kinds of mechanical damage that can result in plant disorders?

What type of damage to plants is associated with biotic factors?

(continued) ➡

REVIEW (*continued*)

How does total plant analysis differ from
plant tissue tests?
What are the limitations of total plant analy-
sis?
Why is soil sampled for analysis?
What is the most important part of soil
sampling?
How can one be sure that the soil is sampled
correctly?
Can you describe how a soil sample is taken?
When and how often should soil be tested?
What is the procedure for analysis of soil in
the laboratory?
What are the limitations of using commercial
soil testing kits?
What kind of soil and root problems can
occur? How can one overcome these?
What are some of the plant disorders caused
by man?

18

Engineering Aspects
of Soils

Although most landscape architects use soils primarily for growing plants, sometimes they need to know how engineers look at
soils. Engineers are not concerned about soil properties that relate to growing plants. Engineers consider soil as a support for
building foundations, use in earthworks, a place for burying pipes
that carry electricity, water, gas or oil, and as a tool for disposing
of hazardous, municipal, industrial, and household wastes. Soil
properties that engineers consider important are hydraulic conductivity (permeability), compressive strength, shear strength, and
lateral pressures. Soil mechanics deals with stress/strain/time
relationships.

PHYSICAL PROPERTIES USED IN
ENGINEERING CLASSIFICATION OF SOILS

Atterberg Limits

Some engineering properties of a soil that describe the relation
of clays to water content were studied by a Swedish scientist,
Atterberg, in 1911. Soil clays based on water content were categorized into solid, semi-solid, plastic, and liquid (Fig. 18.1). The
dividing lines between each of these four states are known as
the "Atterberg limits," that is, shrinkage limit (from solid to semi-
solid), plastic limit (from semi-solid to plastic), and liquid limit
(from plastic to liquid). These points can be measured for individual clays. The Atterberg limits are used by engineers to classify soils based on their moisture properties. These limits are
particularly useful for evaluating soil compressibility, permeabil-

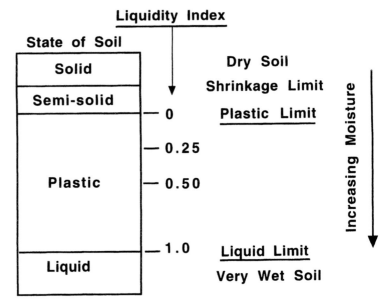

Figure 18.1 Atterberg limits. Atterberg limits of shrinkage, plastic, and liquid can be explained based on the amount of water present in a soil and the state of soil from solid to liquid as the liquidty index.

ity, and strength. The plasticity of a clay soil depends on the type and amount of clay mineral and organic materials present. Plasticity is the reaction a soil has to being deformed without cracking or crumbling.

ENGINEERING CLASSIFICATION OF SOILS

The "liquid limit" is a term indicating the amount of water in a soil between the liquid state and the plastic state.

Soils are first divided into two categories of coarse-grained and fine-grained (Table 18.1). *Coarse-grained soils* are those in which more than half of the material is *larger than a no. 200 sieve*. *Fine-grained soils* are those in which more than half of the material is *smaller than a no. 200 sieve*.

Coarse-grained soils are further divided into two categories of gravels and sands. *Gravels* are those with more than half

Table 18.1 A Key to Classify Soils for Engineering

I. Coarse-grained soils (more than half of material is larger than no. 200 sieve size)	
A. Gravels (more than half of coarse fraction is larger than no. 4 sieve size)	
1. Clean gravels (little or no fines)	
a. Well-graded gravels, gravel-sand mistures, limited fines	GW
b. Poorly graded gravels, gravel-sand mistures, limited fines	GP
2. Gravels with fines (large amount of fines)	
a. Silty gravels, gravel-sand-silt mixtures	GM
b. Clayey gravels, gravel-sand-clay mixtures	GC
B. Sands (more than half of coarse fraction is smaller than no. 4 sieve size)	
1. Clean sands (little or no fines)	
a. Well-graded sands, gravelly sands limited fines	SW
b. Poorly graded sands, gravelly sands, limited fines	SP
2. Sands with fines (large amount of fines)	
a. Silty sands, sand-silt mixtures	SM
b. Clayey sands, sand-clay mixtures	SC
II. Fine-grained soils (more than half of material is smaller than no. 200 sieve)	
A. Silts and Clays (liquid limit less than 50)	
1. Inorganic silts and very fine sands, rock flour, silty or clayey fine sands, or clayey silts with slight plasticity	ML
2. Inorganic clays of low to medium plasticity, gravelly clays, sandy clays, silty clays, lean clays	CL
3. Organic silts and organic silty clays of low plasticity	OL
B. Silts and clays (liquid limit greater than 50)	
1. Inorganic silts, micaceous or diatomaceous fine sandy or silty soils, elastic silts	MH
2. Inorganic clays of high plasticity, fat clays	CH
3. Organic clays of medium to high plasticity, organic silts	OH
C. Highly organic soils	
1. Peat and other highly organic soils	Pt

of the coarse material *larger than a no. 4 sieve. Sands* are those with more than half of the coarse material *smaller than a no. 4 sieve.*

Fine-grained soils are further divided into three categories: (a) silts and clays with *liquid limit of less than 50*, (b) silts and clays with *liquid limit of more than 50*, and (c) highly *organic soils.* The higher the liquid limit the more a soil acts like a liquid. When the liquid limit is zero, it becomes the solid limit. When soil is dry, it acts like a solid, but when it is wet it acts almost like a liquid.

Gravels are further divided into two categories of *clean gravels* (little or no fines) and *gravels with fines* (appreciable amount of fines).

Sands are further divided into two categories of *clean sands* (little or no fines) and *sands with fines* (appreciable amount of fines).

Peats and other highly organic soils are undesirable for engineering but highly desirable for growth of plants. Plasticity of soils is the ability of a soil to be molded or shaped.

This classification by engineers uses size of materials, amount of fine material, and liquidity, all of which are useful for infrastructure. On the other hand, soil scientists classify soils based on easily verified soil physical properties of color, texture, structure, moisture, temperature, and depth and chemical properties of pH, amount of organic matter, clays, minerals, and percentage base saturation. Most of the properties used by soil scientists are related to usefulness in growing plants.

SOIL ENGINEERING PROPERTIES

Engineers consider soil properties of permeability, compression, shear-strength, tensile-strength, lateral pressures, shrink-swell potential, and corrosion to be most important to their use of soils.

Hydraulic conductivity (also called "permeability") is the ease with which water flows through a soil.

Consolidation is the compression of soil under loading, that is, settling or swelling (Figs. 18.2 and 18.3).

Shear-strength is the *ability of a soil to resist movement* and often is associated with landslides (Fig. 18.3).

Tensile-strength is the *resistance* a soil particle has *against a pulling apart* (Fig. 18.3).

Lateral pressure in a soil is directed in a horizontal manner and is important in strength of retaining walls. Lateral

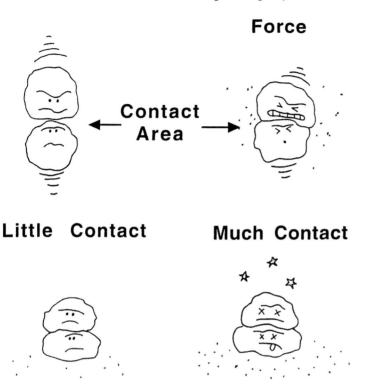

Figure 18.2 Changes in soil contact area. Under load, soil contact area is increased.

pressure is zero at the top of a retaining wall, but increases with depth.

Shrink-swell potential measures the extent a soil volume changes when the moisture content is varied. A soil with a high shrink-swell potential could result in severe damage to building foundations, roads, and other engineering structures. Changes in soil volume is related to the kind of clay present and amount of water present.

Soils can be classified as to extent of corrosion of uncoated steel or concrete. Soil factors that affect corrosion are amount of soil moisture, presence of oxygen, soil reaction (pH), soil solution conductivity (ability of a soil to conduct an electrical current), and activity of microorganisms that operate under oxidation-reduction conditions.

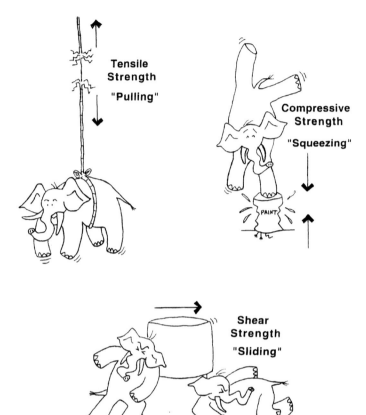

Figure 18.3 Engineering stresses in soils. Tensile (pulling), compression (squeezing), and shear (sliding) strengths of a soil are illustrated.

ENGINEERING GEOTECHNICAL
APPLICATIONS

All failures are related to stability and deformation.

Stability

Stability is related to shear strength; upon failure, the result is sudden and catastrophic. Three examples of this are

1. failure of foundation-bearing capacity,
2. slope stability failures (landslides), and

3. failure of retaining walls, which may overturn or slide
out.

Deformation

Deformation is a functional failure that does not require immediate attention. This occurs when the functionality of a structure
is impaired by deflection or deformation; examples include settle-
ments and heaving.

Correction of Problems

A solution to these problems is to keep the water away from the
structure that might fail. This correction can be accomplished by
proper drainage and insulating the structure from water moving
to it.

GEOTECHNICAL ASPECTS

Engineering projects relating to geotechnical aspects include
foundations, earthworks, and environmental geotechnology.

Foundations

To prevent failures as indicated above, the weight of a structure
must be supported by adequate shallow foundations. For deeper
applications, pilings are driven as a unit to the bedrock. Caissons
can be constructed whereby shafts are drilled, reinforced by metal
rods, and concrete poured. Support for foundations is affected
by the bearing capacity of the soil and settlement under load.
These in turn are influenced by soil density, wetness, texture,
plasticity, and shrink-swell potential. Soils are rated for foundation support based on slope, seasonal wetness, susceptibility to
flooding, and other hydrological characteristics. The amount of
and cost of excavation that is needed depends on soil properties
of slope, wetness, depth to bedrock, and stoniness.

Earthworks

Earthworks involve fills, cuts, and drainage. During construction
of fills, care must be taken to compact the soil by compression
to prevent failure. Engineers consider this compaction to be an
improvement of soil conditions but from an edaphological (use

of soil for growing plants) standpoint, this is extremely undesirable. During construction where the soil is excavated or cut, subsoils may be unstable and could collapse. All movement of soil requires provision for adequate drainage of water around the construction or failure may result. The best soils for earthworks are those that are moderately well drained or better, not subject of flooding, have none or very slight slope (< 8%), deep to bedrock, low shrink-swell potential, low susceptibility to frost action, and have a minimum of stones.

Environmental Geotechnology

Environmental geotechnology is involved any time earth is compacted and used in an artificial way as a liner of a disposal site, such as sites for hazardous wastes, sites for sanitary landfills, sewage lagoons, ponds for industrial purposes, or ponds for containment of pollutants from mining operations. Soils with slow permeability, deep to seasonal water-table, moderately well drained or better, no flooding hazard, and having none or very slight slope (< 8%) are recommended for the base of these environmental structures. The best materials used to cover the sanitary landfills are soils that are friable, coarse textured, thick topsoil, minimum of rock fragments and stones, and better than poorly drained.

SUMMARY

Engineers only consider soils as a material to be used for infrastructure relating to support for buildings, roads, bridges, waste disposal, and corrosion of buried pipes. Soils are classified by engineers based on coarse and fine materials, subdivided into gravels, sands, silts and clays, and organic materials. Further subdivision deals with amount of fine materials and extent of liquidity. All these are related to use of soils for infrastructure, whereas soil classification by soil scientists are based on inherent physical and chemical characteristics, most of which are related to plant growth.

Engineers consider soil properties of permeability, compression, shear-strength, lateral pressures, shrink-swell potential, and corrosion to be most important to their use of soils. Soil instability and deformation problems include foundation failure, landslides, and retaining wall failure. Problems of this nature can be prevented by proper drainage and keeping the water away from the structures that can fail. Foundation support is related to soil properties of density, texture, plasticity, wetness, and shrink-swell potential. Compaction is viewed by engineers as a beneficial soil property as it provides support for infrastructure. On the other hand, soil scientists view compaction as an impediment and detrimental to growth of plants. Engineers use soils as a means of solving environmental problems of disposal of sanitary, industrial, mining, and hazardous wastes.

REVIEW

What is the philosophy that engineers have for use of soils?

How does the engineer's soil classification differ from that of a soil scientist?

Name the soil properties that engineers consider important.

Name some problems of soil instability and deformation. How can these problems be prevented?

What soil properties influence support for foundations?

How is soil compaction viewed by engineers and edaphologists?

For what evnrionmental problems do engineers use soils?

19

Satellite Imaging, Laser Technology, and Computer Programs

Global Positioning System (GPS) is a system using position, navigation, and time distribution based in space and designed for military use on a worldwide basis. The United States sent 24 satellites into orbits approximately 11,000 miles above Earth. At any one moment in time, there are a minimum of five satellites in view anywhere in the world. These GPS satellites are controlled by a master control station in Colorado Springs, Colorado, five monitoring stations, and three ground antennas throughout the world. Those who wish to use the GPS system must have a receiver, a processor, and an antenna on land, sea, or in the air to pick up the satellite messages and thereby compute their precise position, velocity, and time (Fig. 19.1).

This whole system was designed primarily for use in aid to navigation, dredging operations, hydrographic surveying by the Coast Guard and Geologic Survey Departments, and to assist in underwater mine disposal, search and rescue missions of distressed vessels, ice-breaking activities, and environmental assessments and cleaning efforts.

From a civilian standpoint, a GPS can be used in a Geographic Information System (GIS) for scientific investigations, resource management, and development planning. Two examples of this are: GIS could allow emergency planners to easily calculate emergency response times during natural disasters; or GIS could be used to find wetlands that need protection from pollution.

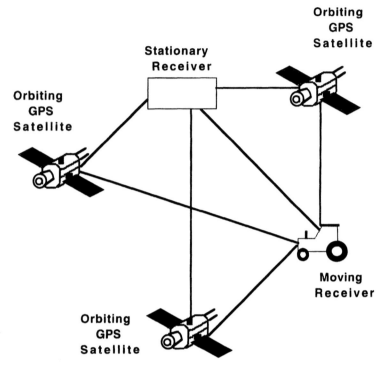

Figure 19.1 Use of orbiting GPS (Global Positioning System) satellites to coordinate exact spatial ground locations connecting to stationary and mobile receivers.

DEFINITION OF GEOGRAPHIC INFORMATION SYSTEM

A Geographic Information System (GIS) is an organized collection of computer hardware, software, geographic data and personnel designed to capture, manipulate, analyze, and display all forms of geographically referenced information (Allender, 1998). A more simplified definition would be: a computer system capable of holding and using data, describing places on the earth's surface, for the purpose of spatial analysis. It is also "intelligent graphics" to aid in the analysis and depiction of complex data sets. Components of GIS include ARC/INFO:GIS software by ESRI (Environmental Systems Research Institute), ARC—graphical features of points, lines/arcs, and polygons, INFO—the relational database component of tables of data of any attribute that ties to a graphical component.

Examples of spatial data (Allender, 1998) are: (1) census/demo-graphics, (2) land use/value, (3) business/finanacial, (4) climatic, hydrologic, and marine features, (5) geographic boundaries, (6) streets and highways, (7) consumer information, (8) environmental (air, soil, ground and surface water, land cover), (9) topographic, (10) natural resources, and (11) aerial and satellite imagery.

Data may be obtained from many sources such as government—USGS, BLM/Bureau of Mines, US Census Bureau, EPA, NOAA/NASA; private—gleaned government data; commercial service—ERDAS, SPOT, and ATLAS; and custom—your data.

GIS can be used to answer a number of questions about various parameters:

Location—"What is at ———?" (coordinates, latitude/longitude, postal addresses, etc.)

Condition—Where is it? or "Find all of the locations where the following conditions are met."

Trends—"What has changed since ———?"

Patterns—"What spatial patterns exist?" or "Correlate alleged cancer incidence to proximity to a plant site."

Modeling—"What if ———?" (linking the GIS database to hydrologic models)

Examples of practical applications in GIS (Allender, 1998) include E-911 mapping—addressing, public information, and hidden data, real-time weather monitoring from continually updated information on temperature, precipitation, barometric pressure, water level, and flood warning systems, and Little League scheduling on specific ball fields. Golf course designing can be accomplished by creating a conceptual computer visualization starting by placing the existing land layout obtained from GIS into a computer program. Data of the designs of the fairways, greens, sandtraps, ponds, surrounding trees, and topography are entered into the program. By manipulation of the data, a conceptualized golf course can be developed and shown on a computer in a three-dimensional fly-through and presented to the owner and investors prior to any construction. Alterations can easily be made prior to any construction saving considerable investment.

OPERATION OF GIS

The GIS is able to capture data, register and integrate it, and relate it to different sources. It is possible to perform complex analyses of data from the GIS to make different kinds of maps and store this information in layers, thereby assisting in information retrieval, topological modeling, networking, and overlays.

Relating Information
from Different Sources

A GIS that can use information from many sources in different forms can help in analyses that may be useful in relating information about rainfall in a particular area to aerial photos of that area providing information as to which wetlands would dry at certain months of the year. Information needed to accomplish this would be the x, y, and z coordinates (e.g., longitude, latitude, and elevation or ZIP codes, highway markers, or other definitely distinguishable characteristics). A GIS system can use data of any variable that can be spatially located and fed into the system.

A number of computer databases produced by federal agencies, private firms, or even data in the form of maps could be entered into a GIS. Existing digital information that may not be in map form can be converted to a form that is recognizable and can be used. Examples of this would be different kinds of vegetative covers that could be coordinated into an integrated map by overlaying data. Other types of layers, such as census or hydrologic, could also be included.

Data from maps of wetlands, slopes, streams, land use, or soils can easily be collected onto individual layers that can be used in an overlay fashion to produce a new map useful in diagnosing and treating problems.

An example of a use of overlays is for site selection. The U.S. Geological Survey cooperated with the Connecticut Department of Natural Resources to use digitized data from 40 map layers that were combined and manipulated by a GIS to locate a potential site for a new water well within ½ mile of a water company service area. Digitized maps of the water service area were entered into the GIS and a "window" was used to view the area within ½ mile of the water service area. Examination of the land use and land cover map for this area showed that the area was only partly developed. This developed area was eliminated as a well site. Since water quality is regulated by the state and some of the streams in the area had nonpotable water, a 100-meter buffer zone around these streams was plotted to prevent water from coming from an undesirable source. To narrow the well sites further, buffer zones of 500 meters were also plotted around point source pollution spots. Geologic maps of earth materials that lie above bedrock were also superimposed on the area with the view showing those areas where sand and gravel were likely to store water that could be tapped for well water. The map layer showing thickness of saturated sediments was created using the GIS to subtract the bedrock elevation from the surface elevation. Areas with over 40 feet of saturated sediments were selected and combined with the previous overlays. The resulting map showed areas that were undeveloped, outside of buffered pollution areas, and underlain with more than 40 feet of water-saturated sand and gravel. Since digitizing limits precision, all very small polygon areas less than 10 acres were screened out by the GIS. The result gave six sites that would be suitable for a desirable well site.

This process of site selection would also work for other common applications such as transportation planning or waste disposal site location. This technique is valuable in a large area where a number of physical factors have to be evaluated and integrated.

Another technique used graphic display in a three-dimensional perspective view in a portion of San Mateo County, California. Common maps on paper show physical objects as symbols and these must be interpreted by users. Similarly, topographic maps only show contour lines to indicate shape of the land surface, but one must visualize the land form in one's head. Graphic displays using a GIS can help make map elements visible and more realistic. A GIS used two types of data to show the three-dimensional perspective view. The first type of data used a digital elevation model of surface elevations at 30-meter horizontal levels with the high elevations in white and low elevations in black. The second type of data used was a false-color infrared image of the same area in 30-meter pixels (picture elements). By combining these two images, a three-dimensional perspective view was shown looking down on the San Andreas Fault.

Precision Farming

Precision Farming is the management of the forms of variability of spatial, temporal, and predictive. Spatial variability indicates how crops vary across a field; temporal variability deals with changes in crops with time (year to year); and predictive variability is a measure of the difference between predicted and actual values. Computerized mapping via GPS can provide data to use in a GIS computer software application that will supply tools to manipulate and display the spatial data so that maps may be developed. Precision Farming goes further in being able to digitally reference diverse types of spatial data to a common coordinate system via real-time georeferencing (Global Positioning System [GPS]). This provides a way of precisely locating, mapping, and managing a variety of variables over a wide area. The data generated can be statistically analyzed for management decisions.

Remote sensing technology, especially AGRICTARS and LACIE, can be used to identify, map, and estimate many agricultural variables. Examples of use include yield and salinity patterns in salt-affected cotton and sugarcane fields and estimating forage production on semi-arid grassland. Plant variables of leaf area, greenness, biomass, and plant cover are easily measured that can be converted into yield potential of a site.

How GIS is Used
in Precision Farming

The GIS for the Precision Farming System may contain layers of topography of the field, types of soils, both surface and subsurface drainage systems, results from soil tests, rainfall data, irrigation data, actual chemical application rates for fertilizers, lime, and pesticides, and yield data. Data for each of these layers may be entered once, annually, or even more frequently depending on those data needed to accomplish the desired objective. The GIS allows a study of these layers of information as a guide to evaluate cause and effect and to be used to make actual farming decisions (Fig. 19.2).

An overview of the Precision Farming System reveals the GIS as the center that forms the knowledge database and makes decisions in the field. This sytem can be used for a number of operations: (1) Variable Rate Tillage, (2) Variable Rate Fertilizer or Lime Application, (3) Variable Rate Planting, (4) Variable Rate Cultivation, (5) Variable Rate Spraying, (6) Variable Rate Irrigation, (7) Harvesting, and (8) Yield Mapping (Fig. 19.3).

Variable Rate Tillage. Tillage depth of plowing or subsoiling can be varied depending on soil type and depth, drainage systems, and localized topography. For example, as a farmer is plowing a field, previously collected data on soil depth in that field can be transmitted from the stationary receiver via GPS satellite to the tractor and plow (moving receiver), allowing plow depth to be deeper or shallower as required.

Variable Rate Fertilizer or Lime Application. Fertilizer and lime applications can be varied as the tractor is progressing across a field provided the data on soil type, soil sampling results, and previous applications are known. For example, results from re-

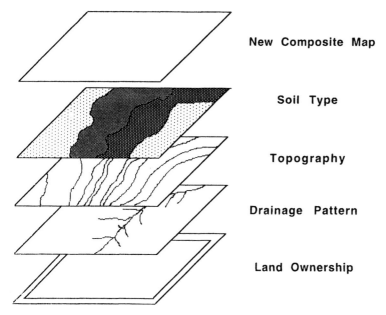

New Composite Map

Soil Type

Topography

Drainage Pattern

Land Ownership

Figure 19.2 Use of overlays of land ownership, drainage pattern, topography, and soil type from GIS data to produce a new composite map in a Precision Farming System.

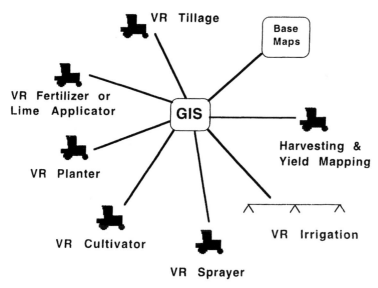

VR Tillage

Base Maps

VR Fertilizer or Lime Applicator

GIS

Harvesting & Yield Mapping

VR Planter

VR Cultivator

VR Irrigation

VR Sprayer

Figure 19.3 Sketch showing how GIS can coordinate data from base maps to variable rate (VR) implementations with resulting yields in a farming operation.

cent soil sampling of known spots in a field can be coordinated via GPS satellite to a moving fertilizer spreader allowing specific metering of fertilizer according to the developed recommendations from the soil tests. This precision farming makes use of data for most efficient use of costly fertilizer.

Variable Rate Planting.   Rates of seed placement as the tractor proceeds across the field can be tied in to data on soil type (inherent yield capability) and recent soil tests for fertilizer elements. The significance of this rate is that the population of plants in a field must be related to the nutrients available for the crop. For instance, seeding rate can be so high as to cause crowding and yield reduction due to competition among individual plants for available nutrients, or seeding rate can be so low that there are insufficient plants to make use of the nutrients present. Therefore, using the GIS a farmer can be sure that at every location in the field optimum economic use is made of the nutrients present.

Variable Rate Cultivation.   Cultivation is used mainly to control weeds. The GIS can indicate how many weeds are present and the cultivator can be instantly adjusted to only disturb that ground where weeds are a problem. If weeds are not a problem in a specific area, the soil structure would not be disturbed at that point, resulting in maintaining desirable soil structure.

Variable Rate Spraying.   Modern agriculture requires use of pesticides to control insects, weeds, and diseases. Often this is accomplished using various chemical sprays. Data on each of these variables can be fed into the GIS to regulate how much spray, if any, is needed for each of these three variables that decrease crop yield. Common soils parameters that are important in pesticide application to land include soil organic matter, fertility, salinity, and compaction. Variation in soil organic matter is often the reason for effectiveness in herbicide application. Soil organic matter also influences crop yield, especially in relation to phosphorus levels in the soil. Soil organic matter can be related to several spectral bands that could be detected by satellite systems.

Variable Rate Irrigation.   Some farmers, often in arid regions, have irrigation systems that can meter the flow of water to different parts of the field. Soil moisture data collected from installed moisture sensing devices can be transmitted to GPS satellites, coordinated by the stationary receiver, and transmitted to a receiver in the field that will operate the valves to send the proper amount of water where it is needed.

Variable Rate Harvesting and Yield Mapping.   For Variable Rate Harvesting and Yield Mapping, data are collected on soil type, field topography, crop cover, and land ownership into a composite map. Superimposed on this composite map are soil sampling and yield mapping. Soil samples are taken on a grid basis at known latitude and longitude locations and the following analysis are entered into a computer in the GIS. Yield maps are developed in the field by devices on the harvesting equipment that measure yield during harvesting and feed this data into a computer linked by GIS to a Differential Global Positioning System (DGPS) via a GPS receiver on top of the harvester. Yield data are recorded every 1.2 seconds and coordinated at that point with the longitude and latitude of the harvester.

Usually, the variability across a field is so great that little sense can be made of the data; therefore, a system of smoothing the data is required to show underlying trends across the field. The yield maps show variability and stimulate the question as to the reasons for the variability. These are likely to be related to permanent field features such as soil type, topology, shading by trees, drainage patterns, and variable features, such as seed, sprays, or fertilizer. The latter generally are uniform. The data can then be analyzed statistically to determine the factors causing the yield differences.

Using GIS to Monitor Crop Conditions and Forecast Yield and Production

Vegetative indices can be calculated from the Advanced Very High Resolution Radiometer (AVHRR) sensor on a satellite. This information has been used to compare data of the current year with that of the previous year, for example, when comparing data between 1992 and 1993 during the Midwest flood and Southeast drought areas. An ASCII legend/key file was created (Table 19.1) in which pixel values used for color assignment for the 1992 season compared with the 1993 season were 1–37 as blue—water, Mexico, and Canada; 38–63 as magenta—much lower; 64–89 as maroon—lower; 90–115 as gray—same; 116–140 as yellow— higher; and 141–167 as green—much higher. The pixel values represented the same for a given year. By superimposing these data on a map of the United States for the two years under study, obvious differences in vegetation were evident for the flood and drought areas.

These types of data can also highlight localized areas under extreme precipitation stresses indicating potential for drought or excess water, with crop yield decreases in such crops as soybeans, corn, cotton, and perhaps could be adapted to pasture and range feed conditions. Therefore, GIS in remote sensing activi-

Table 19.1 Color-Coded Ranges of AVHRR (Advanced Very High Restriction Radiometer) NDVI Differences with an Interpretation of Their Relative Significance (W. Gail et al., 1994)

Color	Label	Current Vegetation Vigor
Green	Much higher	Much higher than previous year
Yellow	Higher	Higher than previous year
Gray	Same	Similar to that of previous year
Maroon	Lower	Lower than previous year
Magenta	Much lower	Much lower than previous year
Tan	Noncrop	Masked out (noncrop areas)
Blue	Water, ex-countries	Masked out (water, Mexico, Canada)

ties can contribute in making crop yield forecasts, acreage estimates, and graphic data presentations. Data from a satellite by GIS can use the imagery by overlaying state and county boundaries, frost isoline data, and monthly precipitation data.

Use of GIS for Landscape Architecture Applications

Example for Designing and Maintaining Golf Courses

Landscape architects can build, analyze, and view from a three-dimensional perspective virtual landscapes by using various computer programs. This is being done on an 18-hole golf course in Switzerland (Internet: www.vrml.sgi.com/basics). A two-dimensional CAD plan is used, along with other computer-generated information, to develop a three-dimensional display using digital terrain modeling. This involves beginning with a two-dimensional CAD project, working in a digital presentation plan, along with detailing of the terrain by Triangular Irregular Networks (TIN), to produce a Digital Terrain Model (DTM). Calculations of earth volumes and automatic profiles from a DTM can be developed into a three-dimensional grid model. By superimposing mapping of textures onto the three-dimensional model, one can create a "virtual landscape" whereby one can view the projected golf course by "flying over the fairways and greens."

Using GIS

The following section shows how GIS can be used for keeping track of individual vegetation on Oregon State University Campus, history of individual trees in an orchard, and management of vegetation on a golf course (Righetti and Jones, 1998).

A graduate student, Dan Jones, working with Dr. Tim Righetti produced a series of slides on a computer file depicting graphics from FieldNotes (a software program by PenMetrics) licensed to the Horticulture Department at Oregon State University. A view of FieldNotes shows a grid map of the area that includes Oregon State University Campus and the surrounding area in Corvallis, Oregon. These maps are generally available in several grid formats or coordinate systems, for example, UTM, Lat-Long, or State Plane. PenMetrics can adapt any of these to FieldNotes.

FieldNotes is an example of a geographical information system. The exact location of each individual piece of vegetation surrounding Milam Hall is shown on a figure zoomed in to a particular area of the campus (Fig. 19.4). This view was accomplished using named zooms that are created on the fly and saved in the project for use at any time. The program also has a zoom feature that will zoom in for any reason at any location. It also

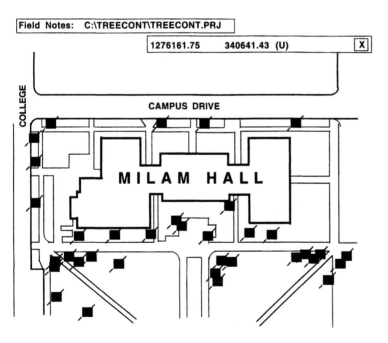

Figure 19.4 A zoomed-in view of FieldNotes using GIS to locate individual vegetation growing around Milam Hall on Oregon State University Campus in Corvallis, Oregon.

will zoom in several times for even closer inspection or accuracy. At the top right portion are shown the grid coordinate numbers. When choosing any one of the data points (in this case, the squares represent individual trees on campus), the coordinates of that point are displayed. These points can be from data downloaded from a GPS (Global Positioning Satellite) or placed in the program manually, standing at the location. Clicking on any particular point will bring up the first page of as many as you design in the data-collecting portion of FieldNotes (Fig. 19.5). This happens to be an oak tree on the campus. The page has been designed for genus, species, and common name that are included in a "code" list and accessed by clicking on the arrows next to each category. The coordinate numbers for the particular tree at this particular location are shown. The program also has the ability to include drawings and photographic images. They can be cropped and manipulated in the program, thereby confirming the identity of a plant or using the information for educational purposes. A data entry page is very important to allow for collection of data in several areas (Fig. 19.6). Once entered, the data can be queried for various parameters and used for any number of tasks, for example, fertilization or use of herbicides.

Use of the same program permits fields to be shown with a border overlay (Fig. 19.7), in this case, an aerial infrared photograph. Superimposed on this field outline photograph was another layer showing the exact location of each individual soil

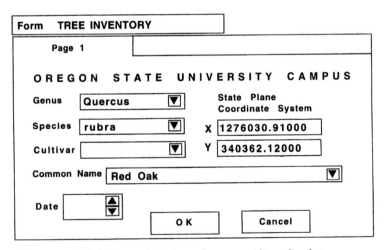

Figure 19.5 FieldNotes data form for a specific red oak tree located at xy coordinates shown.

Form	TREE INVENTORY

		Page 3

Prune memo [   ]

Pruning [   ]

Fert memo [   ]

Fertilizer [   ]

Condi memo [   ]

Date Appl [   ]

Bar Code [   ]

IP Vector [   ]

Ip Memo [   ]

Ip Disease [   ]

[O K]   [Cancel]

Figure 19.6 A FieldNotes data entry page of tree inventory.

Field Notes: Untitled.PRJ   4930745.96   4928580.27   (U)

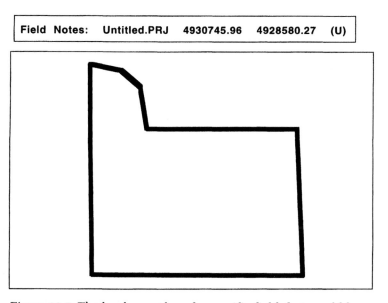

Figure 19.7 The border overlay of a specific field that would be imposed on an aerial infrared photograph in FieldNotes.

sample (Fig. 19.8). Soil samples were secured at each of the locations while the Global Positioning Satellite (GPS) recorded each spot. The GPS information was then downloaded into the GIS program. When the soil sample results were completed and returned, the data were entered for each location, making it available for use. A query menu shows how one can ask specific commands such as "locate any samples with a numerical value of less than or equal to 5.9, possibly a pH value (Fig. 19.9). The answer shows up on the field outline photograph showing those specific locations having a pH of 5.9 or less (Fig. 19.10).

Another application of this program was set up to examine an aerial view of the golf course at Oswego Lake Country Club. Golf courses are intensively managed and may serve as a model for future agricultural projects. The example shows individual features, such as tees, fairways, ponds, and greens, each kept in a separate layer. Detailed recordkeeping about turf status is possible using a blimp-borne camera to record grass condition. Images for past years and seasons within a year can be compared. In this example, all chemical application information has been incorporated into the system. Databases for greens, tees, and other features are automatically maintained. Simply clicking on the green in the lower left portion of the aerial view will allow the

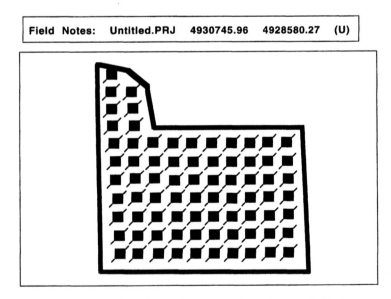

Figure 19.8 Exact locations of soil samples taken in field shown in figure 19.7.

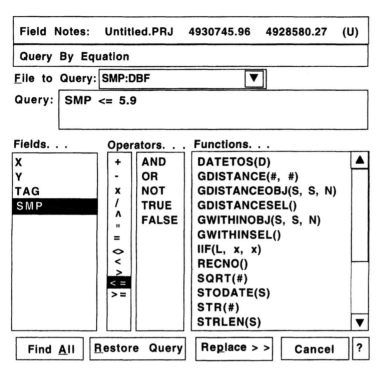

Figure 19.9 A query menu in FieldNotes referring to soil samples in figure 19.8 asking for all soil samples with a pH of 5.9 or less.

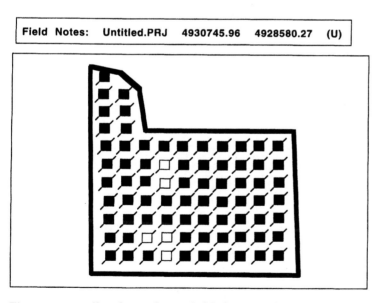

Figure 19.10 All soil samples in field shown in figure 19.8 that have a pH of 5.9 or less (shown in white).

chemical applicator to record what was applied. The form shown (Fig. 19.11) allows for easy entry of information. Any of the three pages are available for information retrieval. Page three of the previous form allows the operator to have access to the fertilizer, herbicide, fungicide, or insecticide history of the selected feature (Fig. 19.12). Queries can also be made to highlight any location that meets the criterion of any choices the user selects. For example, all locations that have been sprayed with "Roundup" and had minimal irrigation in the last month could be found and shown. Finally, a display showing the precise location of each sprinkler and valve, irrigation components, such as laterals and main line pipes, drainageways, fairways, greens, roughs were all superimposed onto a diagrammatical sketch to be used to evaluate plant growth or problems that may arise from each of the above parameters evaluated (Fig. 19.13). The golf course being presented has a computer-assisted automated irrigation system that controls application rates and equalizes irrigation system pressures. Water application rate is determined by ET (evapotranspiration) calculations from independent weather stations on the site, and additional manager-provided information based on past experience. Every sprinkler head (round circles in the image) has been entered into the golf course map. Automatically, archived

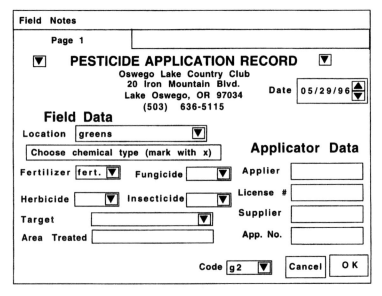

Figure 19.11 Data record in FieldNotes of a specific green of the Oswego Lake Country Club golf course.

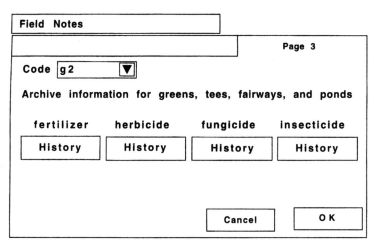

Figure 19.12 A FieldNotes page showing histories of fertilizer, herbicide, fungicide, and insecticide applied.

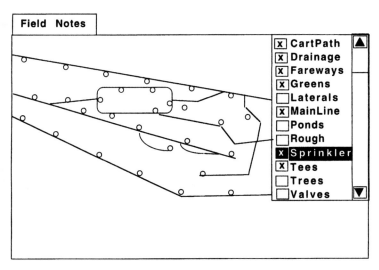

Figure 19.13 A FieldNotes display showing precise location of each sprinkler, valve, irrigation laterals, and mains superimposed onto drainage ways, fairways, greens, and roughs of the Oswego Lake Country Club golf course.

flow rates and volumes can be obtained for any valve or sprin-kler head. This system can also be used to improve sprinkler ir-rigation patterns by overlaying aerial photographs on a map of the sprinkler heads.

Urban Planning

Information-oriented GIS is being used in urban settings. An example is a study (from the Internet: www.riga.fnr.umass.edu/ cgibin/theses.pl?number=761) by A. L. Dorlester at the Depart-ment of Landscape Architecture and Regional Planning, Univer-sity of Massachusetts, Amherst, where GIS was used to assess land use impacts on water quality in the Mumford River Water-shed. A pollution-loading model analyzed annual rainfall data, land use information, and EPA data on pollutant loading to evalu-ate phosphorus, nitrogen, and lead in polluted water.

RECENT DEVELOPMENTS IN THREE-DIMENSIONAL MODELS

State-of-the-art computer programs can be used by landscape planners to develop, analyze, and virtually fly over a landscape. In Zurich, Switzerland, Professor Peter Petschek used digital terrain modeling on an 18-hole golf course project going from a twodimensional CAD plan to a three-dimensional model. This tech-nique involved seven steps: (1) a two-dimensional CAD project was devised; (2) a digital presentation plan was produced; (3) using triangular irregular networks (TIN) from the digital ter-rain model (DTM), the terrain was able to be modeled in detail; (4) volumes of earth were calculated creating automated profiles with DTM; (5) a three-dimensional grid model was developed; (6) texture was mapped on a three-dimensional model for the presen-tation plan; and (7) the three-dimensional model was viewed as a "virtual landscape" using a VRML browser. VRML stands for "vir-tual reality modeling language," which is a standard computer language for describing interactive three-dimensional objects and the world derived across the internet. A browser is a device to scan the World Wide Web.

Use of PolyTRIM Testbed Toolkit

The Center for Landscape Research (CLR) at the University of Toronto (Hoinkes and Lange, 1997) is developing a system of using two-dimensional mapping bases and integrating them into three- or four-dimensional representations called "PolyTRIM." This technique can generate three-dimensional models from physical data of ground water tables, soil-depth models, and other physical attributes producing critical *layers* of information based on the terrain surface. The layers can be easily cut through to see depth relations between the layers. The data that have been studied so far include vegetation, built-forms, and infrastructure (Table 19.2).

The Process of Three-Dimensional and Four-Dimensional Modeling with Two-Dimensional Data

Another application of PolyTRIM is representing a natural environment in a synthetic landscape (Hoinkes and Lange, 1997). This simulation can be accomplished by combining various data sets, for example, in forests (Fig. 19.14). Overlays of this simulation can include satellite image, digital model, forest, single trees, built

Table 19.2 Ways that Physical Data Can Be Represented Geometrically, in Real-World Forms and Three-Dimensional Attributes (Hoinkes and Lange, 1997)

Class of Data	Geometric Representation	Examples of Real-World Forms	Three-Dimensional Attributes
Vegetation	Polygons	Natural forest stands	Density, size, species
	Points	Individual plantings (trees)	Size (height) species
Built-form	Polygons	Building massing	No. of floors, floor to floor height, or total height
		Building density/zoning	Density, type of unit
	Points	Building centroids	Type of cross-section size, type of unit
Infrastructure	Lines	Roads	No. of Roads
		Hydrotower path	Density, type of unit
		Piping	Type of unit
	Points	Lights, towers, etc.	Size, type of unit

FORESTS

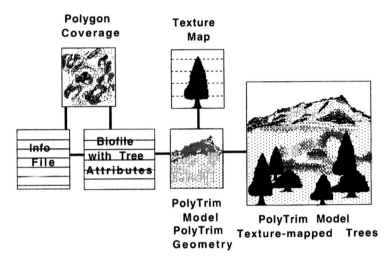

Figure 19.14 An example of a PolyTrim model of a natrual environment in a synthetic landscape by combining several computer datasets as overlays.

objects, and other attributes, when available, eventually creating a dynamic visual simulation elements model.

Dynamic Data Sets as Collaboration in Urban Design

Urban design can use computer applications from data sets on geometric, geographic, and annotative information (McCullough and Hoinkes, 1997). This often involves a need to share data integration, multimedia linkage, and ability to work together with a web browser. The very nature of urban design requires combined efforts of architecture, landscape architecture, and planning along with visualization of changes due to socioeconomic policies (Fig. 19.15). Often urban design needs a wide variety of data and participants; it also necessitates continual striving for accurate data sets.

PolyTRIM can be used to look at two- and three-dimensional constraints for placement of plant and urban structures, environment and behavior changes, historical and environmental options, and urban policy interactions—all related to visual, economic, and microclimate variations. It is imperative that data be accurate and

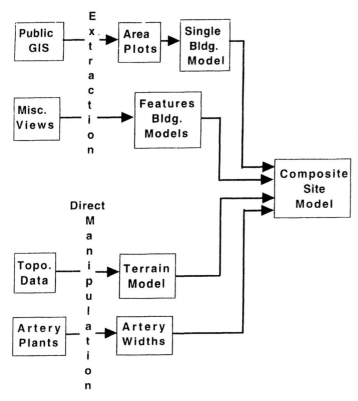

Figure 19.15 Building a composite site model by extraction of public GIS and miscellaneous views to area plots, single building model, and features of building models along with direct manipulation of topographic data and artery plants to terrain model and artery widths.

reliable as data are integrated with a number of collaborative components. A model creation requires inventing new ideas, linking existing components, augmenting existing data, and producing a hybrid consisting of all these components (Fig. 19.16).

REMOTE SENSING USING AN AIRBORNE
LASER ALTIMETER

Complex patterns of micro- and macrotopography, drainage patterns, and vegetation cover can be evaluated using laser technology (Ritchie et al., 1996). The data can be collected quickly, efficiently, and over large areas. Using an airplane-mounted

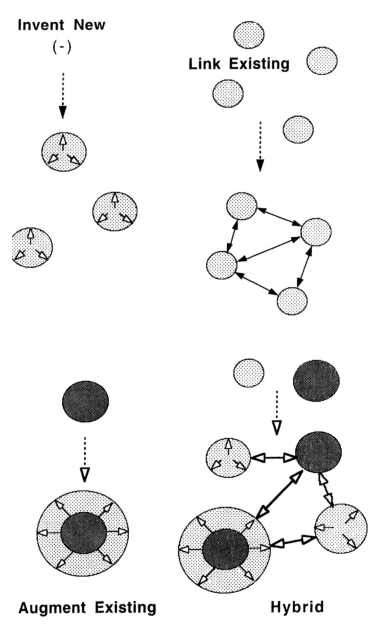

Invent New

(-)

Link Existing

Augment Existing   **Hybrid**

Figure 19.16 Theory of urban design using new information,
linking existing data, augmenting existing data, and producing a
hybrid of all three.

laser altimeter, data can be collected measuring topography, vegetation properties, water depths, erosion channels, and other surface features of the earth. The plane flies over the area to be evaluated and the laser pulses are recorded (Fig. 19.17). By comparing the laser data with survey data, a pattern of the topography and vegetation growing thereon can be shown (Fig. 19.18). By subtracting the survey data from the laser data, the height of the vegetation canopy can be estimated.

Airborne laser altimeters can be used to evaluate landscape topography, gully erosion, stream cuts, and vegetation canopy. This information can be used to quantify movement of water across the landscape, which is affected by the extent of vegetation canopy that is also measured. The laser data collected along with other information can be used to manage natural and agricultural resources on a macroscale for designing, planning, and placing structures on the natural landscape.

SUMMARY

Much of the present information is in a state of flux with new information and ideas being presented constantly. Landscape architects need to be kept up-to-date with the latest technology.

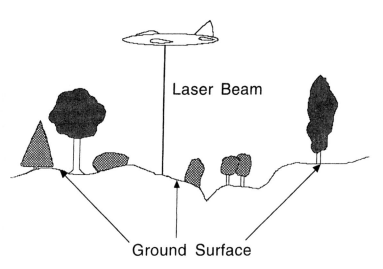

Figure 19.17 Depiction of a laser beam being used by aerial flyover to evaluate ground surface topography and vegetation.

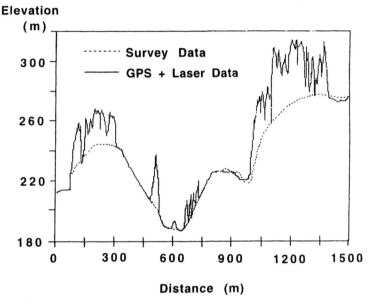

Distance (m)

Figure 19.18 An example of coordinating survey data with GPS and laser data to evaluate height of vegetation over a transect.

One of the best ways to do this is to tap into the Internet regularly for the latest information.

Suggested Internet Web Sites for Resources

www.ced.berkeley.edu/landscape/lawww.html

CLRNet Search for GIS—e.g., PolyTRIM, CAD/GIS, etc.
www.clr.toronto,edu:1080/cgi-bin/clrdb/DB/links?DBReport=search&ANY=GIS

Starting the Hunt: Guide to Mostly On-line and Mostly Free U.S. Geospatial and Attribute Data
www.cast.uark.edu/local/hunt/index.html

GRASS = Geographic Resources Analysis Support System
www.cecer.army.mil:80/grass/

Possible Sources for GIS Equipment and Computer Programs

Corvallis Microtechnology, Inc., 413 SW Jefferson Ave., Corvallis, OR 97333; phone: (541)752-5456

Intermountain Environmental, Inc., 601 West 1700 South, Suite B, Logan, UT 84321 (e-mail: info@inmtn.com website: www.inmtn.com)

MapInfo computer program: Farmers Software Association, P.O. Box 660, Fort Collins, CO 80522; phone: (970)493-1722

FieldNotes by PenMetrics, Corvallis, OR 97333; phone: (541)752-9000

REVIEW

Describe GPS and how it works.
What are some applications of GPS?
How does GIS differ from GPS?
What is meant by the term "precision farming?"
How is GIS used in precision farming?
How are GIS, precision farming, and variable rate operations coordinated?
How does GIS help in monitoring crop conditions for the producer?
How can the Advanced Very High Resolution Radiometer (AVHRR) sensor on a satellite be applied to practical situations?
Name some applications of GIS for landscape architects.
Name several applications that can be evaluated using FieldNotes by PenMetrics.
How can GIS be used in urban settings?
How can two-dimensional data be used to create a three-dimensional model?
What is the purpose of the PolyTRIM application?
How can aerial lasers be used in landscape applications?

References

Allender, W. S. "GIS and its Impact on Land Development Processes." Denver, CO, Berger and Company, Presentation at LAbash '98, West Virginia University, Morgantown, WV, 1998.

Blackmore, Simon. Center for Precision Farming, Cranfield University, Great Britain. Internet: www.silsoe.cranfield.ac.uk/cpf/papers/precfarm.htm 1997.

Brady, N. C. *The Nature and Properties of Soils*. 10th edition. New York, Macmillan, 1990.

Clark, R. L., and R. L. McGuckin. "Variable Rate Application Equipment for Precision Farming." Athens, GA, Department of Biological and Agricultural Engineering, University of Georgia, 1996.

Cowardin, L. M., V. Carter, F. C. Golet, and E. T. LaRoe. *Classification of Wetlands and Deepwater Habitats of the United States*, Washington, DC, Fish and Wildlife Service and U.S. Department of the Interior, FWS/OBS-79/31, 1979.

Das, B. M. *Introduction to Soil Mechanics*. Ames, IA, Iowa State University Press, 1979.

Dorlester, A. L. "Using GIS to Assess Land Use Impacts on Water Quality in an Urbanizing Region: A Case Study of the Mumford River Watershed in Massachusetts." Amherst, MA, Department of Landscape Architecture and Regional Planning. Internet: www.riga.fnr.umass.edu/cgibin/theses.pl?number=761

"Erosion and Sediment Control Handbook for Developing Areas of West Virginia." Morgantown, WV, U.S. Department of Agriculture, Soil Conservation Service, U.S. Government Printing Office, 1981.

Fenska, R. R. *The Complete Modern Tree Experts Manual*. New York, Dodd, Mead, and Company, 1956.

Follett, R. H., L. S. Murphy, and R. L. Donahue. *Fertilizers and Soil Amendments*. Englewood Cliffs, NJ, Prentice-Hall, 1981.

Gail, W., R. Mueller, P. Cook, and P. Doraiswamy. "AVHRR Map Products for Crop Condition Assessment: A Geographic Information Systems Approach." *Photogrammetric Engineering & Remote Sensing*, Vol. 60, No. 9, pp. 1145–1150, Sept. 1994 [Agricultural Research Service Report No. 33074, 1994-09-06]

Goidigasu, M. D. *Laterite Soil Engineering: Pedogenesis and Engineering Principles*. Amsterdam, Netherlands, Elsevier Scientific Pub. Co., 1976.

"Guide for Interpreting Engineering Uses of Soils." Washington, DC, U.S. Department of Agriculture, Soil Conservation Service, U.S. Government Printing Office, 1971.

Handreck, K. A., and N. D. Black. *Growing Media for Ornamental Plants and Turf.* Randwick, Australia, University of New South Wales, 1994.

Harris, R. W. *Arboriculture: Care of Trees, Shrubs, and Vines in the Landscape.* Englewood Cliffs, NJ, Prentice-Hall, 1983.

Hoinkes, R., and E. Lange. "3D for Free-Toolkit Expands Visual Dimensions in GIS." *GIS World*, July, 1995. Internet: www.clr.toronto.edu:1080/links/gisw/origarticle.html 1997.

Horwitze, E. L. *Our Nation's Wetlands*, An Interagency Task Force Report, U.S. Department of Agriculture, Forest Service, Soil Conservation Service, U.S. Department of the Army, U.S. Army Corps of Engineers, U.S. Department of Commerce, National Marine Fisheries Service, U.S. Environmental Protection Agency, U.S. Department of the Interior, and Fish and Wildlife Service, 1978.

McCullough, M., and R. Hoinkes. *Dynamic Data Sets as Collaboration in Urban Design.* Internet: www.clr.toronto.edu:1080/papers/95/caadf95.dynamicdata/caad95/dynamicdata.html 1997.

Page, A. L., T. L. Gleason, III, J. E. Smith, Jr., I. K. Iskandar, and L. E. Sommers. Utilization of Municipal Wastewater and Sludge on Land. In Proc. 1983 Workshop, Riverside, CA, University of California, 1983.

Petschek, P. "Digital Terrain Modeling—Digital Terrain Analysis—Digital Visualization in Landscape Architecture." Zurich, Switzerland. Internet: htpp://vrml.sgi.dom/basics 1997.

Pierzynski, G. M., J. T. Sims, and G. F. Vance. *Soils and Environmental Quality*. Boca Raton, FL, Lewis Publishers, 1994.

Righetti, T., and D. Jones. Personal communication, Corvallis, OR, Oregon State University, 1998.

Ritchie, J. C., M. Menenti, and M. A. Weltz. "Measurements of land surface features using an airborne laser altimeter: The HAPEX-Sahel experiment." *International Journal of Remote Sensing*, Vol. 17, No. 18, pp. 3705–3724, 1996.

Sanchez, P. A. *Properties and Management of Soils in the Tropics.* New York, John Wiley & Sons, 1976.

Sawhney, B. L., and K. Brown (eds.). *Reactions and Movement of Organic Chemicals in Soils.* Soil Science Society of America

Special Pub. No. 22, Madison, WI, Soil Science Society of America, 1989.

"Science for a Changing World: Geographic Information System." Reston, VA, U.S. Geological Survey. Internet: www.info.er. usgs.gov/research/gis/title.html 1997.

"Special Issue on Wetlands." *Journal of Soil and Water Conservation*, Ankeny, Iowa, Soil and Water Conservation Society, Nov./ Dec. 1995.

Staff of Compost Science/Land Utilization (ed.). *Composting: Theory and Practice for City, Industry, and Farm.* Emmaus, PA, J G Press, 1982.

Stevenson, F. J. *Humus Chemistry: Genesis, Composition, and Reactions.* New York, John Wiley & Sons, 1982.

Troeh, F. R. and L. M. Thompson. *Soils and Soil Fertility.* 5th edition. New York, Oxford University Press, 1993.

U.S. Department of Agriculture and Natural Resources Conservation Service. *Field Indicators of Hydric Soils in the United States*, Washington, DC, Fish and Wildlife Service and U.S. Department of the Interior, FWS/OBS-79/31, 1979.

Wentz, W. A. Wetlands Values and Management, Washington, DC, U.S. Fish and Wildlife Service and U.S. Environmental Protection Agency, U.S. Government Printing Office, 1981.

Wischmeier, W. H., and D. D. Smith. "Predicting Rainfall Erosion Losses—A Guide to Conservation Planning." Washington, DC, U.S. Department of Agriculture, Agricultural Handbook No. 537, 1978.

Index

accidents, 192
acidification, 15–6
acidity of soil, 91
  active, 148
  reduced by liming, 148
  reserve, 148, 210
acids, formed during decomposition, 96
actinomycetes (*Frankia*), 24
activated charcoal, absorbs chemicals, 203
activated sewage sludge, 172
active gullies, 55
adenosine triphosphate (ATP), 114
  energy storage, 131
  plant phosphorus, 131
Advanced Very High Resolution Radiometer (AVHRR), 235
aeration of soil, 35
  described, 121
  improved, 40
  phosphorus release, 136
aggregate stabilization, explained, 70–1
aggregation, 62, 184
  from liming, 147
agriculture, variables. *See* remote sensing
AGRICTARS, 232
air, in soil, 22
air pollutants, damage plants, 201
airborne laser
  altimeter for remote sensing, 247
  uses of, 249
alcohols, 184
Alder trees (*Alnus*) nodules, 124

alfalfa (*Medicago sativa*), 122–4
algae, 24
alkalinity, 91
  correcting, 103
alternate freezing and thawing, potassium release, 143
aluminum hydrolysis, described, 96
amines, 118
aminization, defined, 118
amino acids, 113
  in soils, 117
  sulfur in some, 154
amino sugars in soils, 117
ammonia
  air pollutant, 201
  gas toxic
    to *Nitrobacter*, 120
    to plants, 170
  loss from soils by volatilization, 125
ammonification, defined, 119
ammonium, 113, 117, 120
  absorbed by higher plants and soil microbes, 119
  fate of, 119
  fixed by clays, 119, 126
  used in nitrification, 119
  volatilized from soils as a gas, 119, 126
ammonium chloride, 172
ammonium fertilizers
  acid forming, 101
  ammonium nitrate, 170
  ammonium nitrate with lime (ANL), 170

ammonium fertilizers (*continued*)
  ammonium nitrate-sulfate, 170
  ammonium phosphates, 173
  ammonium polyphosphates, 172
  ammonium sulfate, 170, 175
  anhydrous ammonia, 169
  aqua ammonia, defined, 170
Anabaena, 122, 124
anhydrous, defined, 170
animal manures. *See* manures
animal remains. *See* decomposition
animal, damage, 191
ANL. *See* ammonium-fertilizers
antagonisms, 205
apatite, 152
  phosphorus availability, 139
  phosphorus in soil, 134
ASCII legend/key file, creation of, 235
ashes, wood, 149, 174
  as liming material, 150
associations, of soils, 3
Atterberg limits, defined, 217
automobile damage, 192
automobile exhaust damages plants,
    201
auxins (giberellins) in organic matter,
    185
availability of phosphorus in soils,
    factors affecting, 135
available water, factors affecting, 83
AVHRR. *See* advanced very high
    resolution radiometer
azaleas, 158
Azolla (floating fern plants), 124
Azotobacter (aerobic) fix nitrogen, 124

bacteria, 24, 204
  diseases, examples, 204
  effective in nitrogen-fixing
    described, 122
  free-living, fix nitrogen, 122, 124
  specific. *See* nitrification
bark, 40
base-forming factors, 101
basic slag, 169
basin. *See* irrigation
bat guano, 172
bearing capacity of soils, 223
bedrock, 224
biological properties, phosphorus
    availability, 138
biological transformations increased
    by liming, 148

biotite, 141
birds, 192
blood, dried, as fertilizer, 172
blossom end rot, calcium deficiency,
    154
blue-green algae (*Anabaena*), 122,
    124
bone meal, 174
boron, 175
  deficiency in dry weather, 164
  deficiency of shrubs, conifers, and
    hardwood trees, 164
  deficiency symptoms, described,
    164
  foliar sprays, 164
  immobility in plants, 164
  organic complex with sugars, 164
  plants that tolerate, 164
  toxicity symptoms, 164
bottom-up irrigation, 193
brace wires, 199
breast walls, 78
browser, defined, 246
brush layering, 78
buffer, defined, 99
buffering, 148, 210
  factors determining extent of,
    importance of, and order of, 99
buffering capacity, 148, 185
bulk density, defined, 32
burned lime, 149

CAD (computer-aided design) project,
    244
caissons, 223
calcite, 149, 152
calcium
  carbonate, 149
    equivalent. *See* lime, neutralizing
      power of
  cyanamide, 171
  hydroxide, 149
  nitrate, 171
  oxalate, 153
  oxide, 149
  pectate, 153
  phosphates in soils, 134
  in plants
    amounts of, immobility of, and
      uses of, 153
  in soils, amounts of, and fate of,
    152–3
cambium layer, 192

capillaries, 44, 46
capillary movement, 44
carbohydrates (sugars,
    polysaccharides). *See* organic
    matter, composition of
carbohydrate metabolism and
    translocation, 153
carbon dioxide, 35, 161
    gas, toxic, 213
carbonic acid, 119
castor pumice, 172
cation exchange capacity (CEC)
    increased, 184–5
CEC. *See* cation exchange capacity
cell division, 153
cell membranes, functionality
    maintained, 153
cellulose formation, 140
cementing substances, 64
Center for Landscape Research (CLR).
    See PolyTRIM
CH$_2$ = CH$_2$. *See* ethylene
charcoal, activated, absorbs
    chemicals, 203
chelates
    available and absorbed by plants,
        160
    defined and examples of, 160
    foliar or soil sprays, 161
    order of stability, 161
    sprays for micronutrients, 167
    stability, 161
chemical
    injuries, 202
    soil test, 210
    spills, toxicity from, 203
chemicals damage plants, 201
chicken manure, potting mixes, 193
chlorine
    in fertilizers and soils, 165
    leaches easily, 165
    toxicity in soils, 165
chlorites, potassium in, 141
chlorophyll, 140, 153, 184
    defined, 114
    magnesium in, 153
    nitrogen in, 114
chloroplasts, 153
chlorosis, defined, 154
citric acid cycle, 153
Cl$_2$, 201
Claude-Haber process, 169
clays (2:1), protective action, 187

clays (secondary minerals), 15, 21,
    27, 61, 99, 153
clean gravels and sands, defined, 220
climate, 11
Clostridium (anaerobic) fixes
    nitrogen, 124
C/N ratio, 120
    of green manure, 188
    practical importance of, 120–1
color of soil, 184
columnar. *See* structure of soil
compaction, 39
    improvement for engineering, 223
    phosphorus availability, 136
    of wet soils, 212
competition of potassium, 142
composite, soil sample, 209
compost, production of, described, 75
composts, 40, 140, 188
    defined, 188
    for gardens, greenhouses,
        landscaping, and nurseries, 188
    in potting mixes, 193
    sulfur in, 155
compressibility, 217
compression, 220, 223
compressive strength of soils, 217
computer databases for GIS, 230
computer
    program PolyTRIM, 245
    program for virtual fly-over of
        landscape, 244
    software program for GIS, 237
    three-dimensional models, 244
condensation, sugars with amines in
    soils, 118
conductivity of soil solution, defined,
    221
conifers
    boron deficiency, described, 164
    sulfur deficiency in, 154
conservation of potassium in soils, 143
consolidation, defined, 220
constituents of soils, 21
contamination of nitrogen from
    industries. *See* nitrogen added
    to soils
copper, 175
    deficiency in organic soils, 167
    very strongly held by soil, 158
corrosion, 7, 220
    factors affecting, 221
    of steel or concrete, 221

cottonseed meal and cotton gin trash, 172
crop
    monitoring by GIS, 235
    residues, sulfur in, 155
    yield
        forecast by GIS, 235
        patterns, 232, 235
crumb, 32, 62
    formation, 184
    formation from liming, 147
crusts, of soil, 71
cultivation, effect on structure, 71
cuts, 223
cysteine and cystine (amino acids), 154

damages to plants
    animal, 191
    automobile, 192
        exhaust damages plants, 201
    chemicals, 202–3
    dusts, 200
    low temperature, 200
    man-made, 192
    mechanical, 192
    neglect, 192
    snow, 200
data
    comparison by AVHRR, 235
    entry for GIS. See precision farming
    from GIS, smoothing of, 235
    integration, 246
decomposition, of organic matter, 35, 69, 184. See also mineralization
    animal remains (residues), 186–7
    clays, protective action, 187
    defined, 186
    factors affecting rate of, 186
    humus, end product, 186
    microbial, 77
    phosphorus availability, 139
    release of nutrients, 185
    sulfur release, 155
deep rooting stimulated by liming, 148
deer, 191
deficiencies of plant nutrients, diagnosis, 205
deficiency
    of copper on organic soils, 205
    symptoms of boron, described, 164
    symptoms of calcium, magnesium, and sulfur, described 154

symptoms of nitrogen, described, 117
symptoms of phosphorus, described 133
symptoms of potassium, described 141
deformation, soil failures, 222–3
density of soil for foundations, 223
deoxyribonucleic acid (DNA), plant phosphorus, 131
depth to bedrock, 223
depth of soil, 32–3
diagnosis, plant nutrient deficiencies, 205
diammonium phosphate, 172
dicalcium phosphate, in soil, 134
diethylene triamine penta acetic acid (DTPA). See chelates
differential global positioning system (DGPS), 235
diffusion, 36
digital terain
    model (DTM). See PolyTRIM, computer program; see also triangular irregular networks (TIN)
    modeling
        by GIS, 236
        golf course, 244
dihydroxystearic acid, 185
disease vectors killed, 202
disintegration, 15
disposal, of wastes, 217
    site location by GIS, 231
dissolution, 16
dogs, 192
dolomite and dolomitic limestone, 149, 152
drainage, 184, 188, 223
    of soils, artificial, underground, 48
    vs. soil movement, 224
drip line of a tree, 194, 209
drought, 43
    stress observed by GIS, 235
droughty soils, correcting, 212
dry weather, boron in soils, 164
dry well, 195
DTM. See digital terrain model

earth volumes calculated by DTM, 236
earthworks, 217, 223–4
earthworms, 13

economics of potassium fertilizer, 143
egg, as deer repellent, 191
elements absorbed by plants, forms of, 111
engineering properties of soils, 217
environmental
   conditions affect soil testing, 208
   geotechnology, 223–4
   problems, 200
   structures, 224
enzymes activation, 153
   defined, 114
   inactivation, 187
   reactions, 140
equilibrium of potassium in soils, 142
erodibility of a soil (or K factor), 64–5
erosion, 53, 64
   accelerated, 53–4
   mulches retard, 77
   of organic matter, loss of nitrogen from soils, 125
   reduced, 184
   severity, 72. See rainfall erosion index
essential nutrients, defined and listed, 107
esters, 184
ethylene, air pollutant, 202
ethylene-diamine-(o-hydroxyphenyl-acetic acid) (EDDHA). See chelates
ethylene-diamine-tetraacetic-acid (EDTA). See chelates
excavation, 223
excess
   boron, toxicity of, 164
   fertilizers may damage plants, 202
   nitrogen in soil, effects of, 117
   soil drainage, 212
excretion (sloughage), 124

failures, structural, 222
fate
   of ammonium formed, 119
   of nitrogen fixed by bacteria, 124
fats, 184, 186
feldspars, 141, 143, 152
fencing, electric or regular, 191
fertilization, 199–200

fertilizer
   application, methods of, 177
   burn of seedlings, 179, 199
   complete, defined, 169, 175
   elements, listed, 110
   guarantee, defined, 176
   micronutrient, 175
   movement in soils, 179
   phosphorus vs. zinc and iron deficiency, 162
   placement, moisture critical for, 179
fertilizers
   acid-forming, 98
   adding to alkaline soils, 166
   to apply in irrigation, 178
   broadcasting, 177
   chlorine in, 165
   commercial, sulfur in, 155
   compressed pegs for slow release, 178
   elemental vs. oxide forms, 176
   how to use in greenhouses, 178
   for indoor plants, 193
   kinds of, 169–180
   liquid vs. solid, 170, 179
   mixed, 175
   natural organic nitrogen, 172
   residual effects of, 179
   for seeds or perennials, 176
   slow release, 167
   source of calcium and magnesium, 153
   for woody plants, 173
fertilizing, 188
field capacity, 41, 86
FieldNotes (a software program by PenMetrics) for GIS, 237
fill soil, compaction, 212
fills, 223
fineness of a limestone, defined, 150
fires, 192
firing, potassium deficiency, 141
fish meal, 172
fixation
   of iron, manganese, or zinc, on 2:1 clays, 162
   of potassium in soils, 143
fixed-potassium (fixed-K), release of, 143
fizz with dilute acid. See calcium in soils
flocculation, 63
flooded soil, 121

flooding, 224
  stress on plants by GIS, 235
flotation process for KCl, 174
flowers of sulfur. *See* sulfur,
  elemental
fly ash, 18
foliar temperature, 85
forage production estimation by GIS,
  235–6
formation of a soil and factors
  affecting, 11–2
fossil fuels
  burn to release sulfur dioxide, 202
  source of sulfur, 154
foundations, 217, 223
four-dimensional modeling with
  PolyTRIM, 245
frass, defined, 204
freezing and thawing
  potassium release, 143
  release of nitrogen from clays, 126
friable soils, ideal for landfills, 224
functional elements. *See* metabolic
  elements
fungal diseases, examples, 204
fungi, 24, 204
fungicides, may injure plants, 202

gardens, compost for, 188
gaseous exchange in soil, 36
geographic information system (GIS),
  227–8
  aerial view of a golf course, 240
  components of, 228
  computer software program for,
    231, 237
  computer-assisted irrigation system
    for golf course, 242
  data, sources of, 229
  digitizing limits, precision, 231
  examples for using, 227
  FieldNotes, example of, 237
  graphic display by, 231
  information retrieval by, 229
  land use by, 230
  for landscape architecture digital
    terrain modeling, 236
  makes map elements realistic, 231
  moving and stationary receivers
    for, 230, 232
  networking by, 230
  operation of and practical examples
    of, 229

overlaying data in superimposing
    maps for, 230
  for precision farming, 232
  simplified definition, 228
  spatial data for, 229
  spatial variables for, 230
  three-dimensional perspective
    view, 231
  topological modeling by, 230
  transportation planning by, 231
  for urban planning, 244
  use of GPS information, 240
  use of *x*, *y*, and *z* coordinates, 230
  using computer databases, 230
  vegetative cover shown, 230
  waste disposal site location by, 231
  for water quality assessment, 244
  for watering golf course, 242
  for yield mapping. *See also*
    precision farming
geologic erosion, 53
geotechnical aspects, 223
germination, 153
  effects of mulch on, 78
GIS. *See* geographic information
  system
global positioning satellite, 238
global positioning system (GPS), 227,
  232
  civilian uses, 227
  information downloaded into GIS,
    240
  reason for and requirements of,
    227
  satellite, 232
golf course
  aerial view with GIS, 240
  computer-assisted irritation system
    by GIS, 242
  designing by GIS, 229, 236
  digital terrain modeling of, 244
  maintaining by GIS, 236
  vegetation management by GIS,
    237
  virtual landscape of, 236
  watering by GIS, 242
gophers, 191
GPS. *See* global positioning system
granulation, 147, 184
granule of soil, 62
graphic display by GIS, 231
gravels, defined, 218, 220
gravitational water. *See* water

green manure, 188
  sulfur in, 155
greenhouses
  compost for, 188
  how to use fertilizers in, 178
  slow-release fertilizers for, 172
growth-stimulating substances, 185
guano, 174
gullies, 54
  classified, 55–6
Gunneria (aquatic plant), 124
guying, rubber hose for, 199
gypsum
  correcting alkalinity, 104
  potting mixes, 193
  for reclaiming sodic soils, 153
  in superphosphate fertilizer, 175

H_2S. *See* hydrogen sulfide
hardpans, 30, 32, 39, 46
hardware cloth, 192
hazardous wastes disposal, 224
HCl (hydrochloric acid), 201
heavily fertilized soils, 166
heterogeneity of soil, 38
HF. *See* hydrogen fluoride gas
hidden hunger defined, 208
hollies, 158
hormones in organic matter, 185
hornblende, 152
humus, defined, 186
  increased by liming, 148
hurricanes carry salt inland, 203
hydration, 15
hydraulic conductivity, 46, 220
  (permeability) of soils, 217
hydrocarbons, (fats, waxes, resins,
    and oils), 184, 186
hydrogen
  fluoride gas, 201–2
  gas (H_2), 169
  sulfide
    air pollutant, 202
    gas, toxic, 213
hydrological characteristics, 223
hydrolysis, 15
hydrous oxide clays, 19, 64
hygroscopic, 170–1

IAA. *See* indole acetic acid
ice, 15
  damange to plants, 200
ignorance, plant damage from, 192

illites, potassium in, 141
immobilization, 118
  of sulfur in soils, 155
impermeable (impervious), 56
importance of soil depth, 35
improper
  fertilization, 199, 202
  guying or staking, 197
  watering, 192
inaccessibility of substrate, 187
inactive gullies, 55
indole acetic acid (IAA) in organic
    matter, 185
indoor plants, fertilizers for, 193
infectious diseases, defined, 204
infiltration, 30, 54, 61, 64, 76, 184
information retrieval by GIS, 230
infrared photograph, aerial for GIS,
    238
infrastructure, 220, 245
inoculation of legume seed, 123–4
inorganic elements released during
    decomposition, 186–7
inorganic nitrogen in soils, 117
inositol hexaphosphate (phytin)
  plant phosphorus, 131
  in soils, 135
insect damage to plants, 204
insecticides, 202
internal drainage, 44, 49, 211
interrupted water flow, 33
iron
  chelates, 175
  deficiency, 158, 205
irrigation, 43
  acid and base forming, 102
  basin, 86
  bottom up, 193
  drip, 86, 89–90
  fertilizers to use in, 178
  furrow, 86–88
  soils for, 83
  sprinkler, 88–9
  systems, described, 86

K factor. *See* erodibility of a soil
KCl. *See* potassium chloride
kelp (seaweed), 174
kiln dust damages plants, 200

LACIE, 232
land use by GIS, 230
landfills, 6, 18

landscape
  architecture applications using GIS,
    236
  plantings
    fertilizers for, 178
    phosphate fertilizers for, 174
    watering, 194
  plants, when not to fertilize, 178
  projects, aqua ammonia for, 170
  synthetic. See PolyTRIM
  use of urea fertilizer, 171
landscaping
  composts supply organic matter, 188
  slow-release fertilizers for, 172
  use of dried or well-rotted manure,
    188
landslides (slips), 56
laser, airborne
  altimeter for remote sensing, 247
  uses of, 249
laser technology, 247, 249
lateral pressure,
  defined, 220
  in soils, 217
lawn seedings, new, 43
  management, 193
  when to fertilize, 194
lawnmower damage, 192
lawns, how to sample soil, 209
leaching, 97, 161, 164, 179
  loss of micronutrients, 163, 166
  loss of nitrate, 125
  loss of nitrogen from soils, 125
  loss of potassium from soils, 142,
    143
  retarded by organic material, 167
lead (Pb) deposits on plants, 201
leaf drop, premature, 141
legumes, 122
legumes, C/N ratio, 120
legumes, irregular spots on,
    potassium deficiency, 141
light limits plant growth, 200
lightning
  damage to plants, 200
  fixes nitrogen, 125
lignin, 118, 186
  defined, 184
  formation, 140
lime
  base forming, 101
  caustic forms of, 149
  elements, listed, 110

importance of mixing, 152
  kinds of lime: burned, calcite,
    dolomite, hydrated, oxide,
    quicklime, slaked, 149
  for lawn seedings, 152
  in mortar, micronutrients from, 158
  neutralizing power of, 150
  requirement soil test, 210
  source for calcium and magnesium,
    153
  topdressing of, 152
  when to apply, 151
limestone
  amount to apply, 148
  dissolved to leach calcium and
    magnesium, 152
  fineness of, 150
  ground agricultural, 149
  particles do not leach, immobile in
    soils, 152
  soil changes from, 147
liming, 166, 188
  calcium and magnesium in soils,
    147
  materials, kinds of, 149
  for phosphorus availability, 139
  for potassium availability, 143
limiting nutrients, 207
liner for disposal, 224
liquid limit, defined, 217
liquidity of soils, 220
loam, 29. See texture, soil
lombardy poplar damaged by
    lightning, 200
losses of nitrogen from soils, 125
luxury consumption of potassium,
    141–3

macronutrients, defined and listed,
    110
macropores, 38, 46, 61
macrotopography, 247
magnesium. See dolomite
  ammonium phosphates, 172
  in dolomitic limestone, 149
  and organic acids, 153
  part of chlorophyll molecule, 153
  in plants, amounts of, mobility of,
    and uses of, 153
  in soils, fate of, 153
manganese, 175
  chelate, 175
man-made soils, 12, 18

manures, 40, 140, 188
  advantages and disadvantages of, 188
  composition of, 177
  dried or well-rotted for
      landscaping, 188
  farmyard (animal), 176
      composition of, 177
  handling to prevent loss, 177
  as mulches, 72
  nutrient availability in, 177
  residual effects of, 177
  sulfur in, 155
  surface-applied loss of nitrogen
      from soils, 126
material of soils
  size and amount of fines, 220
mechanics of soil, defined, 217
meristematic tissue, 153
mesh. See fineness of a limestone
metabolic elements, listed, 108
metal-complexes, 2-keto-gluconic
      acid, 139. See chelates
metallic sulfides in soils, 155
metals, copper or iron. See
      decomposition
methane gas, toxic, 213
methionine, 154
micas, 141, 143, 152
mice, damage to plants, 191
microbes, increase from mulching, 78
microbial enzymatic oxidation. See
      nitrification
microclimate variations, 246
micronutrients
  amounts required, 157
  anions, 164
  availability, factors affecting, 161
  availability at high pH, 162
  cations present in soils, 157
  deficiency vs. toxicity, 157, 166
  defined and listed, 111
  fertilizers, 175
      when to apply, 178
  in foliar sprays, 178
  management of, 166
  precipitates, 157
  soil management of, 166
  surface adsorption onto soil, 158
microorganisms. See decomposition
micropores, 38, 46, 62
microscopic animals, 22
microtopography, 247
mineral matter, 21

mineralization
  defined, 118
  increased by liming, 148
  of organic phosphorus, 136
  vs. immobilization, 118
mnemonic, essential nutrients, 108
modeling
  3- and 4-dimensional. See
      PolyTRIM
  topological, by GIS, 230
moisture
  by feel, described, 84
  nitrifying bacteria, requirements of,
      121
  phosphorus availability, 136
  in soils, important in fertilizer
      placement, 179
mole drains, 48
moles, 191
molybdate, availability to plants, 166
molybdenum, 166, 175
  organic complexes, 166
  similar to phosphate, 166
mono-ammonium phosphate, 172
mono-calcium phosphate, in soil, 134
muck, 40
mulches, 43, 188, 189
  listed, 72
  rate to apply, 75
  reduce erosion, 74
  time to apply, 76
mulching
  biological and chemical effects of, 77
  disadvantages of, 78
  effects of, 76
  new seedings, 193
  physical effects of, 76
multimedia linkage, 246
muriate of potash (potassium
      chloride, KCl), 174
muscovite, 141
mycorrhizae, 24
  phosphorus from, 133

natural gas, 169
  leaks, 213
natural erosion. See geological
      erosion
necrosis, potassium deficiency, 141
nematodes, 204
  controlling
      by fumigants, 204
      by soil sterilants, 202

netting, bird repellent, 192
networking by GIS, 230
neutralizing power of liming
    material, 150
NH_3. *See* ammonia
nitrate, 113, 117
    lost from soils by leaching, 125
nitric phosphates, 173
nitrification, 148
    defined, 119
    factors affecting, 120
    microbial enzymatic oxidation, 119
    requirements for, 119–22
    soil moisture for, 120–1
    specific bacteria, 119–124
nitrite, 117
    toxic to plants, 120
Nitrobacter. *See* nitrification, specific
    bacteria
nitrogen
    added to soils from atmosphere,
        125
    deficiency, C/N ratio affecting. *See*
        nitrification
    deficiency from mulching, 77
    deficiency symptoms, 117
    effects on plants, 116
    fertilizer may discourage nitrogen
        fixation, 123
    fertilizers, 169
    fixation, 122
        actinomycetes (*Frankia*), 124
        Azotobacter, 124
        blue-green algae, 122, 124
        free-living non-symbiotic
            bacteria, 124
        nitrogen available for plants, 122
        Rhizobium, types of, 122–3
    fixed, examples of, 122, 124
    fixed, practical importance, 122–3
    gas (N_2), 169
    gases, loss of nitrogen from soils, 125
    gases in soils, 117
    losses from soils minimized, 125–6
    metabolism, 153
    organic forms, 113
    oxides air pollutants, 202
    in plants, 113
    in soils, amounts and forms of, 117
    supply. *See* decomposition, release
        of nutrients
    symbiotic bacteria, 122–124
    transformations in soils, 118

Nitrosococcus. *See* nitrification,
    specific bacteria
Nitrosomonas. *See* nitrification,
    specific bacteria
nodules on legume roots, 122
nomograph for soil erodibility, 65
nonmineral elements, defined and
    listed, 109
nonsymbiotic blue-green algae, 124
nonsymbiotic free-living bacteria, 124
nonsymbiotic nitrogen fixation, 124
NO_x. *See* nitrogen oxides
nucleic acid
    derivatives, 184
    phosphorus in soils, 135
    in soils, 117
nucleoproteins, phosphorus in soils,
    135
nurseries, compost for, 188
nutrient
    availability, importance of, 205
    availability improved, 185
    deficiencies of plants, diagnosis, 205
nutrients released by liming, 148

O_3. *See* ozone
ocean spray may injure plants, 202–3
oil, spent
    damages plants, 201
    deer repellent, 191
oils, 184, 186
    synthesis in plants, 153
organic acids, 184
    magnesium and, 153
    phosphorus availability, 139
    sulfate esters in soils, 155
organic complexes
    of boron with sugars, 164
    of molybdenum, 166
organic matter in soils, 21, 30, 64, 65,
    161. *See also* buffering,
        decomposition of, humus
    composition of, 183
    decomposition, phosphorus
        availability, 138
    defined, 183
    importance of, 183
    phosphorus availability, 140
    micronutrient availability, 163
    micronutrients in, 159
    retards leaching, 167
    soil changes from additions, 184
    sulfur in, 155

organic nitrogen in soils
  amounts and forms of, 117
  complexes, 118
organic phosphorus, 184
  forms in soils, 135
organic soils, 12, 29, 166, 219
  copper deficiencies, 167
  for engineering, 220
organic sulfur, 184
  in soils, 155
organisms, living, 11
overlays
  of data. See PolyTRIM
  formed by GIS, 230
  for site selection by GIS, 230
overwatering, 213
oxidation, 16
  potential, 161
  states of copper, iron, and
    manganese, 162
oxidation-reduction of
  micronutrients. See subsoil
  color
oxide of lime. See lime, kinds of
oxygen, 35, 48, 162
  molecular. See nitrification,
    requirements
  required. See decomposition,
    factors affecting
ozone, 201

PAN. See peroxyacetyl nitrates
  from auto exhaust, 201
parent material, 18
  nature of, 11
peat, 40, 140
  Michigan, 72
  moss, 40, 72
  soils for engineering, 220
pegs for fertilizer release, 178
percolation. See infiltration
perennials
  damage to, 200
  fertilizers for, 176
  woody, boron deficiency in, 164
periodical checks for trees and
    shrubs, 194
perlite, 40
permanent wilting point, 41
permeability, 30, 61–2, 64–5, 217,
  220
peroxyacetyl nitrates (PAN),
  201–2

pesticides
  chemical injury from, 202
  movement in air, soil, and water,
    202
pH, 148, 161, 164, 166
  affects phosphorus availability, 136
  defined, 91
  effect on nutrient availability, 95
  favorable. See decomposition,
    factors affecting
  iron deficiency, 205
  optimum for nitrification, 121
  range for plants, optimum, 92
phenolics. See tannins
phosphate
  fertilizers for landscape plantings,
    174
  rock, insoluble phosphorus
    fertilizer (source for
    superphosphates), 173
phosphates of iron, manganese, and
    aluminum in soil, 135
phospholipids
  phosphorus in soils, 135
  plant phosphorus, 131
phosphorus
  availability in soils, factors
    affecting and control of, 136,
    139
  deficiency symptoms, 133
  fertilizer placement, 139
  fertilizers, 173
  fixation by hydroxy-aluminum
    polymers, 137
  fixation by precipitation,
    aluminum, iron, manganese
    hydrous oxides, 137
  fixation by precipitation, calcium,
    137
  fixation by precipitation, soluble
    aluminum, iron, manganese,
    136
  fixation by reaction with kaolinite,
    138
  forms in soils, unidentified, 135
  metabolism, 153
  movement in soils, 139
  in plants, complexes, 131
  in soils
    amount and forms of, 133–4
    main problem of, 133
    toxicity, 133
photography, aerial infrared for GIS, 238

photosynthesis, 42, 107
photosynthetic bacteria fix nitrogen, 124
phytase, microbial enzyme, 135
phytates, insoluble phosphorus, 139
phytin, 139
  (inositol hexaphosphate), in soils, 135
pigments (chlorophyll), 184
pilings, 223
pipelines buried in soils, 217
placement of fertilizer phosphorus, 139
plants
  acid loving, 100
  appearance, 191
  available water, 41
  container grown, 43
  cover, effect on erosion, 72
  diseases, 204
  growth forms acids, 98
  growth habits, 200
  growth requirements, 9
  nutrient availability increased, 148, 185
  nutrient deficiencies and diagnosis, 205
  nutrient requirements, 208
  nutrients from animal manures, 188
  parasites, examples, 205
  parts to test, 208
  remains (leaves, stems, roots). See decomposition
  removal of potassium, 142
  root and top residues, 188
  shade vs. sunlight, 200
  susceptible to wind, ice, snow damage, 200
  toxicities, 205
  toxicity symptoms, 205
  variables for yield measurements, 234–5
  water requirements, 200
  woody, nitrogen fertilizers for, 173
plant tissue testing, 191, 207
  analysis, techniques, 208
  limitations, 208
  reasons for, 207
planters
  raised and step 195
planting, critical factors during, 44
planting hole
  fertilizers for, 178
  potassium fertilizer in, 142

plastic films, for mulch, 74
plastic limit, defined, 217
plasticity, 223
  clay soils, 218
  of soils, 218–20
plinthite, 19
plow pans, 39
pollen tube, growth of, 153
polynuclear hydrocarbons, 184
polyphosphates, 174
polysaccharides, 70, 184. See structure of soil
PolyTRIM
  3- and 4-dimensional modeling, 245
  computer program, 244–6
  for urban design, 246
polyuronides, 70. See structure of soil
ponds
  for containment of industrial pollutants, 224
  soluble micronutrients in, 158
poorly drained soils, 162, 166
pore space, 21–2, 32
potassium
  chloride (KCl), recrystallized, 174
  deficiency symptoms, 141
  fertilizer at planting, 143
  fertilizers, 142, 174
  importance and uses of in plants, 140
  magnesium sulfate, 174
  nitrate, 172, 174
  origin in soils, 141
  in plants, amounts and forms of, 140–1
  problems in soils, 142
  salts, 174
  in soils, amounts and availablity of, 141–2
  sulfate, 174
pot bound, 192
potted plants, 192
  media for, 212
  preventing deficiencies of, 167
  slow-release fertilizer for, 172, 193
potting mixes, use of sewage sludge for, 189
precision
  farming, defined, 231
  digitizing limits, for GIS, 231
prills, defined, 171

primary minerals (rocks), 21
  micronutrients in, 159
  potassium in, 141
  release of potassium from, 143
problems of potassium in soils,
    solutions to, 143
properties, engineering, of soils, 217
protective action, 187
protein
  formation, 140, 153
  synthesis, 153
proteins, 113
  defined, 114, 184
  in soils, 117
  suflur in soils, 155
puddling of soils, 54
  from sodium fertilizers, 172
purple coloration, phosphorus
    deficiency?, 133

qualitative analysis, plant tissue tests,
    208
quicklime, defined, 149
quinones, polymerization of, 118

rain, sulfur from, 175
rainfall
  amount of, 57
  duration of, 57
  erosion index, 72–3
  intensity of, 57
  seasonal distribution of, 58
receiver, for GIS
  moving and stationary, 232
rejuvenation of poor soil structure, 40
remote sensing, 232. See also
    airborne laser altimeter
  by GIS, 235, 247
repellents, 191
replacement of potassium removed
    from soil, 143
representative soil sample, securing
    209
resins, 184, 186
respiration, 35, 107
Rhizobium bacteria
  requirements for, 123
  specific for legumes, 122
rhizosphere, 161, 163
rhododendrons, 158
ribonucleic acid (RNA), plant
    phosphorus, 131
rills, formation of, 54

road salt
  alternatives, 203
  damage to plants, 202–3
rock
  fragments, 224
  phosphate, use on acid soils, 173
rocks (primary minerals), 15
  kinds of, 12
rodents, 191
roots
  abnormalities, 191
  damage, 194
  encircling, 197
  feeder, where located, 194
  girdling, 195
  problems, 211–2
  restriction, 211
rooting depth
  effective, 32
  plants present, 83
rubber hose for guying, 199
runoff, 64
  from mulches, 77

saline soils, 104, 203
salinity of potting mixes, 193
salt
  accumulation damage to plants,
    192, 202
  crusts, 193
  problems, avoiding and correcting,
    203
  problems from fertilizers, 203
  tolerance, plant examples, 104
saltpeter (salt substitute). See
    potassium nitrate
sands, 21, 27, 61
  defined, 218, 220
  potting mixes, 193
sandy soils, 166
sanitary
  facilities, 6
  landfills, 6, 224
sapsuckers, 192
satellite image, 229. See also
    PolyTRIM
saturated flow, 44
saturated soil, 41
sawdust, 40, 140
  C/N ratio, 120
scorching, potassium deficiency, 141
SCU. See sulfur-coated urea
seawater, 175

seaweed (kelp), 172
secondary minerals (clays),
     micronutrients in, 159
seedling stage, critical for watering,
     193
serpentine, 152
sewage lagoons, 224
sewage sludges, 189
     advantages and disadvantages of,
          189
     digested, 172
     potting mixes, 189, 193
     source of organic matter and
          nutrients, 189
shear strength, defined, 220
     examples, 222
     of soils, 217
sheet erosion, 54
shrinkage limit, defined, 217
shrink-swell potential, 220, 223
     defined, 221
shrubs
     applying fertilizers to, 177
     when to apply fertilizers, 178
     where to sample soil, 209
sieves, 150
sign, of plant, defined, 203
silicate clays, 64
silt, 21, 27, 61
slag, 150
slaked lime. See lime, hydrated
slope, 223–4
sloughing, of nodules into soil, 124
slow-release fertilizer, 167
     for plantings, 178
     potted plants, 193
     sulfur-coated urea, 172
     urea-formaldehyde, 171
SO₂. See sulfur dioxide
soap, deer repellent, 191
sodic soils, 104, 203
     defined, 104
sodium nitrate, 171
soil, coarse-grained, 218
soil, coarse-textured, 224
soil, fine-grained, 219
soil, particles, adsorption of sulfur
     by, 155
soil, physical properties affect
     phosphorus availability, 136
soil profile, 16
soil reaction. See pH

soil sampling
     reasons for and technique, 209
     time of, 210
solids in soils, 21
sterilants used in soils, 202
strength of soils, 218
soil testing
     commercial and analysis, 191
     ideal, 210
     kits, limitations, 211
     laboratory procedure, 210
     lime requirement, 148
soluble material. See decomposition,
     factors affecting
sources, of organic matter, 188
spatial variability, defined, 231. See
     precision farming
spatial variables for GIS, 230
sphagnum peat moss, 140
sprays, foliar
     applying fertilizers, 177
     for micronutrients, 167, 178
sprinkler. See irrigation
squirrels, 191
stability of soils, engineering aspects,
     222
starch formation and translocation,
     140
stomates, sulfur dioxide gas absorbed
     through, 154
stones and stoniness, 223–4
straw, C/N ratio, 120
stressed plants, susceptible to
     pollutants, 202
structure of soil, 65, 69, 184
     affects oxygen. See nitrification
     blocky, 30–2
     columnar, 31–2
     crumb, 31–2
     defined, 30
     granular, 31–2
     massive, 30
     platy, 31–2
     polysaccharides and polyuronides,
          influence, 70, 184
subsoil color, related to iron, 158
subsoils, unstable, 224
sugars, 184
sulfate, 154–5
sulfur
     adding to alkaline soils, 166
     deficiency symptoms of, 154

dioxide, air pollutant from fossil fuels, 201
elemental (S), 155, 175
as fertilizer, 100
fertilizers, 175
oxidation, 148
in plants, amounts, forms of, and mobility, 154
in soils, forms present, 155
sulfur-coated urea (SCU), 172
sulfur-containing proteins, 154
Sul-Po-Mag. *See* potassium magnesium sulfate
superimposing maps, for GIS, 230
superphosphate
  ammoniated, 172
  concentrated or triple, 173
  double, 173
  and lime, caution in applying, 177
  main phosphorus fertilizers, 173
  ordinary, 173, 175
surface flow, amount of, 58
susceptibility
  to flooding, 223
  to frost action, 224
symbiotic
  actinomycetes in nonlegumes, 122, 124
  bacteria. *See* nitrogen fixation
  blue-green algae, 122, 124
  nitrogen-fixation by
    nodulated nonlegumes, 122, 124
    nonlegumes (no nodules), 122, 124
synthates, microbial, 64, 183, 186
synthetic landscape with PolyTRIM, 245

tankage, 172
tannins (phenolic substances), 184
temperature in soil
  for nitrification, 121
  for phosphorus availability, 136
  for weathering, 15
tensile strength, 220
tensiometer, defined, 84
terraces, 78
  advantages and disadvantage of, 79
texture, soil, 27–30, 61, 65, 223
  available water, 83
  classes of, diagram, 27

clay, 29
coarse, engineering, 224
coarse-grained, engineering, 218
diagram, 28
loam, 29
phosphorus availability, 136
sand, 29
silt, 29
three-dimensional modeling with PolyTRIM, 245
  objects, interactive by computer model, 244
  perspective by GIS, 231
  view by GIS, 231
  virtual landscapes by GIS, 236
thunderstorms fix nitrogen, 125
tilth of soil, 147, 184
time, geological, 11
tobacco, stems and leaf ribs, 174
topdressing, of fertilizers, 177
topography, 11, 13
topsoil
  organic matter, 17, 32. *See* C/N ratio
  thick, for landfills, 224
total plant analysis, 191, 209
tourmaline, boron in, 164
toxicity
  of aluminum, iron, and manganese reduced by liming, 148
  symptoms of boron and chlorine, 164–5
translocation, 42
transpiration, 42
transplanting, 44
transportation planning by GIS, 231
tree roots, need oxygen, 195
trees
  established, how to fertilize, 178
  small, applying fertilizers to, 177
  when to apply fertilizers, 178
  where to sample soil, 209
triangular irregular networks (TIN), 244
tri-calcium phosphate, in soil, 134
tropical soils, 18

underground drains, 48
underwatering, 213
unsaturated flow, 44
urban
  design, 246
  planning by GIS, 244

urea, 171
-formaldehyde, 171
for landscaping, 171
loss of nitrogen from soils, 126
slow-release nitrogen fertilizer, 171
toxic to *Nitrobacter*, 120
U-shaped gullies, 56

variable rate, by GIS. *See also* precision farming
cultivation, planting, spraying, irrigation, tillage, and harvesting, 232–5
fertilizer or lime application, 232
variability. *See* precision farming
predictive and temporal, defined, 231
vegetation, 13
cover by GIS, 230
indices. *See* advanced very high resolution radiometer
management by GIS, 237
vermiculite, 40
potassium in, 141
vigorous roots, resist disease and insects, 148
virtual
fly over of landscape by computer program, 244
landscape, 244
creation of, 236
virtual reality modeling language (VRML), 244
viruses, 24, 204
vitamins, in organic matter, 185
volatilization, loss of nitrogen from soils, 125
V-shaped gullies, 55

walls, retaining, 195, 200
wastes, disposal of, 217
site location by GIS, 231
water, 15, 22, 40
adsorption by organic matter, 184
gravitational, 41
head, 44
infiltration increased by liming, 148
limits plant growth, 200
logging, 33
movement vs. drainage, 224

quality assessment by GIS, 244
to wet root zone, reasons for, 85
water holding capacity, 83, 184
of soils increased by liming, 148
water table, 224
perched, 48
waxes, 184, 186
weather-induced problems, 200
weathering, 161
biological, 16
chemical, 15
micronutrient release, 159, 162
of minerals to release calcium and magnesium, 152
physical, 15
resistant minerals, 143
of rocks and clays, base forming, 101
of rocks and minerals, 12
weed seeds, killed, 202
weight of the soil solids, 29
wet soils, compaction, 212
wetlands, natural, 49
wetness, seasonal, 223
wetting and drying, release of nitrogen from clays, 126
white clover (*Trifolium pratense*), 122
wildlife habitat and management, 5
wilting, defined, 84
coefficient, 41
severe, 193
wind, 15
damage to plants, 194, 200
erosion, 76
winery pumice (dried), 172
wire cages, with mulch, 200
wood ashes, 149, 174
as liming material, 150
woodpeckers, 192
woody
perennials, boron deficiency in, 164
World Wide Web (WWW), 250. *See* browser
wound dressing, 192

x, y, and *z* coordinates for GIS, 230

yield, mapping by GIS, 232, 234

zinc, 175
zinc chelate, 175